SMART MONEY

The
FALL & RISE
of
BRENTFORD FC

SMART
MONEY

ALEX DUFF

CONSTABLE

CONSTABLE

First published in Great Britain in 2024 by Constable

1 3 5 7 9 10 8 6 4 2

Copyright © Alex Duff, 2024

The moral right of the author has been asserted.

A CIP catalogue record for this book
is available from the British Library.

ISBN: 978-1-40871-940-4 (hardback)
ISBN: 978-1-40871-942-8 (trade paperback)

Typeset in Bembo MT Pro by SX Composing DTP, Rayleigh, Essex
Printed and bound in Great Britain by Clays Ltd, Elcograf S.p.A.

Papers used by Constable are from well-managed
forests and other responsible sources.

MIX
Paper | Supporting
responsible forestry
FSC
www.fsc.org   FSC® C104740

Constable
An imprint of
Little, Brown Book Group
Carmelite House
50 Victoria Embankment
London EC4Y 0DZ

An Hachette UK Company

www.hachette.co.uk

www.littlebrown.co.uk

To my father, and to the memory of Francis Joseph.

Contents

Introduction   1

Prologue   3

Part One: Fall

Chapter 1: 1980s, The Bricklayers Arms, Ealing Road   11

Chapter 2: 1880s, Brentford Dock   37

Chapter 3: 1930s, The Great West Road   59

Chapter 4: 1950s, Bushy Park   81

Chapter 5: 1990s, Griffin Park   107

Chapter 6: 2000s, Griffin Park   137

Part Two: Rise

Chapter 7: 2010, Jersey Road, Osterley   171

Chapter 8: 2000, Bolton, north-west England   197

Chapter 9: 2014, Jutland, Denmark   215

Chapter 10: 2015, Jersey Road, Osterley   243

Chapter 11: 2021, Brentford Community Stadium, Kew Bridge   263

Chapter 12: 2023, Amex Stadium, Brighton   291

Epilogue

Appendix   309

Bibliography   311

Acknowledgements   315

Index   317

Introduction

Internally, it is known as 'The Bible'. The 400-page tome about Brentford Football Club is regarded as close the team has to an official history. It was edited by a match-day press officer, with the help of three fans who dedicated years of their spare time to scour old newspapers preserved on microfilm. That history, *100 Years of Brentford*, was published in 1989 when the club were in a half-century purgatory in the lower reaches of the Football League, playing in an ageing stadium before sparse crowds and a strategy that was sometimes no more ambitious than to avoid extinction.

Smart Money: The Fall and Rise of Brentford FC differs from 'The Bible' on two counts: it is not an exhaustive history, and it is not meant only for Brentford fans.

It recreates key moments of the past and, drawing on new interviews with players and executives, tells the remarkable

1

story of how, after so long as a football backwater, Brentford rose through the divisions to reach the Premier League.

Prologue

The Department of Mathematics and Statistics, Lancaster University, 1997. Undergraduate students hurried between lectures avoiding showers sweeping off the Irish Sea. They sheltered under a covered walkway connecting modernist brick buildings on the campus. Stuart Coles was a statistics lecturer with a line in self-deprecating humour. He specialised in calculating the probability of freak events, such as hurricanes and flooding in Venezuela. Mark Dixon, a graduate in his twenties, helped him out as part of a small research unit.

One day, Dixon became intrigued by an exam paper which asked final-year students to forecast the outcome of a hypothetical football match. He was a football fan and realised the premise of the question was off the mark. It would be too simplistic for students to base their answers on the previous results of both teams. There were too many other factors at play.

Dixon and Coles were inspired to build a model to predict football scores. In their spare time, they got to work. They collected data from three seasons of performances in 6,629 English league and cup games, breaking down home and away form, and attacking and defensive prowess, before coming up with what they felt was a solid model.

Indeed, they were so confident with their creation that, in a delicious twist, they wrote in the draft of an academic paper that bookmakers were getting their pre-match odds wrong. Their model, they wrote, had the potential to make a profit even after factoring in the bookmakers' standard margin of about ten per cent.

At the time, bookmakers like Ladbrokes, William Hill and Coral each had a sort of committee of about a dozen staff to set football odds. These were gambling experts agile with numbers, although few, if any of them, were mathematicians or statisticians. The Dixon–Coles paper was full of complicated formulae and probability theories that were unintelligible to the layman. To show how they would predict a binary scoreline such as 1–0, they presented a series of mathematical equations, one of which was stacked with more than a dozen letters of the Greek alphabet. After satisfying peer reviewers, their academic paper was published over 15 pages of the *Journal of the Royal Statistical Society* under a dull headline.[1] A résumé in a university journal gave the paper a sexier title: 'Beating the Bookmakers'.

---

1 Lancaster University website: 'Modelling Association Football Scores and Inefficiencies in the Football Betting Market'.

The paper generated some publicity. Dixon was interviewed on *Tomorrow's World*, a BBC television science show. In what was a bit of a gimmick, the producers challenged Dixon and Coles to make a profit on the following weekend's ten Premier League fixtures. That was a flawed idea because, with so few games, it was not a serious way to judge a statistical model, but they made a bet on each game using their formula and won a small profit, which was donated to charity.[2]

Most people then forgot about the paper. However, it would change the lives of the two Lancaster University employees, making them far richer than academic life could, and form the baseline of a niche but highly profitable layer of the professional gambling industry focused on football. (In the US there was a precedent: in the 1980s, a fabled Las Vegas-based group had used a mathematician's model to make a fortune from betting on American sports.)

A couple of years after coming across the exam paper that would change his life, Dixon left higher education, where the average annual salary at the time was little more than £25,000. He founded a consultancy that predicted sports results: he picked the name 'Atass Sports' for the business so it would be closer to the front of the *Yellow Pages* phone directory.

Starting out from his home in a country lane in Devon, the company had humble beginnings but grew to such an extent that it hired 80 staff and went on to clear £1 million in profits each year. Dixon came to own an organic farm, run an

---

2 Stuart Coles, *Smartodds* blog, 1 November 2022.

environmental foundation with £9 million in assets, and enjoy holidays water-skiing and trail running in exotic locations.[3]

An innovator in this fledgling sector identified football betting in Asia as the way to get rich – the market in the Far East, according to most estimates, moved hundreds of billions of dollars per year. Tony Bloom, a Manchester University mathematics graduate, realised that applying statistical modelling to this market could be like mining a rich seam of gold. For a couple of years, while developing contacts in Asia, Bloom had been working with a small group of allies on an algorithm that was more sophisticated than the Dixon–Coles model. It was still evolving but over time it would, among other things, challenge the cliché that the football league table never lies by ranking teams on the quality of their goalscoring chances, as opposed to their points tally.

As Bloom set up as an online bookmaker in London that aimed to take Asian handicap football betting to a global audience, he developed a far more lucrative sideline project: a betting syndicate that used probability theory to bet on the other side of the world.

Matthew Benham, an Oxford University physics graduate, applied for a job to work with him as a trader and became involved with the syndicate. After a couple of years working together, Benham and Bloom fell out and they went their separate ways.[4] Both men left bookmaking to set up

---

3 'Atass Ltd, and The Dixon Foundation', Companies House filings for 2022.
4 According to a source close to Tony Bloom.

organisations focusing exclusively on maths-based gambling in Asia. One of the first employees that Benham hired was Stuart Coles. Bloom, meanwhile, hired Dixon's consultancy. That was only the first stage of the ripple effect caused by the 15-page Lancaster University paper: in time its influence would extend even further.

As a young boy, Bloom followed Brighton & Hove Albion Football Club, where his grandfather Harry was on the board in their most successful era. Since then, parlous finances meant the club had sold their Goldstone Ground stadium, forcing them to ground-share in Kent, and had almost dropped out of the league. Making plenty of money already, Bloom decided to get involved.

Benham followed Brentford Football Club, which had spent almost all his lifetime going nowhere in English football's third and fourth tiers. Because of work and family commitments getting in the way, his interest in the club had lapsed. He attended a couple of games per year at Griffin Park, the club's decaying stadium in suburban west London.

In 2005 Brentford had a ballooning overdraft, and an owner who was threatening to put the club into administration unless fans could raise £1 million to pay off a tranche of debt.[5] Benham, who had a modest lifestyle and no taste for fancy clothes or conspicuous consumption, was already making millions of pounds in winnings from gambling. He called Brentford's offices one day, and asked to talk to someone about how he could help.

---

5 Interview with former Brentford deputy chairman Brian Burgess.

Part One

Fall

Chapter 1

1980s: The Bricklayers Arms, Ealing Road

The name of Brentford became well known in the UK in the 1970s thanks to scratchy nylon bedsheets that cost as little as £1. Brentford Nylons was started by Harry Pambakian, an Armenian immigrant, and the company's headquarters were on the Great West Road in Brentford. As well as sheets, the company used nylon and polyester to make everything from shirts and trousers to blankets and dressing gowns, all for less than £2 per item. My mother once drove there in her powder-blue Austin Maxi to buy bed sheets. There was a shop where you get them even more cheaply, straight from the factory floor without any retail mark-up. The factory was staffed with the growing vibrant immigrant population of west London. A picture on a summer's day from that era shows Asian women, wearing colourful saris, emerging from the factory after a shift with the M4 flyover as a backdrop.

There were more than a hundred Brentford Nylons stores across the UK at the time. Those bed sheets took the name of the small west London suburb further than the local football club was able to. Sometimes, when you told a new acquaintance which football team you followed, the stranger would respond: 'Brentford, as in Brentford Nylons?'

On high streets from Southampton to Birmingham and Manchester to Glasgow, Brentford Nylons was spelt out in black or red in bold capital letters on shopfronts. On the M4 you could see the company's name atop a sleek new office tower on the way into London from Heathrow Airport. By 1974 the company was turning over more than £24 million a year.

A couple of hundred metres away was Brentford FC's Griffin Park stadium. Tucked away in a side street, its name on the main entrance of the Braemar Road was hidden at ground level unless you happened to stroll down the street of terraced houses. You could see it better from the M4 flyover. The club had been treading water in the third and fourth tiers of English football since the 1950s. In the 1970s, barely 5,000 supporters came for home games. Match reports merited only a few paragraphs in national media, far less than Queens Park Rangers and Chelsea which were five miles away but a world away in terms of prestige.

On the map of London, Chelsea FC was in Fulham, but the name meant that in the media they were associated with the fashion boutiques of the King's Road. Chelsea won the 1970 FA Cup when it was a jewel of the British sporting calendar: more than half the population watched on the BBC as they beat Leeds in a replay memorable for its brutality. In Shepherd's Bush, Queens Park Rangers came within a point of winning the league from Liverpool in 1976. Brentford, meanwhile, was still best known for a range of discount bed sheets.

Brentford Nylons was not keen on associating itself with Brentford FC. At the height of its fame, the company's advertising director George Smith was taken out to lunch by the football club's top two executives. The football men figured that their successful neighbour might want to do a sponsorship deal worth, say, £1 million.[1] Smith made it clear that was not going to happen: he had already allocated his budget on a nationwide advertising campaign featuring BBC radio disc jockey Alan Freeman. In a television ad you can see on YouTube, Freeman pulled up alongside the company's tower in a sports coupé and introduced some of its products, along with the slogan: 'Brentford Nylons, The Money Savers. (*See Saturday's papers for your nearest Brentford's store.*)'

Brentford Nylons, however, had overstretched itself. In 1976, the company went into administration. It was bought out and renamed Brentfords but remained deeply unfashionable. Years later, after acquiring the dwindling business, Rotherham-based retailer Rosebys dropped the name of the town once and for all. 'The stores' main weak point was the name,' chief executive Michael Rosenblatt explained in 1995. 'People would sooner be seen with a plain white carrier than a Brentfords bag.'[2]

---

1 Jonathan Burchill, *A Pub on Each Corner: Stats and Facts from Griffin Park, the Home of Brentford FC for 116 Years* (1974–75 season).

2 'Brentfords Buyer Insists on a Clean Sheet', *Independent*, 5 July 1995.

My father first took me to watch Brentford in 1978. It was a decision based mainly on geography: it was the nearest league club, two miles from our home in Kew. During that year's summer holidays, I had stayed for a few days with my cousins in Hackney. The highlight was a trip to my first football game, at Orient. It was an 8 p.m. kick-off. I stood on the terrace on a crate to get a better view. The game was against Notts County in the Anglo-Scottish Cup. I was smitten: the evening kick-off, the floodlights, the buzz of the crowd, the players a few feet away. I pestered my father to take me to another football game. He was brought up a short walk from Roker Park on the north-east coast of England; a Sunderland fan with no connection of his own to any of the London clubs. So, Brentford it was.

A few weeks later we walked over Kew Bridge, turned left and past the soot-blackened wall of a former gasworks towards Griffin Park. The 20-foot wall, with a sign – 'Bill stickers will be prosecuted' – blocked the view of the River Thames. I remember passing an abandoned light-industry plant, most of its windows smashed. The area's best days, like the club's, were in the past.

The Braemar Road turnstiles at Griffin Park opened onto a small forecourt. On the roof of the stand was a modest-sized sign in black: 'Brentford FC'. You walked through the tarmacked forecourt, up a flight of stone steps and through a short corridor, passing the club office, which was busy on match days. The office had a sliding frosted-glass window to afford some privacy. At the time there was no club shop. The window was the interface between the club and the rest of the world. On emerging from the corridor, excitement building, you could see the pitch.

I don't remember the game against Bury that day, but we lost 1–0. The next day's *Sunday Mirror* noted in its match report that fans slow-handclapped the performance – the seventh defeat in 11 games – and police escorted the referee off the pitch after ruling a late Brentford goal offside. These were the darkest days of football hooliganism. In east London that day, a police helicopter hovered over Upton Park during West Ham's game against Millwall; police officers with Alsatians on leashes patrolled the perimeter of the pitch.

My father and I became Griffin Park regulars, sitting every other Saturday on the wooden benches of the Braemar Road stand or standing on the stone steps of the paddock below. In 1979 Matthew Benham's father also decided to take him to Griffin Park, the nearest league club to the family home in Eton.

I could recite the Brentford starting eleven from those days. None were household names. One or two lived in the street next to the stadium gates. Players would drink in the pubs, on each corner of the ground, and in the neighbouring streets. After training some reconvened in the New Inn, a low-ceilinged boozer with wooden beams. They would have lunch there, and maybe a beer or two. Sometimes, as can happen, afternoon would turn into evening, and they would still be there after 11 p.m. for a lock-in. In the morning, at around 9.45, a youth-team player would knock on the doors of the players who lived by the ground to make sure they were up for training.

★

Somewhat improbably, Brentford's chairman at the time was called Dobrivoje Tanasijević. More improbably still, he owned a restaurant in Hollywood frequented by A-list stars such as Elizabeth Taylor, Paul Newman and Al Pacino. The restaurant was on Santa Monica Boulevard. From the outside it did not look very fancy. It was a one-storey, yellow clapboard building with green awning. Inside, it looked a little louche. There were red leather booths, red-checked tablecloths and Chianti bottles hanging from the ceiling. The food was Italian, and the vibe was nice and cosy. Since Tanasijević opened the venue in 1964 it had become a home from home for film stars. It was a place for them to wind down, away from the limelight. The owner was the perfect host: polite and friendly but not too in-your-face. He was, according to a profile in *Los Angeles Magazine*, '. . . one of the few men who can carry off kissing a woman's hand. He does it swiftly, smoothly and without hesitation, the same way he lights your cigarette.' There were some movie posters and memorabilia hanging on the walls. But there was nothing too look-at-me, apart from one blown-up black-and-white photo of Tanasijević wearing a suit – no tie – with a broad smile holding a bottle of champagne next to a dozen men sitting in a communal bath wearing little more than jubilant grins. The caption underneath read: 'Brentford Football Club win promotion to the third division'.

Tanasijević's circuitous journey to the Griffin Park changing room began in Belgium.[3] He'd defected from Communist

---

3 Dan Tana's life story is taken from an *Observer Sport Monthly* profile by Rhidian Brook, 7 April 2002.

Yugoslavia when on a tour with the Red Star Belgrade youth team aged 17. On a winter's night, he walked out of a restaurant in Brussels and handed himself in to police, with a vague plan that he would use his talent as a footballer in the West. He secured a contract to play for Hanover in Germany but, less than two hundred miles from the beginning of the Eastern Bloc, he was nervous that he might be bundled into a car, driven over the border and returned ultimately to Yugoslavia. After a few months, he put more distance between himself and the secret police by joining a team in Montreal.

When he and a friend won $5,000 in a poker game, they decided to try their luck in the US even though they did not have a green card. In Los Angeles, his friend *was* bundled into a car while holding the poker winnings, apparently by immigration officials. Tanasijević avoided arrest but was left with less than $10 in change. He took a job in a tuna cannery. After taking acting classes, he got a few roles in Hollywood, playing bad guys in war movies. In 1957 he had a role as a German sailor in *The Enemy Below* starring Robert Mitchum, earning £20,000 for eight weeks' work, far more than he could get from football. For these films, he anglicised his name to Dan Tana. When he acquired his restaurant a few years later, he named it Dan Tana's.

Tana stayed involved with soccer in California first as a player and then as an official but, while life was perfectly pleasant, most Americans did not have the same passion for the game he had known growing up in Yugoslavia. When he went to England to headhunt players for a fledgling US league he met Brentford manager Frank Blunstone, who invited him to Griffin Park. Brentford were in the fourth division. 'They were losing but the atmosphere was tremendous – the crowd was singing, "*We love you Bees*",' Tana, whose English had an American twang, said. 'For me it was love at first sight.'[4]

For most of the previous century, Brentford had a shared ownership model under which a group of well-off directors co-owned and managed the club. The benefit of this model was quickly reinstated in 1967 after the chairman of the time accumulated most of the share capital and came up with a plan to sell Griffin Park to QPR.[5] Tana bought £20,000 worth of shares – about about £180,000 in today's money – and became co-owner alongside a few others, including Eric Radley Smith, a retired surgeon, and Walter 'Bill' Wheatley, a businessman.[6] The directors were older than Tana, then aged 39, and did not seem to have the same get-up-and-go. He persuaded them to appoint him chairman.

It was a relatively cheap investment and allowed Tana to reconnect with European football. He decided to devote the next phase of his life to Brentford FC, moving to a house in Kensington while colleagues looked after business on Santa Monica Boulevard. The restaurant gave him a regular income: the film stars kept coming. Once, Richard Burton was turned away because all 16 tables were booked; he complained on The Tonight Show, to which host Johnny Carson responded that

---

4 *Fulham Chronicle*, 24 October 1980.
5 See Chapter 4 for more on the planned QPR takeover.
6 *Acton Gazette*, 28 February 1980.

Dan Tana's was his favourite restaurant in LA. You could hardly buy better publicity.

Every other Saturday in the Brentford club programme, a picture of Tana's Californian car number plate – 1889 BFC – appeared by the names of half a dozen American companies he had an association with. In a sense, Hollywood was funding Brentford FC.

When Brentford won promotion in 1978, Tana paid for the squad to go on a jaunt to Jersey, putting £5,000 on a tab behind the bar of their hotel. The picture of him celebrating with the squad immediately after they won promotion was proudly put up at Dan Tana's and became a talking point for years to come. Many of his clients knew about Brentford. Many years later, when Rhidian Brook, a writer on assignment for the *Observer*, visited the restaurant, he witnessed Cameron Diaz walk in one evening and, making small talk, ask Tana, 'How are Brentford doing?'[7]

If there was sunny optimism in Hollywood in the late 1970s, life was gloomier and darker in England. There were widespread strikes under Jim Callaghan's Labour government. Unemployment more than doubled in the London borough of Hounslow within 12 months: Firestone, one of the biggest employers in Brentford, shut its factory on the Great West Road not long before Christmas in 1979, laying off 1,500 staff. Then another 1,500 employees were made redundant at the United Biscuits plant in Osterley.

---

7 *Observer Sport Monthly*, ibid.

Hooliganism and racist chanting were common in English football. I remember seeing outbreaks of fighting whenever Millwall visited. Hooligan groups would try to 'take' the home end: a few dozen not wearing club colours would congregate in the Royal Oak stand and, when the match started, sow havoc. Portsmouth supporters, who had arrived in their thousands, threw bananas at Francis Joseph, our black centre-forward.

Most Brentford fans were placid, if sweary, but there were small groups of National Front skinheads who came to Griffin Park that would attack our black supporters, shouting, 'There ain't no black in the Union Jack.'[8] The skinheads made monkey noises at players on the opposing team. It was no wonder the growing Asian population in Hounslow did not come to Griffin Park.

Women and girls at the ground were also rare, and there was little sign that anyone at the club was expecting them: the toilet facilities for them were Victorian, barely more modern than a tin bucket.[9] The ground had seen better days. When, because of a wayward shot or clearance, the ball landed on a roof above one of the terraces, it would dislodge a sprinkling of rust onto spectators below.

Tana wanted to make Brentford's stadium more inviting for families, like the arenas he was familiar with in California: there, families went to matches together, moving around freely to buy hot dogs and sodas, and generally having a wholesome

---

8 *Push Up Brentford!* film interviews with Kenny Raymond and Billy Grant.
9 *Push Up Brentford!* film interview with Jo Whelan.

time. There was no swearing, racism or hooliganism. In 1978, as Brentford were promoted to the third division, he set up a committee to examine plans to modernise the stadium – or move to a site near Kew Bridge, where an indoor fruit and vegetable market had once stood.

One of Brentford's rivals was Watford, whose chairman Elton John was near the peak of his success. He had already several hits including 'Rocket Man', 'Goodbye Yellow Brick Road' and, in a nod to the mood of the times in Britain, 'Saturday Night's Alright for Fighting'. The Brentford board had a smattering of showbusiness stardust itself in Rick Wakeman, the Perivale-raised keyboardist for Yes who lived in Switzerland. Before one game at Griffin Park, the two pop stars had a glass of beer in the boardroom. After both teams were promoted to the third division a sell-out league game was featured on London Weekend Television's *The Big Match*. As players walked out onto the pitch, they passed blonde and brunette models dressed like *Playboy* bunny girls to advertise an Ealing bookmaker. The game finished 3–3. Watford went on to secure another promotion; Brentford finished in mid-table and returned to a more humdrum existence. Wakeman resigned as a director after realising it was not realistic to fly in for board meetings from Montreux.

When Brentford slid down the table the next season, Tana became the target of abuse from fans. The elation of promotion had been replaced by frustration. A small group of supporters stood on the Braemar Road paddock below where the directors sat. During games, they turned towards the chairman, demanding that he spend more money on the club. 'Get your cheque book out, Tana,' they shouted. Tana was not, he told the *Acton Gazette*, a millionaire. He was just a restaurateur with a couple of sideline investments in California. His idea was to have a bit of fun in London, not to bankrupt himself for the sake of the club. He offered to resign.

By 1980 Brentford were losing £3,000 per week and were in danger of being relegated to the fourth division. Tana and the board fired manager Bill Dodgin Jr in March, bringing in Fred Callaghan from non-league Woking. Brentford avoided relegation on the final day of the season, thanks to a 1–0 home win against Millwall. Dodgin was popular with supporters: on a wall of the Haverfield Estate not far from the ground, someone scrawled *Why Sack Dodgin?* It would remain there for years.

As Margaret Thatcher was campaigning to become prime minister on a mandate to clean up Britain, with the election slogan 'Labour's Not Working', Martin Lange arrived for the first time in the Brentford boardroom with his own no-nonsense approach. He wanted to focus on sound business principles, which he felt were lacking under Tana. He had built a Surrey-based commercial property business, and had supported the club since he was a five-year-old boy. He thought Tana's plans for a new stadium were too dreamy for a club of Brentford's means. Tana did not like being challenged by this confident 37-year-old Englishman, whom, he said, had absolutely no experience of the football or entertainment business.

Lange sat across the table from Tana at a few board meetings. There was an awkward status quo between the two young men, the recently arrived Yugoslav who had played for Red Star Belgrade and knew his way around Hollywood, and the commercial property developer who had watched Brentford all his life and knew his way around Ealing. One of these meetings was reaching its conclusion and had got to the 'any other business' part. It was at this point that Lange ambushed Tana, proposing a motion to take over as chairman. He had prepared for this moment, co-opting an ally onto the board whose presence was enough to give him the upper hand: he won the vote 3–2.

In the first weeks after his boardroom coup, Lange fired Brentford's chief scout to cut costs and began a drive to increase revenue. He introduced micro-sponsorship deals that allowed fans and businesses to sponsor a player's socks for £10 per season, in return for a mention in the match programme.

Later, the Ealing Road terrace roof – which could be seen by airline passengers as their planes descended out of the sky before landing at Heathrow Airport – was sold as advertising space to the Dutch national airline: it was painted sky blue with the words, 'Next Time . . . Fly KLM'. Rejecting Tana's idea for a new family stand, Lange instead introduced a family season ticket.

In perhaps the best bit of business of all, he signed Stan Bowles. Bowles had been one of the standout players in the QPR team that had come within a point of winning the league title from Liverpool in 1976. For the first time since I had started to follow Brentford, we had a player who even non-football fans were aware of. He was probably better known that Brentford

Nylons. Bowles was a regular feature in tabloid newspapers that sold millions of copies daily on a diet of football, sex and celebrity gossip. (If they could combine all three in one story, so much the better.) When the *Daily Star* launched in 1978, editor Derek Jameson was asked what the new red-top would cover, he explained, 'It'll be tits, bums, QPR and roll-your-own fags.'

Football players were invited to open everything from nightclubs and restaurants to butchers and hairdressers: the owners of these businesses knew the national tabloids – or at least the local newspaper – would run the photos. Some players liked the attention, even if compensation amounted to little more than a meal or night out. Don Shanks, a close friend of Bowles at QPR, provided greyhound racing tips in a weekly column in the *Acton Gazette* in return for a bottle of Rémy Martin cognac.[10]

Bowles picked up £500 from the *Sun* while at QPR for appearing with a topless model, an error of judgement that he said nearly cost him his first marriage to his wife Ann. For £1,000 he appeared on BBC One's *Superstars*, in which athletes from different sports competed against each other in Olympic events. After a night of drinking with his friend Shanks, Bowles fired a shooting pistol through a table by mistake, was unable to lift anything in the weightlifting, capsized his canoe, and finished next to last in the swimming race. All told, he scored an all-time low of seven points.[11]

---

10 Author interview with Charlie Sale, *Acton Gazette* reporter in the 1980s.
11 Spurling, ibid.

After leaving QPR Bowles had joined Nottingham Forest, but walked out on the club after falling out with Brian Clough, days before their European Cup final win against Hamburg. By 1981 his heyday and five England appearances were in the past. As first division clubs weighed the value of his performance (astonishing dribbling and passing skills) against his off-field behaviour (gambling habit and an anti-authoritarian streak), he dropped down into the second division with Orient and, after falling out with their manager, found himself at Brentford at the age of 32.

On the last Saturday of October, 2,000 more fans than usual turned up at Griffin Park to see him play for Brentford against Burnley; the extra gate money recouped much of the £25,000 transfer fee Brentford had paid to sign him. Bowles arrived with his boots in a plastic bag. (He did not drive and usually came to matches by public transport unless someone offered to give him a lift.) In a 0–0 draw, Bowles showed he had not lost his touch. He was a little disillusioned to be in the third division and did not plan to stay long. 'I have signed a contract for just over a year,' he told the local paper. 'And then I think I'll be off to America.'

Lange gave Bowles a £500-a-week contract – more than other players – and put him up in a two-bedroom terraced house at 38 Braemar Road, abutting the stadium; premises the club had bought and were seeking planning permission to turn into an office. When Bowles walked in Brentford staff were surprised that he was nothing like the troublemaker they had read about who had rowed with almost every manager he worked with. He shuffled shyly into the club reception, saying hello to everyone. 'He was very polite,' Christine Mathews, the club secretary, said. 'A real gentleman.'[12]

Bowles's neighbour just across the road was Terry Hurlock. Each morning at ten Hurlock and Bowles would, after a mug of tea and toast, walk out of their terraced homes in Braemar Road and clamber into the minibus heading to training at Osterley, a couple of miles away, where the club rented pitches. They went with the apprentices, carrying the balls, training kit and boots. The driver was whoever had a licence, ruling out Bowles.

As a schoolboy Hurlock had joined West Ham but, as he grew into his teenage years, he rebelled against the discipline imposed on him at the club. At 15 he was pressured by one coach to lose weight, instructed to wear a woollen tank top while training to lose a few extra pounds. Hurlock was something of a free spirit: although his family lived in a block of flats in Walthamstow, he grew up around gypsies: his father came from a Romany family and another of his close relatives would marry a traveller. Sometimes, he could not stomach the daily routine and would complain of a headache, skip training and go to pubs or nightclubs with friends. If he got into trouble, he would disappear into a traveller camp.

Hurlock was jettisoned by West Ham after one season as a professional. He worked as a labourer and window cleaner while playing non-league football for Leytonstone. He was seen by Callaghan, who offered him a £1,500 signing-on fee and

---

12 Author interview with Christine Mathews.

£300 per week to play for Brentford. For Hurlock, it was a no brainer – more money for less work.

Reporting for pre-season training Hurlock arrived by train at Brentford station one June morning in 1981 and walked to Griffin Park, where he found a few players practising in the forecourt while they waited for the coaching staff to arrive. Hurlock had a mane of untamed curly black hair, a beard and a golden hoop earring in each ear (one hoop was bigger than the other). He was wearing a t-shirt, scruffy jeans and moccasins. Among the group playing keepy-uppy with the ball was Paul Walker. He was a couple of years younger than Hurlock but was already starting his fifth season at the club, having joined as a 15-year-old trainee. Walker had floppy blond hair. He looked up from under his fringe at Hurlock, who was standing there watching them. 'What do you want?' Walker asked. 'The painters are in the other stand.'

'I ain't a painter,' Hurlock replied.[13]

Lange arranged for Hurlock to get a mortgage on a £24,000 two-bedroom terraced house opposite the main gate of Griffin Park where, the chairman told him, club staff could keep an eye on him. Over the coming months teenaged apprentices listened through the fire door at half-time during home matches as Hurlock let rip if he felt any of his teammates were not giving their all. He was a ferocious tackler. Hurlock and fellow midfielder Chris Kamara would intimidate opponents even before the game had started. Kamara was known for his

---

13 Author interview with Terry Hurlock.

sliding tackles that were especially effective at chopping down opponents on a sodden pitch.

On the left flank Bowles remained wonderfully good. He seemed to be a second or two ahead of everyone. He could slalom through defenders, wrong-footing them at every turn; he could trap the ball dead, and then, with the outside of his boot, deliver it to the feet of a teammate. He had, Terry Venables once said, a 'left foot like a hand'.[14] He enjoyed himself even in the third division, although he occasionally lost his patience with Hurlock for not anticipating his beautifully weighted passes.

Quiet off the pitch, Bowles was a showman on it. He liked to play to the crowd, even with only a few thousand people watching him at Brentford. Once, the referee ordered him to move the ball back five yards before taking a free-kick. Bowles made a show of grudgingly obeying the official's insistence to keep retreating, yard by yard. Finally, when the referee was satisfied the ball was in the right place and had turned his back, Bowles winked to the crowd and, as if he was in a pantomime, lobbed the ball back to where it had been at the start.

Francis Joseph was also a joy to watch. He was a striker who could unleash a 25-yard thunderbolt at a moment's notice, with a reasonable chance of finding the net. When he had the ball at his feet, fans would shout, 'Have a go, Joe!' He could also hold his own with the toughest defenders, swearing at them with gusto when they fouled him.

---

14 Or, as Paul Hince, a journalist at the *Manchester Evening News* who'd played with Bowles as a schoolboy at Manchester City, famously noted: 'He could open a can of beans with that left foot.' (Quoted in Rob Steen's *The Mavericks: English Football When Flair Wore Flares*.)

Joseph was among the first group of children born to the Windrush generation, the Caribbean diaspora who arrived in London in the 1950s and 1960s. His mother, who came from the tiny island of Dominica, spoke a French dialect, and did not usually come to matches, preferring to cook and watch television soap operas, but his father and brothers, Lawrence and Roger, came along. The four Josephs were more than welcome at Griffin Park. 'If you played for Brentford,' Joseph said, 'you knew this was your home.'[15]

While Bowles and Hurlock took the minibus with the apprentices, most players drove to training. Sometimes, they congregated beforehand for a bacon sandwich and tea at a café opposite the training pitches. When they had been out over the weekend for a few lagers and a curry, Hurlock would sometimes go over 15 stone on the scales; he would then tear a hole in the top of a black bin bag and put it on under his training top to work up a sweat and lose a few pounds. (Unlike at West Ham, he did this on his own volition.)

The most dreaded part of the year for players was pre-season. Straight after their summer holidays, they had to run around the seven-mile circumference of Richmond Park. To make sure they did not cut corners, coaching staff would stand at the park gates and tick off each player when they passed by. Sometimes they would top it off by sprinting to the top of a half-mile climb that was steep enough to induce vomiting. At the time, sports

---

15 Francis Joseph interview, Brentford match programme, versus Leeds United, 3 September 2022; Roger Joseph would also play for Brentford.

science did not really exist in English football, certainly not at Brentford. The idea you had to hydrate before, during and after physical exercise was not impressed upon players, who for refreshment might drink a pint of milk on any given day. At half-time during games, they ate sliced-up oranges and drank cups of tea.

Throughout the season, there would be surprise weight checks when players had to stand on a set of old-fashioned doctor's scales. The trainer-cum-physiotherapist, Eddie Lyons, would also apply steel callipers to each player's midriff to check their body fat. He had been a lower-league player in the 1950s and, at some point, switched his responsibilities from trainer to physio at Brentford.[16] Some players suspected his methods lacked scientific rigour. It was the era of the so-called magic sponge when physios ran onto the pitch with cold water to treat an injured player. On match days, Brentford would pay a local GP to attend games in case there was a more serious injury.

The uncovered Ealing Road terrace had served as an outdoor gym for decades. Sprinting up the incline boosted power and burned calories. Soon after spraining his ankle one season, Hurlock was instructed by Lyons to build up his fitness again by running up the terrace steps – while giving him a piggyback. The idea was that carrying a load on his back would accelerate Hurlock's return to fitness. While the physio weighed as little as ten stones, it was clear to Hurlock that this was by no means a good idea with a still-tender ankle. He felt like he was on

---

16 Eddie Lyons had played for Crewe and Rochdale among other teams.

completely the opposite route to recovery. 'I'm on the wrong train,' he told himself.[17]

Bowles and Hurlock became friends as well as neighbours. They found there was still a considerable margin for some fun at third division Brentford that had been lacking at first division Nottingham Forest and West Ham. They used to drink at the Bricklayers Arms, less than 100 metres from Griffin Park. The pub was set amid terraced houses on Ealing Road, its name sculpted in stone into the cream façade above a first-floor bay window; it predated the stadium by some 50 years. It was not much bigger than a living room. There was a dart board in the corner. The locals, most of them Brentford fans, treated the pair more like neighbours than footballers. Bowles would sit along one wall, playing cards with friends from his QPR days. The atmosphere was relaxed and convivial, a typical boozer where everyone knew each other, their habits and foibles.

On Wednesday, a day off, the whole squad would gather at the pub for drinks, and later move on to the Princess Royal and the Griffin. The first-team players would pay for the rounds of the apprentices who were earning only a few pounds a week. One fresh-faced recruit joined the midweek pub crawl immediately after signing for Brentford. By the end of the evening he was in no fit state to return to his home north of London, so Hurlock agreed to put him up for the night at his home in Braemar Road, dragging him up the stairs by his legs.

---

17 Hurlock, ibid. In the 1980s Arsenal players were also instructed to run up the terraces at Highbury while carrying a teammate on their backs, according to Paul Merson's autobiography, *Hooked*.

As he lugged him up to the first floor like a sack of coal, the teenager's head bumped on each step. 'Welcome to Brentford,' his teammates joked the next day.[18]

Sometimes, Hurlock would take Bowles to meet his friends in east London. Once, Hurlock borrowed the keys to the team minibus that ferried players to training from Christine Mathews, the club secretary, 'to go around the corner' to fetch something: instead, he drove it around the North Circular ring road to Walthamstow to go out with friends, returning the vehicle to Griffin Park before it was needed at 10 a.m. to take the players to training.

Bowles would take Hurlock to unlicensed gambling houses – or spiels – he went to in Ladbroke Grove, Notting Hill and Shepherd's Bush. The word 'spiel' derives from the Yiddish *spieler*, meaning 'gambler'. Such gatherings were started in 1920s Soho by Jewish immigrants and the Oriental community in Chinatown, before extending to other parts of London. They might be in the backrooms of minicab firms or in basement flats with blacked-out windows, and would typically run around the clock, with a steady supply of tea, alcohol, sandwiches and marijuana.[19] (When they visited, Hurlock and Bowles would stick to tea or beer.) In these places you could get pretty much anything that took your fancy at a discount price. 'If you said, "I could do with a Crombie coat," they would go and get it for you,' one visitor in the 1980s said.[20]

---

18 Author interview with Jamie Bates, who witnessed the episode as a Brentford apprentice.
19 *Independent*, 28 July 1996.
20 Author interview with source who spoke off the record.

On a Saturday afternoon, an hour before kick-off, Bowles could be found in the Bricklayers Arms studying a copy of the *Racing Post*. He would have his breakfast there – coffee and a sausage sandwich. The pub was 50 metres from a branch of Coral, but there was a public phone by the bar from which he could ring in bets to a bookmaker.

At the time, betting on football was dull: by law, to avoid the risk of match-fixing, you could only bet on the outcome of a combination of three games – a treble – and you would have to wait until 5 p.m. on a Saturday afternoon to see if you had won. Horse and greyhound racing, however, gave punters a quick-hit adrenaline rush. You could place your bet and find out whether you had won within ten minutes or so. Bowles was addicted to the buzz. He liked to bet on the 2.30 p.m. horse races and did not see the point of being in the changing room half an hour early. Slightly anxious, a supporter approached him once in the Bricklayers Arms and asked: 'Stan, aren't you playing today?'

Looking up, Bowles shrugged. 'Don't worry, I'll be there.'

At QPR his pre-match ritual had drawn the ire of the manager Dave Sexton. Bowles did not see why Sexton made such a fuss. 'All you had to do was get your fucking kit on and away you go,' he said.[21]

He would arrive in the Griffin Park changing room in his beige Crombie mac with 15 minutes to spare as the rest of his teammates, already wearing their kit, were doing their pre-

---

21 Stan Bowles interview, *QPR Report*, 5 February 2009.

match stretching. The air was thick with Ralgex, a pungent painkiller that players rubbed onto sore calves and thighs still damaged from previous games. Bowles quickly pulled on his team shirt. It was a plain polyester V-neck without any marking save a small logo of the maker, an obscure brand called Osca.[22] Then, under the red and white top, he threw on a pair of black shorts and socks, laced up his black Adidas boots, and trotted down the tunnel and onto the pitch. He got away with his constant tardiness because, well, he was Stan Bowles.

He had made his first bet as a teenager in Manchester: he won £60 from a £5 stake on a horse, more than a month's wages in his part-time job, ironing raincoats in a factory. Even as a Manchester City apprentice, he had widened his knowledge of gambling by working as a runner placing bets for a streetwise group known as the Quality Street Gang. At QPR Bowles used to go to the greyhound races on weekday afternoons at White City stadium with Shanks, his friend who was raised on a council estate across the road. At the oval track there was a bar serving alcohol – and camaraderie among a few hundred punters drawn by idling away the afternoon and the anticipation of a winning bet. As they stood on a terrace exposed to the wind and rain to watch if their pick would come home, betting slips and litter swirled in the breeze.

Once, when feeling miserable at Nottingham Forest and pining for his favourite London dog track, three hours away by

22 Towards the end of Bowles's first season at Brentford, DHL became the club's first shirt sponsor.

car, Bowles hailed a taxi and asked to be taken to White City in time for the afternoon meeting.

Bowles said he may have burned through £500,000 on gambling.[23] He never developed a sophisticated betting strategy. For a bet to be worthwhile, there had to be an element of risk – it had to hurt if you lost, he said. On one occasion when he was flush, he bet £4,000 on a horse at odds of 11/4 at Newbury – it lost in a photo finish. That was indeed painful.

To try and contain his betting losses sucking up all his salary in a single weekend, Brentford would pay Bowles half of his weekly wage on a Friday and the other half on Monday. When Bowles was down to his last few pounds, he would bet as little as £25. When he did not have anything, he would ask Callaghan, the manager, for an advance on next week's wages.

After each home game, Chris Kamara wished everyone well and returned to his family; he lived down the M4 in Swindon, where his wife was from. Before leaving the changing room, Joseph, who was more footloose, would relax on the wooden bench and light a cigarette to help him decompress before heading to the Griffin Park bar. Players would field a few questions from reporters from three local newspapers.[24] Then Joseph would turn to Hurlock: 'What's the plan, Gyppo?' (Hurlock called Joseph 'Black Joe'.)[25]

If they walked into the Bricklayers Arms later, as they often did, the locals greeted them with little fanfare, as though they

---

23 *Stan Bowles, The Autobiography.*
24 *Ealing Gazette, Brentford and Chiswick Times,* and the *Middlesex Chronicle.*
25 Hurlock, ibid.

had just turned out for the pub team. 'All right, boys,' they might say. 'Well done today.' In the pub Joseph had an easy smile, except when suddenly, and without any warning, he would explode into a fit of giggles.

In 1982 Brentford had their best finish in 17 years, coming ninth. The next season they came eighth. To fans used to relegation scrapes, those years felt like they were the best of times. In the early hours of Sunday morning, Bowles would amble back to his home in Braemar Road, by the gates of Griffin Park, his hands thrust into the pockets of his Crombie mac. He never made it to America, settling in Brentford for the next 30 years.

Chapter 2

1880s: Brentford Dock

Today, Brentford is an unremarkable residential suburb
made up of rows of terraced houses, 1920s semi-detached
homes, and the six tower blocks of the Haverfield Estate, home
to the fictitious pirate station Kurupt FM in the BBC comedy
series *People Just Do Nothing*. The newest residential buildings
are several quite swanky riverside apartment blocks. Brentford
has no London Underground tube station, no major retail chain
shops on its humdrum High Street and relatively few attractions
to tempt tourists away from the West End.

There is a fine Georgian square called The Butts, a steam
museum near Kew Bridge, and on the Brentford–Isleworth
border, Syon House, whose gardens were painted in 1749 by
Venetian painter Canaletto for the Duke of Northumberland;
the current Duke maintains the mansion to this day. The
oil painting shows a bucolic summer scene of cows grazing,

and men in tricorne hats and breeches punting upriver from Brentford, then a small and scrappy working town.

The constituency of Brentford and Isleworth has flip-flopped between Conservative and Labour since the Second World War. In 2010 this slither of west London was described by the *Economist* as a Neapolitan ice cream slice of London 'made up of posh Chiswick in the east, predominantly white working-class Brentford in the middle and multicultural Hounslow in the west.' Contemporary Brentford is, for some people, just another layer of suburban London. In 2018 supporters of Queens Park Rangers levelled a chant at Brentford fans: '*You're just a bus stop in Hounslow.*'

In Victorian times, when waterways were the most efficient way of transporting goods, Brentford was an important transport hub because of its position at the confluence of the River Thames and the Grand Junction Canal.[1] At the time, transporting shipments by road and rail tended to be slower and so goods from across Britain passed through Brentford Dock. Cranes loaded and unloaded coal, steel and timber from barges. The wood and metal came by boat from the east and was sent on its way by canal to Birmingham, or by train to the west of England. From the other direction came coal from the Welsh mines of the Rhondda Valley destined for London.

When Brentford Football Club was founded in 1889, the town hummed with activity. It was the most important place for miles around. Apart from the dock, the landmarks of the

---

1 In 1929 the canal merged with other waterways, becoming the Grand Union Canal.

town were industrial: a sprawling gasworks that belched out black smoke across the Thames; a brewery from which wafted the stench of boiled hops; a soap factory's tall chimneys. The High Street stretched for two miles and was packed with pubs and shops.

Eight coal merchants traded on Brentford High Street. (At one stage, the Bricklayers Arms was owned by a coal merchant.) Some of the dirty black lumps powered Brentford's factories and polluted the town. Much of the rest was sent on its way by barge to heat homes in London, then the world's most populous city. A picture from 1896 shows a terraced house in Brentford coated in soot. From the ground-floor window a shopkeeper serves eels and mash. A group of children hang around outside. The girls are dressed in starched white dresses that stand out against the urban grime.[2] Nearby, overshadowed by the hulking machinery of the gasworks, hundreds of workers lived in terraced houses in five parallel streets each as long as 500 feet, where the tower blocks of the Haverfield Estate stand today. The air here would have been dirty and smelly. The rows of terraced houses looked like those in industrial Manchester.

By some accounts, the slums of Brentford by the riverside were more impoverished than those in the East End of London. In the muddy lanes that housed the scruffy clapboard homes of bargemen and eel fishermen,[3] you might have heard off-duty workers singing raucously from one of Brentford's 64 pubs.

---

2 Dan Jackson, *Positively Brentford: A Pictorial History of Brentford, 1896 to 1996*.

3 In Charles Dickens's *Our Mutual Friend*, written in 1865, the home of an orphan is described as lying among 'complicated back settlements of muddy Brentford'.

(When the football club was founded, Brentford had a pub for every 170 residents, three times as many per capita than neighbouring Chiswick.) In these back streets, side by side with the clapboard homes, workers dressed in overalls after a shift at the dock were welcome at ale houses. The establishments were basic: they had stripped wooden tables and floors, and outdoor toilets. There might be a small sign on the exterior, and little more. Men and women stumbled outside in an intoxicated stupor. After travelling through Brentford on a horse and cart to the family mansion at Gunnersbury in 1866, Charlotte de Rothschild wrote to her son, Leopold, that the 'the public houses are full to suffocation and women and children in rags and tatters are far too plentiful'.[4] Brentford was not a desirable place to live. It was noisy, polluted and congested working town. It was the workers who lived and worked there that helped to define Brentford and its football club.

Several of London's other professional football clubs were born by the river when the Thames was the heartbeat of industrial life. West Ham United started as Thames Ironworks and Shipbuilding Company in an inlet of the river at Bow. Arsenal were founded at Woolwich by munitions factory workers before moving north of the river. Millwall started life at a food cannery on the Isle of Dogs.

Brentford was also a stopping place for travellers heading to and from the West Country. On the High Street the pubs, dotted within a few metres of each other, were more luxurious

---

4 Gillian Clegg, *Brentford Past*.

in order to cater for the merchants and moneyed classes passing through. Inns competed for the attention of travellers by embellishing their exteriors with elaborate signs painted in golden hues. Some signs were sculpted into masonry or ironwork, the more elaborate the better. A bay window would filter a warm glow onto the street, inviting passers-by to come in from the cold and enjoy the comforts inside. In the saloon, there might be shiny bottle-green tiles and polished brass fittings. Twinkling lights would reflect off large mirrors. Seats would be upholstered.[5]

In an age before bar service became universal, potboys brought drinkers their beer in pewter mugs on a tray. Popular at the time was a dark malty brew called porter, named after the men who lugged goods to and from their destinations in London. These men preferred the fortifying beer to the watery ales of the time. The strongest version was stout porter, or just stout. While porter would fall out of fashion within a couple of decades in London, it lived on in a similar version by a Dublin-based brewer called Guinness.[6]

In the more upmarket establishments, the name of the brewer supplying each pub's beer was painted on the outside walls, or even chiselled into the stonework. The beer generally arrived in barrels by horse and cart. While the Royal Brewery in the High Street dominated the pub trade, Chiswick-based Fuller's also owned some of the town's taverns and ale houses.

---

5 Paul Jennings, *The Local: A History of the English Pub*.

6 Martyn Cornell's chapter on porter in *The Geography of Beer* (edited by Nancy Hoalst-Pullen and Mark W. Patterson).

In exchange for a modest levy of two guineas, you could even sell beer in pewter mugs from your living room. Often the only mark distinguishing these residential pubs was a sign on the door proclaiming: 'licensed to sell beer'. Pubs were not just a place to carouse. They could be used for almost anything: from eating and drinking; to sleeping and fornicating (in upstairs rooms); idling and working. A few of the larger pubs doubled up as workplaces for magistrates and coroners holding court on criminal cases and death inquests. Others were used by merchants to hand-pick gangs of 'lumpers' to unload coal from barges at Brentford Dock.

On weekdays, there was less pub debauchery. Indeed, Brentford had a fine selection of shops, particularly on the stretch now called Kew Bridge Road. Passers-by would trundle past an array of stores selling fine goods under steep awnings. Today's shrunken retail parade on Brentford High Street of takeaways and grocers does not compare with the bountiful wares the street once boasted. You could buy everything from top hats, straw boaters, cotton dresses and leather boots, to fine glass and chinaware. Indeed, Mrs de Rothschild would send the family driver and a couple of house staff from Gunnersbury to do the shopping. They were the best set of shops for miles around.

The working classes of Brentford who earned only a few pounds each week would not have had enough money to splash out on fine clothes and household goods. Also out of their price range were trips to the seaside and visits to music halls. One of the few entertainment venues in Brentford was a small theatre in a yard behind a jam factory off Ealing Road. The entrance fee was one penny (or two empty jam jars). Other than that, the pub trade had a virtual monopoly on the leisure time of the town's working classes. Going to the pub was one of the few treats of a life dominated by work. But even the sanctity of the pub was not completely safe from the virtuous middle classes. Magistrates decided there were too many pubs in Brentford. Armed with government powers they closed more than a dozen, removing the licence of landlords in return for financial compensation. Among the reasoning for their unilateral decisions, they cited drunken clients and poor hygiene.

Then, quite unexpectedly, towards the end of the Victorian era there was a shift in the habits of pub-goers. The fast-growing popularity of a new sport taking hold in London had begun emptying pubs of customers on Saturday afternoons. On a wooden door by the takeaway fish, eels and mash shop in 1896, where the group of young children were hanging around, a fly-poster appeared, advertising a game between the Second Grenadier Guards and a recently founded sporting association: Brentford Football Club. The entrance fee was 6d, or 2.5 pence, roughly the price of a pint of ale.[7]

Long before football arrived, rowing had been one of the most popular sports in London. The skill and athleticism of oarsmen who ferried passengers across the Thames in narrow wooden boats evolved into sporting competitions. The watermen were proud of their agility commanding wherries, which looked

---

7 Jackson, ibid.

like stripped-down gondolas. These rowers were perhaps less elegant and did not sing in the same rich baritone, but they were London's answer to the gondoliers of Venice.

There were several watermen in Brentford, some living above riverside pubs, who could be called on by travellers, sometimes raising them from their slumber, at short notice. The Watermans Arms at Ferry Lane dates to 1751 and still bears the coat of arms of the watermen's guild.[8] Also operating in Brentford, further to the east, were the lightermen who carried goods across the Thames in flat-bottomed boats, sometimes by royal appointment to Kew Palace.

In 1715 the watermen who worked around London Bridge held the first recorded race, a contest that still survives today. Later, the Oxford–Cambridge boat race, first held over a four-mile stretch of the Thames between Putney and Mortlake in 1845, drew massive crowds each spring, far more than it does today. There was a carnival atmosphere for this free sporting day out for Londoners. Days in advance, working-class women with no affiliation to either university would pick a side and wear a ribbon in their hair: dark blue for Oxford, or light blue for Cambridge. Middle-class men in suits sported navy or sky-blue handkerchiefs in their breast pockets; strips of one of the two shades were even displayed on dog collars.

When the big day came, spectators crowded along the riverbank to watch the race, risking injury for the best vantage point. Young men crawled onto the girders beneath Barnes

---

8 Gillian Clegg, *Brentford and Chiswick Pubs.*

Bridge to see the boats pass underneath them. On Hammersmith Bridge, they shimmied up an iron stanchion high above the crowds to get a bird's eye view. Along the course, watermen took to their wherries and tried their best to keep in sight of the eight oarsmen in each university boat. Steam-powered boats were laden with revellers who brought beer, wine and whisky to wash down their picnics. Friends and colleagues had small bets on the outcome. As the winning crew crossed the finishing line, top hats were tossed into the air.

In the era before radio and television, newspaper reporters devised ways to get the news of the winning boat out quickly, tying a light-blue or dark-blue ribbon to the leg of a carrier pigeon so that the bird could get the result to a telegraph office at Barnes or Richmond. Illustrators sketched the image of the winning moment and reporters on the press boat filed written reports by tossing them into watertight tin boxes to messenger boys in dinghies.[9]

Brentford held its own, more low-key regatta in August. The organising committee based themselves at the Oxford and Cambridge pub by Kew Bridge. The pub was a grand place with a bar, dinner service, boathouse and a fleet of boats for hire. In the summer months, just over the way from Kew Gardens and far enough from Brentford's polluted riverside, it would have been a pleasant spot to mess about on the water. When the site was excavated some 120 years later, builders found beer-

---

9 Christopher Dodd and John Marks, *Battle of the Blues: The Oxford & Cambridge Boat Race from 1829.*

bottle caps from a local brewery – Brentford's Royal Brewery – embedded in the riverbank, the traces of idyllic summer evenings by the waterside. When the day of the Brentford regatta came in August, bunting was put up, Brentford Rowing Club's claret and light blue flag was raised at the pub, and a banner was unfurled: 'Prosperity to the B.R.C.' As spectators massed on Kew Bridge in their best summer suits and dresses, a brass band played popular songs. The amateur rowing crews were not always highly skilled and, with the Thames at low tide, some of them ran aground on the mudbanks. But the regatta was a good day out, rounded off with prize-giving and, after dusk, a firework display.

As well as rowing, rugby was also popular. By the 1880s, match reports appeared in the thrice-weekly *Middlesex Independent* about amateur clubs, including Harlequins, London Scottish and Rosslyn Park. With contemporary sports still developing, rugby reports in its inky pages were laid out under the subheading of the sport's name at the time: 'football'.

It was in a meeting room at the Oxford and Cambridge in 1889, not long after the end of the summer, that a group of Brentford Rowing Club members turned their thoughts to winter. Several of the young men were the sons of small business owners. The middle classes tended to live in houses to the west of Brentford, as far away as possible from the stink and smoke of the gasworks. At the pub, they discussed taking up a sport to keep them fit in the colder months. Among them was Bill Dodge, one of four children from a Brentford family that lived on the bustling High Street. He was 23 years old. His father was in the building trade and had a small business as an undertaker, giving him and his wife enough to afford a live-in servant. Bill had trained as a surveyor and was an enthusiastic sportsman, if not particularly talented: he'd participated in the Brentford regatta that summer, without winning any prizes.

After some back and forth on the merits of rugby and football in the pub's large meeting room, Dodge and the other rowing club members held a vote on which one to pick as their club's winter sport. Football was still unfamiliar to many Londoners. The rules of Association Football were written in a pub in Covent Garden in 1863, but the game had spread much faster in the north and the Midlands than in London. In the capital, football tended to be the preserve of amateur teams, many of whose players had attended private schools. Dodge cast his vote for rugby, but football won out by eight votes to five. A note appeared on page two of the *Middlesex Independent* two weeks later, inviting members to join Brentford Football Club. The note said that gentlemen wishing to join the club should register by sending five shillings to the club secretary.[10] The word 'gentlemen' was loaded with meaning. In the lexicon of Victorian English this inferred men from the working classes were not welcome. Nevertheless, among the club's first draft of middle-class football players – schoolteachers, a merchant's clerk, a railway works manager and a solicitor – was a humble porter. This would set the tone of the new club. Within four

---

10 *Middlesex Independent*, 26 October 1889.

years, the local newspaper noted that the growing 80-strong membership 'was representative of all classes in the town'.[11]

The club's inaugural match was the following week against Kew on parkland alongside the terraced homes of Windmill Road in Brentford, where cattle owned by a local butcher grazed. After the cows were removed, Dodge and a friend cleared the field of cowpats with a shovel and pail. Most players lived within walking distance and ambled along the dirt roads of the town to meet before games at the Griffin pub in Brook Road, where they would exchange gossip while changing into their football gear: collared shirts, thick woollen socks and heavy boots.

Dodge played at full-back in Brentford's historic first game, a 1–1 draw against Kew which, in keeping with the hard-charging style of football at the time, was described by a newspaper report as 'fast and furious'. Eschewing short passing, players would boot the ball forwards and give chase. If they looked from afar like a band of wild Celts rushing back and forth on the battlefield, when you got closer you might have seen they were hardly warriors, wearing pomade to keep their hair in place and sporting pressed claret shirts. Their Brentford kit was based on the colours of the rowing club: claret, light blue and salmon.

Association Football was easy to follow and generally more entertaining than rowing. Flush with their weekly wage, Brentford's workers got into the habit of downing a few ales

---

11 *Middlesex Independent*, 8 March 1893,

in the pub and heading over to watch the match. Part of the attraction was cheering on their workmates or neighbours. As more members joined the club, the standard improved and Dodge lost his place in the team; he was appointed captain of a new second team.

Using the harsh vocabulary of the dockyards, spectators swore merrily, and hissed at the opposing goalkeeper of a rival neighbourhood team, Fulham. At one point, a fan – perhaps after an ale or two at lunchtime – got into a fight with a linesman. A few middle-class women who were watching left in horror, and extra police were called in to keep the peace.

The games were on the edge of the town, where the soot-stained houses of workers met lush meadows, tree-lined paths and grand townhouses with steps leading up to the front door. The Butts, set among orchards, was the grandest residential location: a square whose residents included a civil engineer and a retired admiral. Most fields were rented out to market gardeners growing apples, pears, cherries, plums, raspberries and strawberries – landowners preferring to let fields to gardeners rather than a football club that attracted some rowdy spectators. One man letting a field to the growing band of players decided to withdraw his offer at the last minute, leaving the amateur enthusiasts looking for another pitch. For the first fifteen years, Brentford Football Club was bounced around from field to field.

While the club may not have had a permanent home, it had a following that would turn up every Saturday. The men who came to games, dressed in suits and flat caps, could now be classed as fans. They were proud of the team – known as 'the Bs' – and wanted them not only to beat Fulham but also prevail over Hounslow, Southall, and Hanwell, which all had their own teams. In 1893, 72 Brentford supporters travelled by train for a match at Kensal in north London. On Boxing Day that year, the club arranged train travel for a friendly at Ipswich.

To encourage their team, the travelling Brentford supporters cried, '*Buck up, Bs!*' The Bs would become 'the Bees' because of a mistake by a newspaper reporter, who thought spectators were shouting, '*Buck up, Bees.*'[12] Whether by coincidence or not there was a brewery in the town called The Beehive, owned by the Gomm family. Harry Gomm was one of the first captains of Brentford Football Club. William was chairman of Brentford Rowing Club. Undoubtedly, the Gomm brothers would have liked the nickname, the Bees.

For a couple of decades London's neighbourhood teams were eclipsed by behemoths from the Midlands and the north. No clubs from the capital were in the inaugural English Football League. Aston Villa and West Bromwich Albion were the southernmost of the 12 founding members. By the time Brentford began playing on a public park cleared of cowpats in front of a few spectators, Bolton Wanderers were attracting 8,000 fans to their matches. The Bolton folk were even able to read a match report a couple of hours later in a Saturday evening sports paper. From 1898 to 1920 Brentford entered an amateur team in the second tier of the Southern League, competing against the

---

12 Eric White, with Graham Haynes, Rob Jex and Ian Westbrook, *100 Years of Brentford*.

likes of West Ham and Queens Park Rangers. On the fringes of the professional game, like other London teams, Brentford did not enter the FA Cup for the first 35 years of the competition. Brentford's management committee did not seem to mind much about not playing in the Football League: they saved on travel costs by playing in and around the capital, and London derbies generated more than enough interest among spectators.

The only major drawback to the north–south divide was that the financial might of northern clubs meant they could scoop up the best players. As an amateur club, Brentford repeatedly lost talent. To keep their standout players, Brentford went into the red by paying wages disguised as expenses. In the season that ended in 1899 the club's total travel expenses rose to £318 – almost eight average annual UK salaries.[13] In another dodgy deal, the club bought a barrel of Scotch whisky for a local employer in exchange for releasing a player on Saturday afternoons.

As professionalism flourished in the north, the London FA and the Middlesex FA were among the last guardians of amateurism in football. Sharing an office in Chancery Lane, both associations were overseen by posh administrators who had a deep dislike of professionalism. They enjoyed nothing better than to call out anyone dirtying the reputation of the amateur game: the London FA's address for telegrams was: OFFSIDE.[14] Brentford played in competitions organised by both associations but, in the event, it was the Middlesex FA who picked apart

---

13 Average income per head in Britain in 1900 was £42.70, www.nationalarchives.gov.uk.
14 London FA website.

Brentford's iffy finances. Brentford board members panicked, destroying accounting records, but the club was found guilty of subterfuge and suspended for a month. The punishment, handed down just before the Christmas of 1899, was embarrassing. In a subsequent home game against Upton Park only 180 spectators turned up, providing gate receipts of three pounds. Post-festive cheer was thin on the ground. At the end of January a meeting was held to decide whether the club should continue as a going concern. The rendezvous was at the Castle Hotel in Brentford High Street. The hotel, topped with three pitched gables, and a hall that was big enough to stage boxing matches and Christmas pantomimes, was where Brentford Rowing Club had held an annual banquet one autumn, its 75 members having a singalong around the piano. In a more sombre mood, the football club's members decided to persevere, on a miserly budget of four pounds a week. A few years earlier, a club photo taken in a walled garden had featured a cheerful array of 33 players, men in bowler hats and young boys in caps. Everyone wanted to be in the picture. Now, in front of a plain redbrick wall, there were just 11 players and three managers in flat caps. Professional football was a tough business.

Still, deciding to make their way cautiously at the roulette-wheel of the transfer market, Brentford secured permission to become semi-professional (transfer fees for players had existed since 1890). One of their first player signings was Lanarkshire-born inside-right Roddy McLeod. The Scots were the South American players of their time, known for having superior short passing and ball skills than the English – the imminent arrival of a Scot down south would create a *frisson* among fans, much like Brazilian and Argentine players arriving in England a century later. McLeod had played in two FA Cup finals with West Bromwich Albion. For the Bees to sign a Scotsman was a sign they were willing to take a tentative step towards full professionalism.

By the summer of 1901 Brentford had cut their amateur roots once and for all and the club became a limited liability company – Brentford Football and Sports Club Ltd – whose shareholders included three builders, a wine merchant, a town hall clerk, a merchant and the manager of a brewery. The ten directors included Bill Dodge and one of the other founding members, Harry Blundell. All of them were men and lived in Brentford, apart from one who resided in Twickenham.

The directors did not receive a salary but had the right to a season ticket and, if the club made a profit, a dividend payment. In an innovative financial move at the start of the season, the board gathered £300 in loans from members of the public with the promise that they would be repaid through ticket revenue during the season. An experienced football administrator called Dick Molyneux, who had worked at Everton, was hired as manager and, in a pre-season roadshow in the north of England, he hired a dozen players. During the 62-match season, which was packed with games to maximise ticket sales, attendances peaked at 3,834 for the visit of Tottenham Hotspur. The loans were paid back by February, long before the end of the season.

The club had a wealthy benefactor in Leopold de Rothschild, whose mother had written to him about the drunken behaviour in Brentford's slums when he was a child. Every Christmas, the Rothschilds sent 900 brace of pheasants to the London United Tramways Co., whose drivers and conductors wore the dark blue and gold colours of the family's racing silks for a week in January. The family also gave the land for a local school in Brentford. In Leopold's honour, Brentford FC abandoned the rowing club colours that had latterly seen them resembling Aston Villa's claret and blue and instead adopted the navy and gold stripes of the Rothschilds. (Brentford would not use red and white stripes until 1925.) The fabulously wealthy Rothschilds had a household staff of 25 at Gunnersbury House, where they entertained foreign royalty and ambassadors. The mansion's interior had glass chandeliers, marble fixtures and frescoes on the ceiling. The grounds were no less intricate, with a Japanese garden containing pretty bamboo bridges across streams. When motor cars first became readily available Leopold acquired a small fleet – made in Twickenham by Orleans – which his chauffeurs used to ferry guests to and from central London.[15]

In 1904 Brentford finally found a permanent home of their own: a five-acre orchard owned by Fuller's, the brewery, was secured on a 21-year lease by the club. Named Griffin Park – the Fuller's logo was a griffin – the new ground soon took shape over the summer. Apple trees were cut down, turf was laid, and embankments made of ash cinder and reinforced with timber were built around the pitch to improve the sightlines for spectators. The wall running along the New Road stand was,

---

15 Gillian Clegg, *Brentford Past.*

in a design flourish, topped with flowerpots. The pitch was set amid terraced houses and had a pub on each corner – which would prove handy for a pre-match drink and for conducting business: one of the four pubs, the Princess Royal, was used for club meetings. In their first game at Griffin Park in 1904, Brentford played out a draw against Plymouth Argyle in front of a crowd of 5,500.

The transformation of Brentford FC from a community team to a professional club coincided with the dawn of commuter transport when tram and train lines began to criss-cross the outskirts of London. Workers no longer had to walk to work, allowing residents to escape the filth of Brentford's riverside. The Dickensian slum homes in side streets running down to the Thames were cleared. Families moved to newer housing in neighbouring districts like Ealing and Hounslow. Businesses followed their customers to these areas, which were more aspirational. All this change meant that Brentford was losing its dominant position in the region, and gradually melting into the suburbia of west London. As commerce left Brentford, so did some of the pubs. Boozers in the town were shutting down at the rate of almost one a year until the mid-1930s. Among those to close was the Black Boy and Still, which had served beer on the High Street since the 1700s.[16]

Not all was lost, though. The expanding train and tram network that allowed working men to move away from

---

16 Brentford High Street Project, research published on www.bhsproject.co.uk. Under licensing rules aimed at restricting the number of pubs in west London, brewers had to get permission to switch licences from one address to another.

Brentford also brought them back to Griffin Park on Saturday afternoons. The children and grandchildren of the first supporters continued to follow the same team. Football fans were, it would turn out, a loyal bunch. As Chelsea, QPR, Fulham and Brentford established themselves as professional clubs in west London, other teams without established working-class backing faded.

In their first two decades as a professional operation, Brentford were hardly a powerhouse: they advertised for new players in the local press, relied on more than a few journeymen and, for a couple of games at the start of 1914, called up a vicar to join their forward line. (Reverend Herbert Farnfield's parish was in Highbury.) For the twelve seasons until the outbreak of the First World War, they finished no higher than mid-table in the Southern League Division One. Then they were relegated to the second tier, which meant facing off against faraway teams from the Welsh valleys. However, for FA Cup ties and local derbies, Brentford could still be a draw and pull in as many as 14,000 people to Griffin Park.

One of those local clubs to fade was Barnes FC, which was located in a crook of the Thames, a much quainter setting than the rough riverside at Brentford. Barnes was the foremost football club in south-west London in the earliest days of Association Football, playing in 13 of the first 14 years of the FA Cup, long before Brentford entered football's oldest cup competition. Indeed, Barnes co-founder Ebenezer Morley, a solicitor, wrote in looping handwriting the original 13 rules of the game for the FA in a booklet of meeting minutes that is today valued at £2.5 million.[17]

Morley also organised one of the earliest football matches recorded – a trial match against Richmond at Barnes Elms that finished 1–1 – but the importance of Barnes as a football pioneer in south-west London is often forgotten. Then, as now, football was about the survival of the fittest – and with a management committee tied to amateurism, and few loyal supporters, Morley's club dropped into local leagues before disappearing into the mists of time.[18]

---

17 British Library press release, August 2013.
18 In 2021, about 60 years after disappearing, Barnes FC were re-established.

Chapter 3

1930s: The Great West Road

Not long after the dawn of mass-produced motor cars, drivers zipped down a new four-lane highway cutting through Brentford past pristine factories housed in white, low-slung art deco buildings. Companies on the Great West Road, some of them American, were attracted by cheap land, good transport links and proximity to London. They used their buildings to present their brands as the cutting edge of cool. They made everything from perfume and toothpaste to swimwear and car tyres. At night neon lights lit up the company names: Gillette, Macleans, Firestone and Coty, a cosmetics maker.

The stretch of the road at Brentford became known as the Golden Mile and had an air of the American dream. It was a pantheon of consumerism, supplying the growing list of essential accoutrements of suburban life in southern England. To the author J. B. Priestley, visiting in 1933, the Great West

Road 'did not look English. We might suddenly have rolled into California.'[1]

One of the first companies to move in, around the time the road was opened by King George V in 1925, was Firestone. As the tyre maker opened a new factory in Los Angeles, it chose Brentford for a UK base, building a grand whitewashed facility where hundreds of workers, some dressed in white shirts and ties, sculpted rubber for cars. Inside, there was a lunch canteen and drinking fountains.

A few hundred metres east towards Chiswick, the front of Henly's car showroom looked a little like today's Formula One pit lanes. It had a sweeping forecourt with 22 petrol pumps offering a range of fuels. Through the window were rows of gleaming Jaguar and Studebaker motor cars. Next door, with its façade featuring pavement-to-roof colonnades, was the headquarters of Smith's Potato Crisps. The company founded in 1920, nine miles away in Cricklewood, was the purveyor of a new fad: packets of crisps (with a blue sachet of salt) that were a suitable accompaniment to pints of beer. These were becoming Britain's premier pub snack.

This new cleaner era of electricity began to mark a slow change from the dirty coal that had powered industrial Brentford. At first, there was only a smattering of cars on the Great West Road at any one time. With the speed limit abolished in 1930, few road markings and inexperienced drivers, there were many accidents. But the road changed Brentford. The building of

---

1 J. B. Priestley, *English Journey*.

the highway meant that travellers no longer had to squeeze through the High Street, which was only a few metres wide in the narrowest sections and frequently congested with horse-drawn carts and trolleybuses coming and go, not to mention the activity that spilled over from the dock and factories. From now on, the new highway meant the importance of the river and canal would dissipate (Brentford Dock would shut down completely in 1964). The axis of Brentford had shifted, about half a mile to the north.

Amid an interwar house-building boom, new suburban homes were developed in outer London, and the Piccadilly Line was extended to Osterley and Hounslow. Owning your own house had never been more affordable: an annual salary of £200 was enough to secure a mortgage. Among the new homeowners in Hounslow, Osterley and Cranford at the time were a railway station foreman, a toolmaker for car parts, a metal-plate engraver and a carpet salesman.

Some of the biggest private landowners on the fringes of Brentford made way for this new suburban landscape. The Rothschilds sold their mansion and grounds – including the land on which the Brentford stadium stands today – to public authorities. Another family, the Clitherows, who had also grown wealthy from banking, sold their Jacobean mansion, along with its elegant furniture and a couple of oil paintings by Dutch masters that decorated the walls.[2]

2 Janet McNamara, 'Brentford's Jewel: Boston Manor House', www.brentfordandchiswicklhs. org.uk. The Clitherows left the house in 1924, and it fell into disrepair. The house was opened to the public in 2023 after being restored.

Brentford may have changed, but the football club remained important. They had joined the Football League in 1920 and, after remaining in Division Three (South) for more than a decade, were finally starting to gain some momentum. In fact, the art deco factories on the Great West Road and tens of thousands of new suburban homes gave Brentford FC a new audience. Many of the workers clocked off from the factories at lunchtime on a Saturday and headed straight to the football. (The start of matches was adjusted to align with factory shifts, with kick-off sometimes at 2.45 p.m. or 3.15 p.m.) Hundreds, if not thousands, of men massed waiting to cross the road to get to the match. Police stopped the traffic and, through loudspeakers, directed the crowds towards Griffin Park.

From the new suburbia, came more Brentford fans. From Hounslow, they packed into cars and minibuses. From Ealing and Hanwell, they arrived by trolleybus. By the mid-1930s, football was ingrained into the lives of Londoners: it was the talk of factory floors. The size of Saturday afternoon crowds at Griffin Park was comparable with the attendance at Liverpool's Anfield and was bigger than the throng at Leeds United.

To meet demand, Brentford enlarged their ground to sell more tickets. They extended the Brook Road terrace, building a roof over it, and increased Griffin Park's capacity to 30,000. An Ealing furniture store paid to paint its name on the roof of the New Road stand, and there were billboards around the perimeter of the pitch for Oxo, Bovril and Rizla. The cheapest ticket to stand on the terrace cost a shilling, less than the price of a pack of cigarettes. The most expensive tickets cost two shillings and six pence for the wooden flip-up seats in one section of the Braemar Road stand.

As football in London boomed, so did the pools. In the ensuing gold rush, more than a hundred pools operators started up; soon British households were spending as much as £20 million a year (£1.2 billion in today's money) on a weekly flutter. Sacks of coupons would arrive by post at the whitewashed art deco headquarters of Littlewoods, the biggest operator, which was based in Liverpool. Women, sitting side by side on benches, sifted through the coupons one by one to check who was entitled to a share of the winnings. At the time off-course gambling was illegal and so, in something of a charade, win or lose, pools players did not send in their stake of a penny or two until the following week, allowing the game to exist in a grey area, somewhere between betting and bingo.

In suburban London, winning the pools was seen as a conduit to a new semi-detached home, a Baby Austin motor car and a seaside holiday. Housewives not normally interested in football would sit next to the transistor radio on a Saturday afternoon listening to the results to see if they had won a share of the spoils. Their dreams were fomented by tabloid newspapers which covered the life-changing stories of winners. The *Daily Mirror*, which sold more than one million copies a day, appeared to have an inside line from Littlewoods about the biggest winners. In 1937 a 52-year-old carpenter from Tottenham found out from a reporter that he had won what the *Mirror* called a sum that was 'a world record in football pools'. Reuben Levy was due £30,780 – the equivalent of £1.7 million today.

A picture in the paper showed him standing outside his home on a council estate pointing to a six-pence – the amount he had staked. Levy handed in his notice at the cabinet factory where he worked and told his manager, 'You can keep my tools.' His wife, wearing a pinafore, and apparently informed of the news while doing household chores, was 'trembling with excitement' as she looked through the pages of a fashion magazine, picking out dresses she fancied.

To keep fans, who were predominantly boys and men, coming back to Griffin Park every other Saturday, Brentford sought to build a team that was successful – a task the board had handed to general manager Harry Curtis.[3] Louis Paul Simon – later the Brentford chairman – had been impressed by his quick mind when Curtis held the corresponding role at Gillingham.[4] After agreeing to an initial 12-month contract, Curtis arrived with his wife in Brentford on a May evening in the spring of 1926. They planned to go house-hunting near Griffin Park. When they got off a tram on the Ealing Road, it was pouring with rain, and they could smell the stench of the gasworks nearby. It was not the most inviting place. 'I wondered,' Curtis said, 'if I had made a mistake.'[5]

The stadium was more welcoming. Griffin Park had a full-size billiards table, a stove to make tea and warm the changing

---

3 His official title was 'secretary-manager'.
4 *Brentford and Chiswick Times* journalist Alan Hoby, in the foreword to *The 'Bees' Sketch Book, 1936–37*.
5 David Lane and Mark Croxford, *Harry Curtis: Brentford's Golden Era*.

room, as well as showers with hot water. Curtis and his wife moved into a terraced house at 258 Windmill Road in Ealing, a 15-minute walk from Griffin Park and far away enough to avoid the worst of the smell from the gasworks. He turned up to work at the ground every morning in suit, tie and waistcoat. His role was all-encompassing: he recruited players, negotiated with advertisers, paid the utility bills and ensured the stadium was well-maintained. His wife also got involved when necessary, acting as an emergency midwife when the wife of a player went into labour. One of the few things Curtis did not do was coach – that was the task of the trainer, Bob Kane, who had come with him from Gillingham and whose main job was to oversee training and try to ensure players were healthy, relaxed and rested.

At the time, Brentford were in the lower reaches of Division Three (South) and short of cash. Curtis had a good eye for talent and went about signing up young footballers, instead of splashing out in the transfer market. If they were too young or inexperienced to turn professional, they might be offered a job helping the groundsman or club secretary, a role they could combine while training with the reserves. Players would typically sign for a season, no more, but they were generally a talented bunch. 'Gone were the days,' a club history said, 'when Brentford signed almost anything in boots.'[6]

The pay at Brentford tended to be way below the £8-per-week maximum wage for professional footballers. Joe James, a

---

6 White, et al, *100 Years of Brentford*.

19-year-old centre-half whose previous job had been working at a chemical factory, was spotted by Curtis while playing for a team representing a church in Battersea. He was paid £3 per week, with an extra £1 for every first-team appearance.

James would become team captain, and an expert in shutting down attacks. Because of the ultra-attacking style of play of the era, Brentford continued to leak an average of more than a goal per game, but James limited the damage by chasing down forwards and heading away crosses. His income increased a little over the coming seasons, eventually allowing him to move into a terraced house in Ruskin Avenue, Kew.[7] As he settled into life at Brentford, Curtis worked hard but also had a taste for a good time. In his office at Griffin Park he studied the form of racehorses and greyhounds, reportedly using one of the phones on his desk for football business and the other for betting.[8] He owned a couple of greyhounds himself and would sometimes take Brentford players on an afternoon team-bonding trip to one of London's 20 dog tracks for a bet and a beer.

By the late 1920s Arsenal were turning into the premier team in London by some distance. They had been the first club in the capital to enter the Football League in 1893, even if in those early years they could not compete with the likes of Aston Villa and Newcastle United. To increase crowds Arsenal relocated from Woolwich in south London to a strategic spot in north London, one with a bigger catchment area, next to

---

7 Copy of James's contract shared with author by club historian Rob Jex.
8 Lane and Croxford, ibid. Undated interview in the People with Jack Chisholm, who played for Brentford in the 1940s.

Gillespie Road underground station in Highbury. After hiring the manager of league champions Huddersfield Town, Arsenal transformed themselves into a match for the clubs from the north and Midlands. Herbert Chapman led them to their first league title in 1931, when they became the first team from London to be crowned champions. The Gunners won again in three of the next four years, becoming so well established that the tube station got a new name: Arsenal. In keeping with the fashion of the time, they built an art deco façade to the East Stand, along with a terrazzo hallway and cocktail lounge.

In west London, Chelsea were as rich as Arsenal, if not as successful. In 1904 a property developer called Gus Mears had wanted to build London's pre-eminent sports stadium on the site of an athletics arena close to Walham Green tube station, now Fulham Broadway. When Fulham declined his offer to move from Craven Cottage to play at Stamford Bridge, he started his own team, naming it after the adjoining and posher neighbourhood of Chelsea.

While Brentford had dallied in regional divisions for decades, Chelsea walked straight into the big national championship, the Football League. Thanks to their new stadium, and good transport links, they were an instant attraction: for one of their first home games in the league – against Manchester United – 67,000 people turned up. When Gus died, his brother Joseph Theophilus took over, adding a royal box at Stamford Bridge.[9]

---

9 Rick Glanvill, *Chelsea FC, the Official Biography, the Definitive Story of the First 100 Years.* One of the first members of staff Chelsea hired was Brentford club secretary William Lewis.

Joseph lived in a gothic mansion called Royston House, opposite Kew Gardens. He had business interests including Ford car dealerships, cinemas and Thames steamboat cruisers and, in today's money, was a billionaire.[10]

Brentford chairman Louis Paul Simon was from an entrepreneurial family of somewhat humbler origins. He was the son of Camille, a French chef who as a young man had emigrated to the UK. In a book published in 1872 a visiting Frenchman in Britain said that unless a restaurant had a Gallic cook, the diners could 'take no pleasure in eating'. He came across tasteless fare including greasy meat and bland vegetables without seasoning or sauce.[11] Camille added some French techniques to West End restaurants. After toiling in London kitchens for a while, he started a laundry business at Strand-on-the-Green on the north side of Kew Bridge. Clients of the family business, which was in a building called Pier House, by the Thames, included hotels and restaurants. Two hundred staff worked there, some of them Brentford residents, and there was a laundry drop-off point at 273a Brentford High Street.[12] The service was advertised in the club's match-day programme, along with that of a local mechanic, and a Great West Road tea bar.

Louis Paul Simon was co-opted onto the club's board, becoming first treasurer and then chairman. In middle age,

---

10 Glanvill, ibid. Joseph Mears left a will of £30 million.

11 Hippolyte Taine, *Taine's Notes on England*.

12 The façade of the Pier House building is listed and leased for office space; among recent tenants was the sports management company IMG; a paved area and small garden stands on the site of the original laundry building.

he had a distinguished aura: with his olive skin, silver hair and well-cut suits, he could have passed for a Parisian solicitor, or statesman. He wore the same wing collar favoured by the political elite. When he handed over silver tea sets to players at an end-of-season ceremony, he looked much more formal among them than Curtis, who usually wore a smile on his face.

Back then, nobody at the club held out much hope that Brentford could compete with the might of Arsenal and Chelsea, both of whom frequently commanded gates of more than 50,000 and had teams stocked with internationals. In an interview in 1930, Curtis warned that London's biggest clubs might one day kill off the smaller teams like Brentford, Orient and Queens Park Rangers.

Nevertheless, by his fourth season, he had built a consistent team on a modest budget, and crowds were coming to home games from miles around. West of London there was no professional club until Reading, some 35 miles away in Berkshire. Brentford won every home match of the 1929–30 season, just missing out on promotion to join Reading in the second division. They finished second to Plymouth Argyle – at the time only one club went up. The fine job Curtis was doing attracted the attention of Tottenham Hotspur, but he ruled out a move, cementing his loyalty to Brentford.

He installed a gifted player in each position, and there was often a budding understudy waiting in the reserves. Whenever someone moved on, Curtis found a replacement, spending, if necessary, the odd thousand pounds on transfer fees. With an average age of 25, the team's energy and efficient style of play made them the team to beat; they were promoted as champions in 1933. They tarried just two seasons in Division Two, their winning mentality helping them to end the 1934–35 season undefeated again at Griffin Park. Within a decade of stepping off a tram in Brentford, Curtis had led the team to the first division. Along with Arsenal and Chelsea, the Bees became the third London club in the top division, Tottenham having been relegated the previous season. The only other club of the 22 teams that was from south of Birmingham was Portsmouth.

A journalist who covered the club for the *Brentford and Chiswick Times* at the time, put the club's ascent down to a clear strategy shared by the chairman and manager. He noted the successful recruitment of young players by Curtis based not only on talent but also on their character, and how his management had engendered a healthy team spirit.[13] It was some achievement: on the way to the first division, Brentford had spent less than £5,000 on transfer fees.[14]

During the summer of 1935, nobody at Griffin Park knew quite what to expect from the first division. On the eve of the new campaign, Curtis said they would stick with the policy that had served them so well. They would continue to develop talent, rather than spending in the transfer market. For the first game of the top-flight season, Brentford fielded seven players who'd helped the club win promotion from the third division two years earlier (they opened with a 2–0 win at Bolton). Building

---

13 Hoby, ibid.
14 White, ibid.

work to expand the stadium in time for the visits of Arsenal, the league champions, and Chelsea was still ongoing in a corner of Griffin Park when their first home game – against Blackburn Rovers – kicked off at 2.45 p.m. on 5 September 1935. The New Road terrace was given extra standing room and a new roof; the upgrades increased the ground's capacity to almost 40,000, making it among the biggest stadiums in the south of England. With crowds milling in the streets outside, the gates had to be closed ten minutes before kick-off. The terraces were packed with men in trilbies and flat caps, and boys in shorts squeezed their way through to the edge of the pitch, from where they watched on their knees. Brentford won again, 3–1.

After those two early victories, Brentford won only two of their next 17 matches. During that run was the visit of Arsenal: a meeting billed by the local newspaper as the first between the league champions from north London and 'the Cinderellas' from west London. Such was the demand for tickets that there was a proposal mooted to hold the derby match at Wembley stadium. Curtis said no to that, favouring home advantage over extra cash from gate receipts.

Some 35,000 fans turned up at Griffin Park for the game. Brentford went 2–0 up before, with ten minutes to go, Arsenal pulled a goal back. The noise at the end was deafening as home fans willed on the Bees, who held on for the victory. It was a rare success: that autumn, the club lurched from one defeat to another, making home games uncomfortable viewing. One Brentford fan, observed by a writer in the press seats, watched a match against Liverpool in a state of nervous panic: his 'stomach turn upside down' when the game began, he was fearful each time the opponent pressed forwards.[15] By late November Brentford were in the relegation zone.

Sometime after 9 p.m. on a November evening that season, Harry Curtis, a short and stocky man with a pleasant disposition, walked through the hall of Euston train station, beneath its square panelled roof befitting a Renaissance chapel. Above a doorway was a white marble sculpture of Britannia sitting by Mercury, the god of travellers and commerce. Curtis had a cheque for £5,500 in his pocket.

Steam from the locomotives rose upwards towards the station's glass roof. Porters idled, waiting for the train from Edinburgh. On the incoming *Flying Scotsman* was Hearts centre-forward Dave McCulloch who, at age 24, had just broken into Scotland's national team. McCulloch had set off at lunchtime on the seven-hour journey to London.

With Brentford facing a quick return to the second division, Curtis had made a volte-face on his pre-season recruitment plans. A couple of days earlier he had persuaded the board to sanction £15,000 to spend on new players. It was an extraordinary amount of money for Brentford, three times as much as they had spent in the previous five years.

Curtis had watched McCulloch play for Hearts at Chelsea and was confident he would bring more goals to his ailing team.

---

15 Match report, 'Brentford 1, Liverpool 2', by Lionel Louch, *Middlesex County Times*, 21 December 1935.

He'd spent all week on the phone haggling over a transfer fee with the Edinburgh club. Hearts had financial difficulties and needed to sell, but there were other suitors. Hearts eventually agreed to cede him to Brentford for £5,500. The Hearts general manager had travelled with McCulloch on the train down to London with a view to picking up the cheque. By the time the pair arrived the evening papers across the country were reporting that Brentford had signed McCulloch. To his annoyance, Curtis found a huddle of newspaper photographers and journalists had gathered, waiting to photograph the striker as he stepped off the train – even though he had yet to agree personal terms.

Curtis and McCulloch convened in a refreshment buffet off the main hall at Euston. The photographers snapped away, their flashbulbs lighting up the hall. Sitting across the table from one another, Curtis lit a cigarette and tried to get down to business, but they were disturbed by the media's presence so retired to a nearby station hotel to continue their discussions. At one point, perhaps as a negotiating tactic, McCulloch said he wanted to return on the next train to Edinburgh – but the deal was eventually closed at 1.20 a.m.[16]

The following afternoon, hundreds of miles from home and after only a few hours' sleep, McCulloch rolled up the sleeves of a cotton shirt in red and white stripes, pulled on a pair of baggy black shorts that, even on his big frame, reached his knees, and laced up some sturdy brown boots. As the crowd cheered,

---

16 Lane and Croxford, ibid.

Brentford's record signing ran onto the pitch at Griffin Park to play Leeds. By the end of the afternoon, he looked like he would be a good investment, scoring the second goal in a 2–2 draw.

There were no restrictions on signing during the season and in a matter of weeks Curtis had also brought in Wales left-half Dai Richards, from Wolves, and winger Bobby Reid, from Hamilton Academical. With their new firepower Brentford stormed up the league, McCulloch leading the charge. He had the attributes of a comic-strip striker: he was fast, dominant in the air and possessed a fearsome shot. It was necessary to give the stitched brown leather ball a good thwack, especially when it became weighed down with rainwater. McCulloch scored 26 times in as many games, ending the season with more goals than the great Dixie Dean of Everton. Between Christmas Day and the end of the season, the Bees lost only two of 22 games.

Brentford ended their first season in the top division in fifth place – two points off second place. They were the highest-placed team from London, ahead of Arsenal and Chelsea. Their transfer outlay was offset by trading players to other clubs, and ticket sales from bumper attendances. If the league table looked spectacular, the bottom line was not bad, either: Brentford ended the season with a profit of £584.[17]

Following big-spending Arsenal and Chelsea, Brentford's team was increasingly made up of some of the best players from across

---

17 White, ibid. Brentford's 2–1 home win against Chelsea brought record ticket sales of £2,205.

Britain. By 1937, in a sign of the club's growing status, all five first-team forwards were internationals for England, Scotland and Wales.

Ever bigger crowds came to Griffin Park to see Brentford, and the press were effusive in their praise of how they played. The Bees had, the *Daily Herald* proclaimed, a 'magnificent combination of high-class footballers'. As their target man, McCulloch finished as the second-highest scorer in Division One in the 1936–37 season with 31 goals, including a hat-trick in a 4–1 home win against Middlesbrough. In that game he intercepted a back pass for his first goal, flicked in a header for the second, and sprinted onto a pass to rifle in the third. Brentford, who were 2–0 up within nine minutes, were, the *Sunday Dispatch* reporter wrote, 'swift as a Bentley and more determined than two dogs over a bone.'

In their squad crammed with internationals was a spotty teenager from Ealing called Leslie Smith. Smith had gone to St Dunstan's School in Brentford with Gordon Curtis, the son of Harry.[18] He was a talented sprinter and played football for a team of boy scouts. Curtis, spotting his talent in a low-key game, arranged for him to start work as an office boy at Griffin Park at the age of 16 while gaining experience as an amateur player with Wimbledon and Hayes. When Scottish winger Bobby Reid was recovering from appendicitis in September 1936, Curtis called up Smith to the first team. In his second game, he was named in the team to play Arsenal at home in

---

18 St Dunstan's is now called Gunnersbury Catholic School.

front of a crowd of 31,000. He was up against some of the best-known players in the country including his opposite number Cliff Bastin, who played on the left wing for England.

Side-stepping his markers, and throwing them off balance, Smith darted into space with the ball and whipped in dangerous crosses, setting up both goals in a 2–0 win. Schoolboys – some of whom he would have known – crept nearer the touchline. A policeman ordered them to move back. When the game ended, they ran onto the pitch to mob him. His performance made headlines in the *Daily Mirror*. In the evening, his mother Ethel-May took him to a local cinema, perhaps to calm him down. As the reels were being changed, the manager came onto the stage. The lights were turned on. 'I believe,' the manager said, 'we have young Leslie Smith with us tonight.'

Smith, red-faced, stood up. The audience cheered. Soon, the Brentford teenager was being tipped to one day play for England.[19]

When Reid recovered from appendicitis, Smith was left out of the team, but he got another chance, on the right wing when Idris Hopkins left for international duty with Wales. The teenager was the perfect stand-in: a handful for defences on either wing.

In May 1937, as part of Smith's turnaround from boy scout to big-name star, and after Brentford had finished sixth in Division One, he found himself on a post-season tour of Adolf Hitler's

---

19 In 1939 Smith would become the second Brentford player to represent England, in a friendly game against Romania in Bucharest; the first was Billy Scott in 1936.

Germany. Brentford were treated as special guests on the four-match tour. 'Hamburg Welcomes Brentford,' one newspaper headline said. Before each game, captain Jack Holliday was presented with a bunch of flowers. The team had some time for sightseeing, posing for a group photograph in summer suits before Sanssouci Palace in Potsdam.

In the 1930s there was growing international diplomatic disquiet about Hitler's anti-Semitism. For the previous four years, under a veneer of legality, Jews had been removed from public life, their assets confiscated; a law against 'overcrowding' limited the number of Jewish students in universities. During the 1936 Berlin Olympics, Hitler had sought to camouflage this stealth Aryanisation movement: *Der Stürmer*, an anti-Semitic tabloid, was removed from street stalls.[20] At the opening ceremony, the British team had made a conscious decision not to respond to Hitler's stiff-armed greeting. Athletes merely turned in his direction as they walked behind the Union Jack and made no gesture of respect. It was 'very embarrassing', Joseph Goebbels, the Nazi propaganda minister, noted in his diary.[21] The long-jump duel between Jesse Owens – the son of a sharecropper from Alabama – and Luz Long, a blond German, helped to paint a rosier picture of Germany. After Owens won the battle, he left the arena arm in arm with Long. According to a Jewish visitor leaving on a boat back to New York, American

---

20 Oliver Hilmes, *Berlin 1936: Sixteen Days in August.*
21 The American team took off their straw boaters to acknowledge Hitler, while the French made a stiff-arm salute to cheers from the crowd, although the French delegation later claimed it was an Olympic salute, not a Nazi salute.

visitors came away from their trip to the Olympics thinking 'how nice everything was in Germany'.[22]

Before Brentford's opening game against Hertha Berlin, club staff were asked if players would perform a Nazi salute when the German national anthem played. With little forethought, the players agreed. 'Quite frankly,' Curtis said, 'we thought that to do this would just be a matter of courtesy.'[23] In a distinctly unmilitary looking salute, Brentford players held their right arms out at different angles. When a rendition of 'God Save the King' followed, they were upset to see the Hertha players failing to respect the British national anthem, instead continuing their Nazi salute. After that, Brentford did not repeat the Nazi salute. When the tour ended, without further controversy, Smith returned to his mother's cooking and other home comforts in Ealing.

The next season, Brentford were in the unprecedented position of leading the first division for a full 16 weeks. After beating defending champions Manchester City 2–1 two days after Christmas in 1937, supporters opened the newspaper the next morning to see their club still atop the first division after half of the season, ahead of the chasing pack of Leeds, Arsenal and Wolves. The prospect of Brentford becoming league champions was now 'something more than a mere dream', according to the *Daily Herald*.[24] In the FA Cup Brentford were also on a roll, beating second division Manchester United to

22 Paul J. Karlstrom, *Peter Selz: Sketches of a Life in Art*.
23 Lane and Croxford, ibid.
24 *Daily Herald*, 28 December 1937.

move within two matches of the final. But the excitement petered out by the start of March. They were dumped out of the quarter-finals by Preston North End, losing 3–0 at home before a record crowd of 39,626, and their formidable start in the league tapered off. Nevertheless, they finished only seven points behind champions Arsenal for their third top-sixth finish in as many seasons. In a few short years Brentford had become an established power in English football, and were now surely not far off winning one of the biggest domestic trophies. At the club's annual dinner in Marylebone, FA secretary Stanley Rous – later the FIFA president – paid tribute to Brentford for their rise from Division Three (South). 'The football of your players, your club, and the way you manage it, are a matter of respect to very many people in this country,' Rous said. 'You are sowing the seeds of a very great tradition.'[25]

---

25 *Middlesex County Times*, 16 April 1938.

Chapter 4

1950s: Bushy Park

In post-war Britain, the English breakfast was among everyday pleasures still affected by a weakened economy. Tea was rationed until 1952, sugar until 1953, and bacon and butter until 1954.[1] Britons had to skimp and save and, along with a pack of cigarettes and pint of beer, Saturday afternoon football was one of the few luxuries to look forward to. To avoid the cost of the train fare, many Brentford fans arrived at Griffin Park on bicycles, some having pedalled for hours from as far away as Windsor or Staines. Rather than risk losing their bikes, they could pay three pence to leave them in the Price family's backyard at 92 Brook Road before taking their place on the Royal Oak terrace. The yard had space for 150 bicycles. When fans came to fetch theirs after the match, they

---

1 Peter Hennessy, *Having it So Good: Britain in the Fifties*.

would curse if an accessory was missing: 'Where's my bloody lamp gone?'[2]

On the packed terraces, supporters cheered on their team as individuals, shouting, '*Come on, Brentford.*' The communal terrace chanting was not yet prevalent and would not take hold in Britain until the 1970s.[3] There was an escalation of noise the nearer the team got to the opposition's goalmouth that, if they scored, culminated in a roar which could be heard for miles around. Fans went home happy if the Bees won. If there was a north-westerly wind, they would get back home for tea with a sulphurous smell clinging to their clothes. The gasworks that flanked both sides of the eastern part of the High Street continued to dominate the Brentford skyline. At the wheel of perhaps a Ford Anglia or Morris Minor, drivers would accelerate on this stretch, today known as Kew Bridge Road, until they had passed the worst of the smell. As the 657 double-decker bus between Shepherd's Bush and Hounslow trundled past, passengers on board held their noses.

Bizarrely, while most people scurried away, the gasworks drew people suffering from asthma under the popular misconception that the polluted air was beneficial to their health. In harsh and sometimes dangerous conditions, the workers at the gasworks loaded coal into furnaces that emitted methane and sulphur, and was cooled, filtered then stored for

---

2 Stan Price quoted on www.brentfordhistory.com, 18 February 2013.
3 The roots of some of chanting we know today began around this time. According to Hennessy, ibid, eight years after the war, England fans sang to the Hungary team at Wembley, '*If it wasn't for the English, you'd be Krauts.*'

distribution by underground pipes across west London. At the Barge Aground, a pub abutting the gasworks, black sulphate particles repeatedly settled on the bar and tables, no matter how many times staff cleaned the surfaces.[4]

The Second World War had brought a rare piece of silverware to Griffin Park. Brentford won a watered-down version of the FA Cup in May 1942. In front of 72,000 fans at Wembley, some wearing army and navy uniforms, they beat Portsmouth 2–0 with both goals by Leslie Smith to win the London War Cup. In the match programme, spectators were instructed to shelter in corridors under the stands if the air-raid siren sounded, or leave the ground to seek refuge elsewhere. On the way to the stadium from his RAF Hornchurch base Smith's car broke down and he had to get a lift from police, finally entering the changing room just as his substitute was getting ready.

Harry Curtis said leading Brentford out at Wembley was the proudest moment of his career. He chain-smoked his way through the match. While archive footage shows Portsmouth dominating periods of play, Smith's goals were enough to cap his Brentford journey from local schoolboy to Wembley match-winner. Just as captain Joe James received the silver trophy, the lid toppled off. Later the cup was filled with drink, perhaps champagne or beer, and passed around, first to players and then supporters.

Curtis was still at Brentford when the war ended and, approaching his third decade in the club's employment, was by then living in a five-bedroom house in Boston Gardens,

---

4 Jean McMillan, daughter of landlord, quoted on www.bhsproject.co.uk.

Brentford, with a fireplace in the hallway and a garden lawn the size of a penalty box. Few of the other key figures of the club's heyday were still around. Players, board members and staff had grown old, moved on, retired or died. Chairman Louis Paul Simon had passed away at age 72, soon after the London War Cup success; Bob Kane stepped down after 20 years as first-team trainer. A few months after the war, even former local schoolboy Leslie Smith – by then aged 28 – requested a transfer and joined Aston Villa for a fee of £7,000.

Without the backbone of the team that had given Brentford three top-six finishes in the first division, the Bees lost their way. A pre-season tour of Denmark in the summer of 1946 in which they were beaten in all three games against players drawn from amateur teams in Copenhagen was a precursor to what was to come: they won just one of their 15 first division games between mid-September and Christmas Day, and then lost seven in a row from 1 February to 4 April. They looked beaten and forlorn. The *Daily Herald* sighed: 'They are a dispirited side for which nothing seems to go right.' Harry Curtis tried everything to shake off the malaise, making several signings, including Scottish international Archie Macaulay, who arrived from West Ham in November. He gave a debut to a 17-year-old apprentice printer from Twickenham called Wally Bragg but the teenager 'was a bag of nerves' when he came on as a substitute forward in a 1–0 loss against Grimsby.[5] Nothing Curtis tried seemed to

---

5 *Kensington Post*, 5 April 1947. Bragg went on to play 168 times for Brentford, mostly as a central defender.

work: Brentford were relegated in that first post-war season. Surveying what had gone wrong, the manager bemoaned the lack of unity that was the hallmark of Brentford in the 1930s. Interrupted by six years of war, that illustrious era was now a distant memory. Supporters even turned against Curtis, for so long a hero at Griffin Park. He received abusive letters at his office, sent anonymously. Enduring sleepless nights and stress, Curtis, 59, announced the following season would be his last. In his final months in charge, the club began preparing Jackie Gibbons – a senior player – to take over as the general manager.

In post-war Britain, professional football players typically earned less than a skilled tradesman such as a plumber or electrician. Jimmy Hill, Brentford's left-half, got £7 per week (about £200 today) during the season, and £5 in the offseason.[6] Hill shared a semi-detached home belonging to the club in Whitton Manor Road, Isleworth, with striker Billy Dare – Hill had the first floor with his wife Gloria; Dare lived with his spouse on the ground floor.

Most players arrived by public transport for training each weekday morning, although Hill drove his dark blue Morris Ten, with Dare cadging a lift in the passenger seat. The first thing players did when they arrived each morning was head to the tea hut located in the forecourt of the ground for a cuppa. (They had to pay for the tea themselves.) To earn some extra cash after training Hill and another teammate Johnny Paton called

---

6 Jimmy Hill, *The Jimmy Hill Story: My Autobiography.*

door to door at the factories of the Great West Road selling light bulbs for a company called Accessories Electrical Supplies.[7]

Although attendances for league games at Griffin Park were holding up at around 20,000 in the second division, the club was in the red: fans coming through the turnstiles paid only one shilling to stand on the terraces – about £2 in today's money. Inflation, meanwhile, was ratcheting up costs for everything from football boots to train tickets and hotel rooms. Speaking to journalists, Jackie Gibbons painted a gloomy picture about the coming years for Brentford. 'The future's bleak,' the new manager said, 'unless we get more revenue.'[8]

Unable to afford players in the transfer market, Gibbons sent scouts to scour amateur football for talent they would not have pay a fee for. He had a free-and-easy approach to signing players on short-term deals: in his first season in charge he fielded 26 players, among them Kevin O'Flanagan, who ran a dental practice in Ruislip and had played rugby union for Ireland. Renewing the squad constantly was relatively successful: Brentford finished ninth. However, the following season, Brentford won only nine of 29 games and were just above the relegation zone.

One day at the end of January 1951, one of Brentford's scouts went to run his eye over the local RAF team, which played at Bushy Park, by Hampton Court Palace, to see if he could uncover some new talent. During the war London's royal parks

---

7 Hill, ibid.
8 Jackie Gibbons interview, the *People*, 25 March 1951.

had been taken over for the war effort. Some 400 huts made of brick topped with corrugated roofs were erected as barracks. They lined the road that cuts through Bushy Park, their iron roofs disguised by rows of horse chestnut trees and a layer of camouflage. To allow the RAF men to let off steam one section of the park was set aside for sports fields.[9] Even six years after the war, some of the huts and sports fields were still being used by the RAF.

As the scout watched the team of amateur players chase the ball around the pitch, he saw their coach scribbling into a notepad by the touchline. The RAF coach was logging shorthand notes about passes, throw-ins and corners: he was stress-testing his theories about the best means of attack and defence. The basis of his thinking was that it was important to punt the ball forward as swiftly as possible to avoid losing possession before having a shot at goal. He also believed it was fundamental to disarm the opposing team deep in their own half before they had a chance of launching an attack.

As Charles Reep, a Wing Commander by rank, glanced up and down from his notebook to the pitch, the RAF team's aerial bombardment continued. As soon as the other team regained possession, they were set upon by the air force men. The scout returned to Griffin Park to recount the methods of Reep, who in civilian life was an accountant with a gentle face and jug ears protruding from either side of his flat cap. 'There's some crazy

---

9 In 1944 General Eisenhower moved his centre of operations to a corner of Bushy Park to plan the D-Day landing.

fellow who stands on the touchline with bits of paper making notes,' he told Gibbons. 'But, well, his game plan seemed to work.'[10] The RAF team looked almost unbeatable.

Even when they were near the top of the first division, Brentford had not given much thought to match tactics. Like other teams of the era, they stuck to a 2–3–5 line-up: two full-backs, three midfielders and five forwards. Altering this classic English football formation was seen as a peculiarity of people who did not know the game of Association Football. At the height of the club's success, Harry Curtis had explained that the Bees did not bother strategising before a game. In his mind, smart player recruitment and team bonding were infinitely more important than faffing around with team formations. 'Brentford,' he said, with some pride, 'is not one of those clubs which plan their games beforehand around a blackboard.'

Most training sessions involved some light fitness work, running a few laps around the pitch, maybe some weights, and little else. Practising with the ball was done sparingly. Coaching was almost an alien concept. When players asked to practise corners or free-kicks, the manager or trainer would shrug, as if there was no point. 'Everyone believed,' Hill said, 'that great players, or even good players, were born, and there was no way you could improve upon God-given talent.'[11]

A grammar schoolboy from Balham, Hill had been bemused by this torpid attitude to performance on his arrival at Brentford

---

10 Rob Haywood, BBC website, 2 June 2022: 'Charles Reep: The military accountant who brought data analysis to English game'.
11 Hill, ibid.

at the age of 21. When he asked to be coached about how to head the ball, Brentford manager Gibbons gave him a side-eyed look, as if to question why this young man was wasting everyone's time with a daft request. He threw a couple of balls at a 38-year-old veteran player and told him to give Hill a quick demonstration.

Even the fitness work was gentle, with players expected to conserve as much energy as possible for the next game. A middle-aged man with white hair, longstanding trainer Bob Kane said he had never asked players to do physical exercises that he could not do himself.[12] Once, before a fourth-round FA Cup game, he took them to Southend for sea air, brine baths and long walks. When they returned to Griffin Park they played golf and billiards and listened to gramophone records.

But as Brentford faced the prospect of relegation to the third tier, listening to a Bing Crosby record or two at Griffin Park was not really an option any more for Gibbons. He had to try something new. He went to meet Reep. Two days later, the 46-year-old RAF accountant took a day off work and found himself on board a train with Brentford players heading to a midweek game at Doncaster Rovers.

On journeys to away games, most Brentford players gathered in groups to play cards. They would play poker or brag, betting with stakes of a few pennies to while away the time. Whether Reep interrupted the card schools to expound his football analytics theories on that first train journey is not

---

12 Burchill, ibid; Kane had recently retired after two decades of service.

clear, but Gibbons appeared to take his advice, and results were transformed. Booting the ball to the wings and harrying opponents relentlessly, Brentford overran Doncaster 3–0. That weekend at Griffin Park they thrashed Bury 4–0.

Over the next couple of months, Brentford blew away promotion candidates one by one: Cardiff, Manchester City and Sheffield United were all ambushed. Reporting on the 2–0 'smash and grab' victory over Manchester City, the *Sunday Mirror* said Brentford's football was not pretty, but it worked. The team's goals-per-game average during this period rose to 2.9 from 1.3, with striker Freddy Monk going on a club record ten-match scoring streak. Reep later described the tactics he had introduced at Brentford as an 'unbelievable and instant' success.[13]

Irrespective of what the RAF man's tactical analysis told him, there was a certain logic to bypassing the midfield at Griffin Park. The pitch was in such poor shape that the fire brigade were sometimes called to pump off water. Passes along the ground rolled to a halt in three-inch mud. An hour before the mid-February game against Preston North End the referee announced he would take the ball into the penalty area to see if it would bounce – it did not. Perhaps fearing the wrath of the crowd who had gathered to see the great Tom Finney, the referee ordered play to go ahead on a surface which the *Sunday Dispatch* described as looking like 'a farmyard after a downpour'.

---

13 Haywood, ibid.

In the last 14 games of the season Preston were the only team to beat Brentford at Griffin Park; in a performance remembered for years to come, Finney used the yard or so of grass on the fringe of the pitch to dance pass defenders, setting up or scoring each of the four goals in a 4–2 win.[14]

The Bees avoided relegation comfortably, finishing in mid-table. All these years later, how much of the turnaround was down to Reep is difficult to gauge based on match reports, goals scored and results. News of his consultancy work with Brentford only emerged years later, after he had gone on to work for bigger clubs, and was based on his own version of events.[15] Neither Gibbons nor the players were quoted by newspapers about Reep's impact. The *Middlesex County Times* told of the 'amazing form' of Brentford, without mentioning him.

From those days in Bushy Park, Reep would go on to annotate, in his shorthand, more than two thousand games in English football, storing bundles of notepads in his garage in Haverhill, Suffolk, and later in retirement in Cornwall. In what Reep thought proved his theory about the efficacy of long-ball football, Ken Bray, a visiting Fellow in the Sport and Exercise Science Group at Bath University, found some 80 per cent of goals came from moves of three passes or less.[16] For every new pass, the chances of losing possession increased, Reep argued, and therefore careful build-up play was not a good idea.

---

14 Hill, ibid.
15 Haywood, ibid.
16 Jonathan Wilson, *Inverting the Pyramid: A History of Football Tactics.*

In the modern era Reep, who went on to work for Wolves, Sheffield Wednesday and Coventry, has been blamed for damaging English football with his long-ball tactics. In his book on the evolution of football tactics, *Inverting the Pyramid*, Jonathan Wilson wrote that Reep's analytics were flawed because, in what he calls a 'horrifying' mistake in his philosophy, the RAF man failed to factor in that 91.5 per cent of *all* moves of the era had three passes or less. Therefore, he writes, the three-pass or less goalscoring theory of Reep does not hold water: a fuller data set suggests more elaborate passing moves were, in fact, more likely to lead to a goal. However, Wilson does concede the theory might have an element of truth 'at a low level' of the game, in which players were not as skilful, such as in an amateur RAF team – or second division Brentford.

Partly thanks to Wilson's book, perhaps Reep has been unfairly pilloried for contributing a negative influence on the development of English football, and some of his more innovative thinking has been overlooked: he was also an early proponent of what today is described as high pressing. Most goals, he found, came from winning the ball back in the opponent's final quarter.[17] Today, this technique is applied by some of the most successful clubs in Europe.

Reep also understood goals were frequently the result of arbitrary events, such as a deflection in the penalty box.

---

17 Christopher Anderson and David Sally, *The Numbers Game: Why Everything You Know About Football is Wrong.*

'Potential goals can be obtained by random chance,' Reep told his local paper, the *Haverhill Echo*, in 1971.[18] This line of thinking would be employed, 50 years later, by Brentford in how they took corner kicks and long throw-ins in the Premier League. There is an argument that the problem with English football was not Reep but a paucity of other contrarian tacticians willing to channel their energy into changing British football's lazy thinking.

Charles Reep's successful four-month stint at Brentford ended abruptly when he was transferred 140 miles away to the RAF base at Bridgnorth, Shropshire. The same summer, Jimmy Hill, then aged 23, volunteered to spend a week in the West Midlands for a new football coaching course – an almost alien concept in English football at the time. He went with a couple of older teammates, including the Brentford captain Ron Greenwood.

It was the first course of its kind in the grounds of Lilleshall Hall – a former private estate which the government had bought to turn into a centre of sporting excellence. The course was taught by England manager Walter Winterbottom and proved inspiring for the Brentford group. For some of the Brentford squad's most inquiring minds, it provided evidence that there was much more potential to football tactics than many people imagined. In the weeks and months after the course, Hill, Greenwood and Johnny Paton, a Glaswegian, gathered on train

---

18 *Haverhill Echo*, 14 October 1971.

journeys to away games to discuss tactics, while other players joined the usual card schools. Sometimes, the trio prolonged their discussions at the team hotel, long into the night.

Aged 29, Greenwood was the most respected player at Brentford. He had gone to school not far from Brentford in Alperton, leaving at 14 to become an apprentice sign-writer. (He once painted the changing-room signs at Wembley stadium.) Jackie Gibbons, only a few years older, had played with him at Bradford Park Avenue and persuaded him to join Brentford. At Griffin Park Greenwood was the first name on the teamsheet; a commanding centre-half with a presence on the pitch. He had played every league game for the previous two seasons before going to Lilleshall. He had the ear of the manager and, on some days, he even led training sessions while Gibbons attended to the administrative tasks that were part of his job. As the season got underway Greenwood persuaded Gibbons to jettison Reep's long-ball tactics and experiment with some of the techniques he had picked up from Winterbottom during the summer. Whenever Brentford lost possession, Greenwood said, the midfield and defence should drop back and soak up the pressure in their own half before regaining possession and moving up the pitch as a unit. This was a radical about-turn on the tactics of the previous season that had been so effective, but Gibbons agreed to give it a go.

By the halfway stage of the season, the Brentford scoring rate had dwindled to barely one goal per game – from almost three when Reep was there – but the defence marshalled by Greenwood had the best defensive record of any club in the top two divisions and, as Christmas approached, Brentford found themselves second in the table, level on points with leaders Sheffield United.

In west London there was heavy rain on Christmas morning. The Griffin Park pitch was as muddy as usual in mid-winter, virtually devoid of grass. In a festive mood supporters crowded into the ground for the 11.15 a.m. kick-off against mid-table Southampton and would be home by lunchtime for turkey and roast potatoes, and to listen to King George VI's Christmas message on the radio.[19] For the players it was a more stressful week: they had to play three matches in four days. As was typical at the time, in a Christmas double-header, they would host Southampton on 25 December then travel down to play the same team on the south coast on Boxing Day afternoon. And then they would have another game two days later.

As their first match got underway, Brentford scored first but Southampton rallied, levelling before half-time. The home defence led by Greenwood did not look as solid as usual. In the second half Southampton forward Frank Dudley collected the ball in his own half and began running across the mud. Greenwood backtracked. He did not lunge to make a tackle, instead hoping to pressure the striker into a mistake. Dudley kept going forward. 'He kept running with it, running with it, running with it,' an eyewitness recounted.[20] Then Dudley looked up, saw a narrow gap, and squeezed the ball into the

---

19 The King had recently undergone surgery for lung cancer and would die a few weeks later.
20 Johnny Paton interview in Jon Henderson, *When Footballers Were Skint: A Journey in Search of the Soul of Football*.

net, giving Southampton a 2–1 lead. Brentford tried in vain to equalise. As the Brentford players walked into the dressing room at the end of the game, Gibbons 'went berserk'.[21] 'Why the hell didn't someone go and tackle Dudley?' Gibbons yelled. 'Ron Greenwood: you're the captain.'

Greenwood felt the tactics he had introduced, not to mention his captaincy, were under attack. He pointed out his defensive approach had worked fine until now: only 18 goals conceded in the previous 21 games. But there was tension in the air. As the other players kept quiet until Gibbons had calmed down, Jimmy Hill could not resist piping up to support Greenwood, his friend. 'You don't know what's going on,' Hill, in his whiney voice, said to Gibbons. 'You don't even come in for the team meetings on a Friday.'

'Shut up,' Gibbons snapped back.[22]

There and then, Greenwood vowed to hand in a transfer request. 'Everything we were doing was suddenly wrong,' he said later. 'The criticism mattered to me deeply because I believed in what we were doing.' Out of loyalty to his friend, Hill also handed in a transfer request, delivering a handwritten letter a few days later to the house of chairman Frank Davis, who lived in Hanwell.

After the Christmas Day bust-up, Brentford's defence lost its shape, leaking twice as many goals in the second half of the

---

21 Henderson, ibid. Paton's account has the argument taking place at half-time, but Dudley's goal was in the second half. There may also have been tension at half-time caused by Southampton's first goal.
22 Henderson, ibid.

season, and they ended the campaign in tenth place. Greenwood and Gibbons patched up their differences, but Hill's relationship with the manager had broken down irreparably. Before the end of the season, he had left to join Fulham.

On a foggy afternoon in November the following year, Hill and Greenwood went to Wembley stadium where they saw Hungary trounce England 6–3; it was the first time the English national team had lost a home match against opposition from outside Great Britain. The defeat prompted a moment of introspection about the tactical inferiority of English football. The Hungarians were more inventive than the English, allowing one forward to drop deeper to disrupt the defence. The visiting Magyars were also supremely talented, none more so than Ferenc Puskás, who once said he could 'feel the ball as a violinist feels his instrument'.[23] Hungary moved the ball around the pitch with ease, tricking the English with back-heels and feints.

Hill was so fascinated by the performance, as he watched among a Wembley crowd of 105,000, that afterwards he obtained a copy of a Hungarian coaching manual which included training methods that he had never heard of before: for example, two-touch passing drills in small grids to improve reaction speed. There were enough diagrams for him to understand the basic tenets, without having to learn Hungarian. Invited to lead Fulham's pre-season training at age 27, Hill used the manual as his guide as he put his teammates through

---

23 *Guardian*, 16 November 2022.

their paces for ten days, before centre-half Gordon Brice lost his patience with the constraints of one-touch football and led a revolt to liberate practice sessions from this young technocrat. In his spare time Hill coached Oxford University, whose students were more open to his innovation, although they were not gifted enough to play like the Hungarians.

For Greenwood, the game at Wembley was also an epiphany. He was sure by now that he wanted to become a coach. After he left Brentford he also spent time coaching Oxford University before ending his career as a player with spells at Chelsea and Fulham, where he was reunited with Hill. He seemed surer than ever that Reep's style of football was not the future. Football, he said, 'had more to offer than the average league club's performance on a Saturday afternoon'.[24]

Greenwood went on to manage West Ham for 13 years, building a passing style started by his predecessor Ted Fenton, with players including Bobby Moore, Martin Peters and Geoff Hurst, who combined to help England win the 1966 World Cup. After becoming general manager in 1974 he took a special interest in the youth team and remained fascinated by tactics, sitting in a car park with first-team coach John Lyall into the early hours of the morning to talk football. Years later, Greenwood coached England at the 1982 World Cup.

At Brentford, on Greenwood's recommendation, Hill had become Brentford's union representative at the age of 22. A decade later, as chairman of the Professional Footballers'

---

24 Ron Greenwood, *Yours Sincerely.*

Association, he would go on to end the wage cap for players in 1961. It was a landmark moment in the history of British football and would mean that many more players could afford their own car, even if it was more likely to be a second-hand Sunbeam than a brand-new Bentley.

While Greenwood and Hill made a name for themselves after leaving Brentford, the club would gradually drift into obscurity. Paton – their companion when discussing tactics on away trips – claimed, decades later, that the Christmas Day argument in the dressing room at Griffin Park was a seminal moment in Brentford's history. From pushing for promotion back to the first division, they began sliding down the Football League. That dressing-room row, Paton said, 'ruined Brentford Football Club'.[25]

Brentford could not get out of their downward spiral. Once they had dropped out of the upper echelons of the game, some match-goers preferred to switch allegiance and follow Arsenal or Chelsea. Gates at Griffin Park fell below 12,000, not enough to cover the players' wage bill. Where once terraces were packed now there were gaps in the crowd. This negative spiral was difficult to reverse: as ticket sales fell there was less money to sign players and performances suffered accordingly. Meanwhile, away from the pitch there was a new form of entertainment to compete with live football: television.

---

25 Henderson, ibid. Paton became a professional snooker referee and ran a snooker club in Ealing.

Frank Davis, the Brentford chairman, blamed falling match attendances at Griffin Park on this new technology, which was available under hire-purchase agreements. The BBC's Saturday afternoon programming included a sports show featuring horse racing, rugby and football scores. This was not the only reason for falling gates. Because of the cost of meeting monthly payments for TV sets, the working man could no longer afford to go to games, according to Davis.

In 1954 Brentford were relegated to Division Three (South), joining QPR, Millwall, Orient and Crystal Palace. Brentford downsized accordingly: with money tight, staff painted the offices themselves and, in the summer of 1956, manager Bill Dodgin, shirt soaking with sweat, was seen with a wheelbarrow and shovel re-tarmacking the forecourt in Braemar Road.[26]

By the start of the 1960s the attendance at Griffin Park had dropped to as low as 5,000: instead of a clutch of local rivalries Brentford found themselves playing in the new third division against the likes of Hartlepool, Rochdale, Crewe and Darlington. In 1962 Brentford were relegated again, this time to the fourth division, becoming the first club to drop to the basement of the Football League from the first division. The descent had taken just 15 years. Only the most loyal of fans remained. 'Anyone can follow the fashionable or successful teams,' Jack Dunnett, the new chairman proclaimed in a club handbook, 'but it takes

---

26 Burchill, ibid.

greater character to stick out your chest and proclaim allegiance to Brentford FC.'[27]

The Bees were promoted back to the third tier as champions immediately, but there would be no further upward momentum: they remained stuck, impecunious, in the lower reaches of the league. In 1966, when England won the World Cup with a squad including players from West Ham, Arsenal, Tottenham, Chelsea and Fulham, Brentford were relegated again to the fourth division. In the space of a generation they had gone from the highest to the lowest-placed league club in London. When a few years later *Time Out* magazine published a feature on fan culture in the city it divided up the capital's boroughs into teams. Hounslow, Ealing and Richmond were coloured Chelsea blue, with dashes of Arsenal red. Brentford were not on the map.

In the first weeks of 1967 the Brentford chairman Jack Dunnett decided it was an insurmountable task to lead the club back up the divisions and announced he was in advanced negotiations to merge the club with QPR in order to take on the might of Arsenal and Chelsea. Under his proposal, QPR would take over Griffin Park, a better facility than they had in Shepherd's Bush, and Brentford would disappear.

It was a bombshell nobody had seen coming. For decades Brentford had existed with a group of minority shareholders, none of whom had really considered the possibility of the club being a business that you could make money from or sell. But Dunnett had accumulated 89 per cent of the shares

---

27 Burchill, ibid.

and suddenly was threatening to do a deal that would make him richer while leaving Brentford fans without their club. On the morning of Friday 20 January the *Daily Mirror* ran the headline 'Goodbye, Brentford'.

★ ★ ★

Jack Dunnett was a Cambridge-educated solicitor with a Mayfair office and a property portfolio that had made him wealthy. He also had an offshore investment company based in the Bahamas. (He was often cited by the press as being 'in the Caribbean for business'.) He had joined the Brentford board in the summer of 1961 to promote his fledgling career as a Labour MP and present himself as man of the people, rather than a champagne socialist. He was a bright young man, and both Brentford board members and fans found him charismatic. They liked his enthusiasm for turning around the club's fortunes, but his personal marketing strategy soon went off course: instead of being picked by Labour to stand in the Brentford and Chiswick seat, he was assigned to stand in Nottingham Central.

On the campaign trail in Nottingham he would swap his Rolls-Royce for a Ford Capri and drive around the city centre with a megaphone on the bonnet, issuing the message: 'Vote Labour, vote Dunnett.' He stopped off to sup pints in working-class pubs, dropping football gossip into the conversation.[28] Most men he talked to were far more interested in chatting

---

28 Jack Dunnett's *Guardian* obituary, 14 November 2019.

about football than politics, and this helped him win their approval. Dunnett won the Nottingham Central seat from the Conservative incumbent in 1964. A chauffeur would drive him in his Rolls-Royce between Nottingham and Westminster while Dunnett sat on the back seat eating grapes. He survived on five hours' sleep a night and frequently had to multitask: in 1964 he finalised Brentford's £15,000 signing of Ian Lawther from Scunthorpe in the House of Commons.

By 1966, as Brentford dropped into the fourth division for the second time in four years, Dunnett's enthusiasm for his football project was wearing thin. The club were losing £500 per week and doing little to help his political career in Westminster. He was taking anxious calls from his bankers about the mounting overdraft when he began secret talks with the QPR chairman John Gregory about a takeover of Brentford.

On the day of the 'Goodbye Brentford' headline, a picture showed Dunnett, in a deserted Griffin Park, chatting to a sombre-looking captain Bobby Ross. The next day a crowd of 10,650 – double the average gate – turned out for a Saturday afternoon match against Southend waving banners ('Leave Us Alone Rangers') and milling in the forecourt of the Braemar Road stand waiting to vent their fury on Dunnett. How dare he shut down their club? Most of these men (and they were almost exclusively men) would have had ties to the club since childhood. Some had had that bond with the club passed down by their grandfather and father. Dunnett did not turn up to the game but, chastened by the public reaction, he was soon backpedalling. The deal, he told reporters, might not go ahead and, even if it did, he would not profit personally.

On the Monday, Brentford Supporters' Club chairman Peter Pond-Jones – described by the local paper as a 'bearded militant' – called a crisis meeting. Some 3,000 fans turned up at Griffin Park. Among them was Alan Simpson, a scriptwriter for the popular BBC sitcom *Steptoe and Son*. Pond-Jones asked the supporters to do their bit to contribute to a fighting fund. Factories on the Great West Road were asked to donate £1 per week. Six current and former Brentford directors mobilised, racking their brains and contacts about how to reverse the doomsday plan. They managed to secure backing from Ron Blindell, an Ascot-based millionaire who knew the football business. Blindell, who had been chairman of Plymouth Argyle, arranged a bridging loan of £104,000 (£1.6 million today) to buy out Dunnett. The plan was to sell shares to a supporters' trust but, by the end of the season, the trust had acquired less than ten per cent of the club. The new board, meanwhile, reined in costs. They shut down the youth and reserve teams, laid off a groundsman and steward, and reduced hotel and travel costs. The club became profitable and began to pay off Blindell's loan.

Dunnett flitted from Brentford to Notts County, where he joined the board. Flush with the proceeds of his Brentford sale, he provided the fourth division club – which was also losing money – with interest-free loans. Over the next 14 years, he led the club up the league to the first division, helping to burnish his credentials with voters in Nottingham. To support his political cause, Notts County players canvassed door to door for him in neighbourhoods near the Meadow Lane stadium – apart from striker Les Bradd, who idled on a street corner. He had been raised as a Conservative.[29]

Two years after providing his emergency financial aid, Blindell fell seriously ill and died in a Windsor nursing home aged 63. He left a long-standing legacy: he had kept Brentford Football Club alive.

---

29 *Guardian* obituary, ibid.

Chapter 5

1990s: Griffin Park

By the 1990s Brentford had become a backwater of suburban London. The once-bustling dock where coal and steel and timber had arrived in barges from across the UK had fallen silent a quarter of a century earlier and the town had acquiesced into a peaceful if eerie hinterland inhabited by mudlarks, herons and the residents of a few narrow houseboats. Wharves had been left derelict, accumulating weeds, graffiti and bird droppings.

Apart from one or two boatbuilders, there was little industry left. The river and canal had become an unknown part of the city to everyone bar a few urban dwellers and explorers. I lived for three years in The Ham, a road that followed the bend of the Grand Union Canal past a patch of wasteland, a timber yard and a mechanic who serviced black London taxicabs.

On the other side of the canal was a housing complex that resembled the Brutalist apartment blocks at the Barbican, but with riverside views. The site had been converted into flats by the Greater London Council in the 1970s after the dock shut down for business. Where the gasworks once stood by the Thames, Hounslow Council later built the Watermans Arts Centre.

However, private developers had generally left Brentford alone. The High Street was an unloved district with an internet café, a post office and a couple of convenience stores and takeaways. The smell of fried food lingered even early in the morning. The only surviving family member of the High Street's pomp was Stanley Goddard, who was in his eighties and came from a fifth generation of Brentford shopkeepers. His ancestors had sold a wide selection of products spanning umbrellas, snuff boxes, china and glassware, before specialising in furniture. The family shop was cluttered with pinewood wardrobes, cupboards and beds. Rusting, light-blue Goddard's delivery vans were parked haphazardly around Brentford.

Typically, between 5 a.m. and 7 a.m. Stanley wrote down his childhood memories in a series of letters. He remembered the clip-clop of horses pulling carts of vegetables to Brentford Market; catching the ferry to Kew Gardens for a penny; fish and chips for three pence; girls travelling by canal boat to work on market gardens; a man selling rabbits from a barrow for sixpence; the squeal of tram wheels as they turned off Ealing Road; people sporting new gloves and hats on Christmas Day; all the men going to Griffin Park on Boxing Day.[1]

---

1 Brentford High Steet Project: www.bhsproject.co.uk, December 2008.

On the Great West Road some of the biggest art deco factories had shuttered long ago: Firestone tyres, Macleans toothpaste, Smith's crisps and Coty perfume made way for a proliferation of nondescript office blocks. Many of the workers here no longer had any roots in Brentford and would commute to work from other parts of London and the Home Counties. No longer did hordes of men clock off on Saturday lunchtime and stream towards Griffin Park. Of the neon light displays that had once lit up the road at night, one landmark sign remained at Brentford: a bottle of Lucozade being decanted into a glass with the accompanying slogan: 'Lucozade Replaces Lost Energy'.[2]

In its tenth decade Griffin Park was as threadbare as ever. The changing rooms looked like they belonged in an outdoor municipal swimming pool, with their stone floors, wooden benches, whitewashed walls and low ceilings with four strip lights and a single splash of colour: a strip of wood painted red with pegs to hang clothes on. There was only one decent-sized office, which could accommodate three or four people. Staff had to find new ways to carve out more space in the rabbit warren of rooms built into the main stand.[3] After home games Eric White, the press officer, presided over the manager's news conferences in a plain windowless room that looked like a storeroom.

---

2 The sign was removed in 2016 after the factory was demolished, and put on display in Gunnersbury Museum.
3 The plan to turn 38 Braemar Road, where Stan Bowles lived in the 1980s, into a club office did not come to fruition.

As well as a shortage of office space, there was a deficit of parking places. There were two marked out with white lines in the forecourt of the main entrance. David Webb, the manager, parked his silver Mercedes 450SL in one berth, after commuting from Southend during the week. Chairman Martin Lange, who lived in Ashtead, Surrey, parked his red Ferrari in the other spot. Everyone else parked in the side streets or arrived by public transport.

More than a decade after retiring, Stan Bowles would still stop by for a cup of tea at the club's offices. He was the town's most famous resident, along with two BBC television journalists. Anna Ford – who read the *Nine o'Clock News* – lived in a seven-bedroom Georgian house with wine cellar and bucolic garden in The Butts, the handsome town square that had once stood among orchards but was now surrounded by suburban sprawl. Kate Adie – an international correspondent famous for war reporting – lived in a boxy riverside house where Brentford dock once stood, conveniently near Heathrow Airport.

To pay off his gambling debts Bowles had, long ago, sold the family home in Ealing he had bought with his first wife Ann. After his career as a player ended, he relied on friends for somewhere to sleep in Brentford. Like the club, he seemed too comfortable and broke to move anywhere else. In 1993, while sleeping at a friend's house in Clayponds Lane, he was discovered in bed with his host's blonde girlfriend Diane and was chased into the street wearing only his boxer shorts.[4] She became his

---

4 *Middlesex Chronicle*, 31 March 1994.

third wife: they moved into a council house about a hundred metres from Griffin Park. Years after he had retired, fans arriving for games on a Saturday afternoon would shout through the window: 'We're a man short – put your boots on, Stan.'

Middle-aged men spoke with reverence when Bowles's name came up in conversation. Recalling a game for QPR against Middlesbrough, the *Guardian* journalist Ed Vulliamy wrote of Bowles performing 'voodoo with the ball'. Once, I saw Bowles standing outside Coral, the bookmaker, in his trademark Crombie mac, looking artfully dishevelled – he still had the aura of a star. He would fix his tousled hair in the mirror before sitting down in the pub for a drink and a chat.

Brentford spent 14 consecutive seasons in the third tier until the spring of 1992. By winning 1–0 at Peterborough with a goal from Gary Blissett on the last day of the season, the Bees were promoted as champions to the second tier for the first time in 38 years. The ground was so heaving with Brentford fans that day – perhaps 5,000 or more – that dozens were escorted out of one of the home stands to join the others. It felt wonderful to finally taste some success. I toasted the rare success with cans of Stella Artois lager on the train home. The next season we were relegated.

The style of football was formulaic. It was based on decades-old patterns: big centre-halves, tough midfielders, fast wingers. Once, the Brentford manager would confide to his chairman, 'All you need at this level is one good goalkeeper, two centre-halves and a centre-forward.'[5] Week after week, as the clock

---

5 Author interview with Greg Dyke, recounting a conversation with Martin Allen.

ticked to 3 p.m. on Saturdays, Brentford would get matches under way by passing the ball back from the centre spot, and – as if enacting rugby union's playbook – firing the ball out to one of the flanks for the winger to chase. Defenders were instructed not to pass the ball in their own half, but instead boot it to the forwards. These were boilerplate tactics in England, mostly in the lower leagues, but even among some first division teams.

Wimbledon's team of bruisers, including Dennis Wise, Vinnie Jones and John Fashanu won the FA Cup final in 1988, beating Liverpool after seeking to intimidate them in the tunnel before the game. Millwall battled their way to the first division, finishing above Manchester United when managed by John Docherty, a former Brentford player and manager. Terry Hurlock joined Docherty at Millwall, where his wild hair and hard tackling made him a talismanic figure as the scrappy south London club challenged the British game's aristocracy. Docherty had no time for the passing game played by Liverpool and Tottenham, calling their artistic endeavours 'fanny football'.

Tottenham, for one, were operating in a different sphere. Once on a tour of Russia, Bill Nicholson's team were inspired by the Bolshoi Ballet.[6] The Spurs way was to pass the ball all day long. When Brian Statham arrived at Brentford from Tottenham, where he had spent his teenage years, he had to learn a new way of playing football that bypassed midfield.

---

6 Henderson, ibid.

His mandate was simple: to win the ball and launch it forward to Dean Holdsworth or Gary Blissett.[7]

Brentford leased a couple of training pitches next to a lawn tennis court at Osterley, but there was little in the way of short passing each morning. The only day of the week they played five-a-side games was on Friday mornings, when they used the patch of lawn to sharpen their first touch; they were, nevertheless, full-blooded sessions with thunderous tackles flying in, some of them by Webb, then in his forties but a veteran of some ferocious battles with Leeds as a defender at Chelsea in the 1970s. By mid-winter the tennis court was ruined. On the eve of matches, Webb did not impart tactical advice to players about the opposition, preferring they focus on their own game.[8]

In the lower leagues, Swindon played like Tottenham. They had played under Glen Hoddle in the Premier League before dropping down the divisions, while retaining their passing game. When Swindon dominated possession during a 2–0 win at Griffin Park, Webb was asked why Brentford did not play the same way. His players were, Webb said, better suited to the no-nonsense style most of them were familiar with. Countless times over the years I remember the ball being dispatched with such ferocity by defenders that it would fly into the air, clear the tin roof of the New Road stand and disappear, presumably into someone's back garden. Sometimes, a wayward shot meant the ball would end up bouncing past traffic in Ealing Road.

7 Author interview with Brian Statham.
8 Author interviews with Barry Ashby and Brian Statham.

Because of all these flying balls there was a ready supply of half a dozen replacements on hand at the start of each game.

Brentford's players were dependable professionals, mostly raised in London: Kevin Godfrey, a hard-working utility player; Marcus Gayle, a lightning-quick forward whose first touch sometimes let him down; Jamie Bates, a centre-half with a Desperate Dan jawline who would play more than 500 times for Brentford. One day, in a throwback to the times when players still travelled by the railways, Bates gave me a big smile as he hopped off the train at Brentford station – he lived in Croydon – with a sports bag slung over his shoulder.

By then, the Wednesday pub crawls around the local boozers which Bates had experienced as a wide-eyed apprentice had been discontinued, although players still socialised, playing golf, or meeting at a wine bar in Ealing or Kingston. Brentford's family atmosphere remained.

When the pressure was off, it was easier for players to share a joke with Webb after training. There was mutual respect between them. For a few weeks, Webb invited Bowles – whom he had played with at QPR and who was also in his mid-forties – to come out of retirement to train with Brentford. Bowles impressed the players with his deft touch, and his reunion at Brentford with Webb and another former QPR teammate Dave Thomas made a full-page spread in the *Evening Standard*. To the players, he gave passing tips. 'Why don't you hit it in there?' he would tell them. But, in truth, he was probably not suited to coaching: what he did with the ball could not be taught.

For a couple of years while working on the news desk of the *Brentford and Chiswick Times* newspaper, I got closer to the inner workings of the club. In the windowless room under the stand, I listened to the news conferences of Webb who, still raw after the tensions of a game, would snap back at any perceived slights, especially by a young journalist who had never played professional football. Every now and again, as he sat behind the wooden office table in the press room facing half a dozen of us reporters, Webb would drift into reverie about the East End, where he was brought up. He spoke whimsically about playing football as a schoolboy on Hackney Marshes.

His East End heritage extended to knowing the Kray twins, gangsters who terrorised London with armed robberies and protection rackets, until they were imprisoned for murder – and who, for all their violent crimes, were considered by some to be caring of their community. Webb went to the funeral of Ronnie Kray in Bethnal Green and, a few years later, paid his respects before the coffin of Ronnie's brother Reggie. When asked why, he said he knew convicted criminals and police chiefs, and did not judge the people whom he was familiar with because of what they did for a living.[9]

The office of the newspaper where I worked was in Duke Street, Richmond. The pay was poor – £7,500 per annum – but you could supplement your income by selling stories to national newspapers. You could get £75 for a page lead in the

---

9 *Daily Telegraph*, 16 October 2000.

Evening Standard and as much as £500 for a back-page splash in one of the national dailies. There was a spike where old press releases were speared, and a giant ashtray overflowing with cigarette stubs.

Generally, national newspapers did – unlike today – report on third-tier games, although they rarely sent their own staff to Griffin Park, using a few paragraphs of copy filed by a news agency in Sunday editions. There was the odd exception: when Brentford played Tottenham at home one evening in a League Cup second leg, the *Sun* and the *Daily Mirror* dispatched reporters. With not enough room in the press seats – which amounted to desk space for about a dozen journalists – the pair of tabloid hacks sat in the stands and, without bothering to take notes, filed their copy by phone as Spurs rounded off a comfortable 7–3 win on aggregate.

Occasionally when there were few other games in London, Brian Glanville, a long-time football correspondent for the *Sunday Times*, who had lived in Italy for many years, would cycle to Griffin Park from his home in Holland Park to cover a game and lecture us over tea and custard creams at half-time about Italian football. For Fleet Street journalists, Brentford was rarely anything but a footnote on the sport news agenda.

Webb was charming and expansive when I first interviewed him about Brentford in the office at Griffin Park. (He gave me his mobile phone number but, a few months later, hung up on me when I asked a frivolous question – in my defence, I was young and inexperienced. But he never took my calls again.) Lange, meanwhile, returned my calls to politely explain the club's plans. While players found Lange easy to talk to, a few of them were intimidated by Webb. When he was launching a half-time tirade, they stared at the stone floor. If you caught his eye, you risked becoming part of the rant.

When Webb's team picked up just a single point from the last three games to miss out on automatic promotion in 1995, he laid out plans for the eight days before the first game of the two-leg play-off semi-finals against Huddersfield. 'We are going to have a mini pre-season,' he announced, conjuring up images of Richmond Park's hills.

The players stared at the floor. Only captain Jamie Bates responded. 'Are you serious, gaffer?' he asked.

'Too fucking right, I am,' Webb said. 'If you were all fitter, you would have been fucking promoted already.'[10]

A decade earlier, searching around for ways to raise extra revenue for lower league clubs, Martin Lange had come up with the idea of the play-offs while sitting on a Football League panel that included the Crystal Palace chairman Ron Noades. As in US sports, the play-offs would be a series of end-of-season cliffhangers. At a meeting in a hotel by Heathrow Airport, Lange's proposal was adopted. BSkyB liked the drama that culminated with a finale at Wembley and agreed to air all 15 of the end-of-season games across three divisions. While a good commercial idea, Lange's brainwave turned out to be bad for Brentford. Webb's team would have already been promoted in second place in the pre-play-offs era but, instead, due to a

---

10 Author interview with Jamie Bates.

restructuring of the league that year which meant only one team was automatically promoted, they were pitched into the knock-out competition. After preparing by running up hills in Richmond Park, they lost on penalties in the play-off semi-final to Huddersfield, leaving them rooted in the third tier.[11]

After a decade in charge, Lange's ambition for Brentford seemed to have largely petered out: he had presided over all but one season in the same division. Since signing Stan Bowles, he had adopted a cautious approach. His strategy, by and large, seemed to revolve around trying to remain a solvent business, without undercutting his personal fortune. He had a house with a gravel drive in Surrey, a vacation home on the Côte d'Azur, and a collection of Ferraris, but owning Brentford had made a £1 million pound hole in his finances.[12] Nevertheless, he remained a fan at heart. He would drive up to Griffin Park from Surrey on match days in one of his Ferraris, sometimes taking his personal assistant Christine Mathews, the former club secretary who had gone to work for him.[13]

In the boardroom, club directors liked to have a drink and a chat but there was little innovation or appetite for financial risk. On match days, food was made in a ground-floor kitchenette and carried up on trays covered in tin foil, where it was set on a table in one corner of the room near a display cabinet that illustrated the club's lack of success: there were one or two obscure silver trophies; a porcelain cup presented

---

11 Between 1991 and 2020, Brentford fans endured nine playoffs, each one unsuccessful.
12 Dave Twydell, Mark Chapman and John Hirdle, *Brentford 1989–1999: Ten Traumatic Years*.
13 Author interview with Christine Mathews.

by Stoke City to Football League clubs to commemorate the coronation of King George VI, some obscure East German club pennants; and a Sikh sword that was a gift from the Mayor of Hounslow.[14]

In truth, if Brentford stayed in the third tier and maybe had a good cup run, supporters were happy enough. Expectations were low: only a minority remembered the time, half a century earlier, when the club was in the first division. Ever vigilant of the club's bottom line, Lange hired a hard-working executive called Keith Loring to run the commercial department – yet, despite his best efforts, Brentford consistently posted annual losses. In a deeply unpopular move, in 1986 Lange paid off the club's debt that was eroding his fortune by selling the rear of the Royal Oak terrace to developers. The land was converted into flats and an ugly two-tier stand – nicknamed 'the Wendy House' – replaced the terrace, reducing the stadium's capacity by about 8,000. The cash windfall from the deal paid off the debt, but soon it began to rise again.

Two miles away, on the site of a former biscuit factory near the Great West Road, BSkyB was pumping money into the Premier League. As the teams in the top division got richer, Brentford and other lower league clubs were left with dwindling ticket income and only a rare cheque from broadcasters willing to pay to show a cup game or a play-off final. It was increasingly unsustainable to be a small football club in the modern era. Even

---

14 The London War Cup won by Brentford was on display in Chelsea's club museum following their participation in a later edition of another war tournament; in 2015 a petition by Brentford fans on www.change.org to return the trophy to Griffin Park garnered 388 signatures.

hospitality was meagre: Griffin Park may have had a pub on each corner, but their beer sales did not flow into the club's coffers.

On the flip side, being a Brentford fan was relatively stress free. You could stroll through a gap in a row of terraced houses in New Road to the turnstiles at 2.55 p.m., five minutes before kick-off – there was barely ever any queue – and walk up the stone steps into the stands just as the players jogged onto the pitch and 'Hey Jude' came on over the PA system.

The Beatles song had become a Saturday afternoon ritual: it had been played to stir up the crowd at home games since it came out in 1968. As match-day disc jockey, Peter Gilham first selected the tune back then. The song starts with Paul McCartney's gentle call – *'Hey, Jude'* – before gradually building momentum, adding tambourine, drums and cymbals, progressing from sadness to positivity, and finally erupting into a joyful crescendo. The song signalled the start of a match and the beauty of football: anything could happen.

By 1997 Lange and Webb had worked together for four years. They spoke on the phone regularly, sharing updates about the team. Around this time Brentford's centre-forwards were Nicky Forster and Bob Taylor. They were the team's axis. Taking the first letter of their surnames David Webb gave them the nickname 'the FT Index'.

'How is the FT Index doing today?' Martin Lange would ask him.

Webb had some success at identifying talent which he sold on, helping to shore up Lange's finances. During pre-season

Fall

entford High Street heaved with traffic in the early years of the football club because of the town's
sy dock and position on the road to the West Country. *(Popperfoto/Getty Images)*

entford scrambled to expand Griffin Park's capacity to 40,000 when the team was promoted to
First Division and demand for tickets soared. *(Photo by J.A. Hampton/Stringer/Getty Images)*

General manager Harry Curtis congratulates Billy Scott, the first Brentford footballer to play for England, after he was selected to face Wales in 1936. *(Photo by David Savill/Stringer/Getty Images)*

On a pitch with more mud than grass, Brentford striker Dave McCulloch heads at goal in a 6-2 home loss to the 1937 league champions, Manchester City. *(PA Images/Alamy Stock Photo)*

(above) One of the art deco factories on the Great West Road – this one produced Pyrene fire extinguishers – from where workers flocked to Griffin Park on Saturdays. *(INTERFOTO/Alamy Stock Photo)*

(right) Owner Jack Dunnett arrives at Griffin Park to explain to minority shareholders his plan to merge with Queens Park Rangers and effectively shut Brentford. *(PA Images/Alamy Stock Photo)*

(above) Described by a newspaper as a bearded militant, Peter Pond-Jones, chairman of Brentford Supporters' Club, rallies fans against the merger plan.
(PA Images/Alamy Stock Photo)

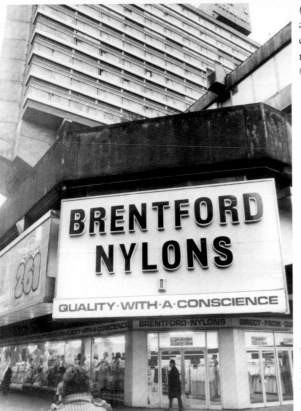

(left) Brentford Nylons, which made bedsheets, was more prominent than the football club in the 1970s thanks to stores like this one in Manchester.
(Photo by Manchester Evening News/Mirrorpix/Getty Images)

iffin Park's forecourt, with barbed wire, uneven tarmac and overflowing litter, in 1985 during a
-year stretch in the third division. *(Express/Freelancer/Getty Images)*

n Bowles, who mixed supreme skill with an anti-authoritarian streak, brought some glamour to
ntford when he arrived in 1981. *(PA Images/Alamy Stock Photo)*

When Terry Hurlock first reported for pre-season at Brentford, he was mistaken for a painter; he became a fearsome midfielder and captain. *(PA Images/Alamy Stock Photo)*

Dan Tana, whose Hollywood restaurant served Paul Newman and Elizabeth Taylor, became chairman after investing £20,000 in Brentford. *(Photo by Evening Standard/ Hulton Archive/ Getty Images)*

meron Diaz, who chatted to Dan Tana about Brentford, in his restaurant with entertainment
:utives and former L.A. Laker Jerry West. *(Photo by Smallz & Raskind/Contour by Getty Images)*

d Webb, who became manager in 1993, went on to oversee a fire sale of players as owner that
ted in relegation to the fourth division. *(Photo by Professional Sport/Getty Images)*

Ron Noades bought out Webb and appointed himself manager but sold up to fan group Bees United for £2 after failing to sell Griffin Park. *(PA Images/Alamy Stock Photo)*

training he would bring in as many as 20 trialists to see if they were good enough. Among them in 1994 was Carl Asaba, a young forward then at Dulwich Hamlet. Asaba signed with Brentford but struggled in his first season as a professional. After hiring a personal trainer – the club did not have a fitness coach – he flourished, scoring 24 goals the next season. He was transferred to Reading for £800,000, burnishing Webb's reputation as a talent spotter.

Part of Webb's remit from Lange was to control Brentford's wage bill. He set the salaries of players, and there was little room for negotiation. Typically, players took the contract they were offered or moved on. When Webb had been a player, most footballers did not have an agent to do the back and forth with management. But by the mid-1990s even a few lower league players had their own representatives. Once, one of these agents, who was still in his twenties, called Webb on his mobile and asked to come round and have a cup of tea and a chat about a salary rise for his client. He was seeking no more than an extra couple of hundred pounds a week. Webb said there would be no tea, no chat, and if the agent came knocking on his office door, he would chase him out of Griffin Park.[15]

During his career as a tough defender, Webb developed a sideline in small businesses, selling clothes and, during a brief fad when they were fashionable among women, wigs. He bought a hair salon in Chelsea in 1969 to sell more of the hairpieces, but they went out of fashion within a couple of years, leaving

---

15 Author interview with agent.

him with declining sales.[16] As his time as a player wound down, he became attracted to the idea of owning a football club. He tried to buy Bournemouth while a player-manager but failed to meet a deadline to raise the asking price, then, for a few months, he multitasked as player, manager, co-owner and managing director of Torquay United. Money was short and not only did he run daily operations, and play in games at the age of 38, he also picked the starting eleven and drove the team bus.[17] In between subsequent management jobs at Southend and Chelsea, he sold second-hand cars and mountain bikes near his home in Essex.

By the age of 52 Webb decided he wanted to have another go at football club ownership. In 1998 Lange agreed to cede him control of Brentford. Webb would pay £1 million for a 51 per cent stake, giving Lange enough to recoup his loans to the club over the years. To help finance his acquisition, Webb sought out other investors. Among those he invited to discuss the possibility of buying a minority shareholding was Greg Dyke, a well-known television executive.

Dyke had grown up watching Brentford in the 1950s, when his elder brother was in the reserve team. As a schoolboy he'd caught the bus from Hayes to watch games in Division Three (South); the bus he caught had a circuitous route across suburban west London and it would take him about an hour and a half to reach Griffin Park. By 1997 Dyke lived nearby in

---

16 David Webb interview, Leicester City website, 25 June 2020.
17 David Webb interview, *Southend Echo*, 16 September 2021.

Twickenham and still went to some Brentford games, taking his three children, the youngest of whom brought along a Gameboy to keep him entertained.

Dyke had received £7 million three years earlier under a share bonus scheme while chief executive of London Weekend Television, and Webb wanted to know if he would invest some of the cash in Brentford.[18] When Dyke arrived for their rendezvous on a summer's day, he found Webb in a hospitality suite at Griffin Park sawing a plank of wood.[19] Dyke did not see much upside in bankrolling a money-losing third division club where the chief executive carried out DIY improvements. While he was fond of the Bees, they had perpetually bounced around the bottom two divisions and there seemed little prospect of that changing. A few weeks later he became a non-executive director of Manchester United, then the richest club in the world.

Webb had more success with Tony Swaisland, another boyhood Brentford fan who was now a property investor based in the Channel Islands: Swaisland agreed to become a co-investor in the third division club.

Webb stood down as manager, appointing himself as chief executive and awarding himself a management fee for the year of more than £330,000.[20] That summer, as though he was flogging cars and bikes, he raised £1.2 million in trading players who had taken the team to the play-offs for the second time in

---

18 Size of payout cited in *The Times* profile of Dyke, 29 January 2004.
19 Author interview with Greg Dyke.
20 Brentford Football and Sports Club Ltd accounts for year to May 1998, Companies House.

three years. As well as transferring Asaba, he sold three more first-team regulars to Gillingham: Barry Ashby, Brian Statham and Paul Smith.

Off the pitch, Brentford finished the 1997–98 season with net income of £350,000, one of the biggest profits in their history.[21] On the pitch, they won only 11 of 46 games, burned through three managers and, on the last day of the season, were relegated to the fourth division.

With his money on the line, the prospect of playing in the Football League basement and perhaps sinking even further spooked Webb. He looked out of his depth. He sold the club at a 25 per cent discount on the price he had paid, to someone with more experience.[22]

With the Bees languishing in the lower leagues, they became a second team for some – thanks, perhaps, to a loyal father, uncle or cousin – but many residents of the suburb now supported Chelsea. In the history book published to mark Brentford's centenary in 1989, roughly half of the 725 fans who paid £10 to be name-checked had addresses within a five-mile radius of Griffin Park: Chiswick, Acton, Hanwell, Isleworth, Twickenham, Heston, etc.[23] As well as being local, the demographic of supporters was ageing and white. For the Asian population in Ealing, Hounslow and Southall, with no

---

21 Companies House, ibid.
22 *Middlesex Chronicle*, 7 May 1998.
23 White, ibid.

family connections, there remained little motivation to visit Griffin Park of a Saturday.

Since the 1960s the Asian population of outer west London had swelled as new arrivals from India and Pakistan arrived at Heathrow. Some found jobs in a rubber plant in Hayes, or a margarine factory in Southall, others at Brentford Nylons. Cricket was more popular among Asian families. There were more cricket pitches locally than in other parts of London.[24] Osterley Cricket Club, near Brentford's training ground, had six teams and fields spilled over with cricketers in summer. But there were still some for whom football had always been their sport.

At Chanchal Saroya's school in a village near Amritsar in India, he had played football, kicking a ball about in the schoolyard and then, in a district league, on a threadbare grass pitch dried out by the sun. In 1963 Chanchal Saroya had arrived at Heathrow, eventually settling with his family in Southall. Two or three families crammed into suburban homes. It was cold and it was difficult to find Indian spices for cooking: there was one shop which received weekly deliveries from the subcontinent to remind him of home cooking. But the waft of curry eventually emanated from terraced houses – the burgeoning of the UK's love affair with curry. Saroya remembers thugs from far-right groups fighting. As he walked down the street, white youths would shout: 'Go home, Paki.'[25]

---

24 In the London borough of Hammersmith and Fulham there is one cricket pitch for every five football pitches, compared to one in three in Hounslow, according to 2022 data in the app Playfinder.
25 Author interview with Chanchal Saroya.

Saroya was good at maths and landed a payroll job with the Greater London Council. When he discovered that some of his colleagues at work played in a local football league in Whitton, near Hounslow, he tagged along. He did not make the first GLC team – they had as many as eight teams, maybe more – but he did not aspire to greatness; he just loved the game. On a black and white television he watched Bill Nicholson's Tottenham Hotspur, one of the most exciting teams of the 1960s, and adopted them as his own. Aged 19, he and a friend went to White Hart Lane to see if they could get hold of tickets for the next weekend's game. They had a scout around the stadium and were walking through the car park when a man came out of one door and approached them. 'How can I help you?' Bill Nicholson asked them. Meeting a man of Nicholson's stature by chance was akin to walking around the grounds of the Vatican and meeting the Pope. He had won the league with Tottenham as a player in 1951 and, more recently, as manager, he had led them to the league and FA Cup double in 1961. 'We are looking for tickets for Saturday's game,' they explained. Nicholson looked back at them kindly. 'If you come back on the day, you should be able to find them,' he said, with a smile.

The Saroya family moved to Hayes, where they were the only Asian family in their street. Chanchal carried on playing football in Whitton, taking along his two sons. When they were older, he took them with him to watch Tottenham. They rarely saw any other Asians in the crowd at White Hart Lane. While watching his younger son Nevin play football for West Drayton Boys Club, his father overheard another parent say, 'He'll never make it as a footballer because he's Asian.'

One day, his father dropped by former Tottenham captain Steve Perryman's sports shop in Hayes to ask his advice on helping Nevin become a professional footballer. Perryman had managed the shop while still playing for Tottenham, and while player-manager at Brentford. For the Saroyas, Brentford was their local club and had a Youth Training Scheme for apprentice players, even though it had never taken on an Asian before. Here was a cultural barrier that Nevin would need to cross to fulfil his ambition. Perryman gave Mr Saroya some club programmes as a gift and some advice for his son: stick with it.

Ronald Geoffrey Noades was one of a new generation of football club owners who emerged in the 1980s, who saw ownership as a business rather than a public service.[26] For decades the businessmen who had co-owned Brentford ran the club benevolently, with little hope of receiving a return on their investments. At best, they would get most of their money back and enjoy a few perks, mixing with players, enjoying a nip of whisky after games, and maybe the thrill of briefly meeting a first division manager like Brian Clough after an FA Cup tie.

Noades, however, flipped football clubs in the same way property speculators flipped houses. He bought them cheaply, increased their value, then sold them for a higher price. He bought Wimbledon for £2,782, selling the club five years later for £100,000. He acquired Crystal Palace for £600,000,

---

26 The other most notable example was Chelsea's Ken Bates.

disposing of that property 17 years later for £23 million.[27] In 1998 he bought just-relegated Brentford from David Webb for £750,000 and set about turning it into an asset which he could one day sell on.

Noades had made his fortune from property and golf course development – he owned four golf courses in the Surrey commuter belt. He lived with his wife Novella in a seven-bedroom, six-bathroom mansion in Purley, with an indoor swimming pool with a slide and the club crest of Crystal Palace embossed on the bottom. His fleet of cars included a classic sports car, a 4x4, and a Mercedes saloon with a personalised number plate: RGN 3. At the start of the new millennium, when players in the Premier League were earning more money, and their lifestyles were being scrutinised, Noades rented out his home for filming of the television drama *Footballers' Wives*.

At Brentford he spun off the stadium from the club. Making them two separate companies was his way of trying to maximise his return on investment. Because Griffin Park was ageing, had two parking spaces, and was hemmed in by rows of terraced streets, there was little scope for redevelopment. He worked on a plan to sell the ground to homebuilder Wimpy and began talks about ground-sharing on a temporary basis with non-league clubs Woking and Kingstonian. He felt that moving to either site in Surrey would encourage Hounslow Council, which was responsible for planning permission, to accelerate efforts

---

27 He initially received only part of the £23 million sale price and, as a result, retained Selhurst Park stadium for a time, renting it out to both Wimbledon and Crystal Palace's new owner Mark Goldberg.

to help find a place for a new stadium in the borough. This kind of hard-nosed approach, of course, horrified supporters. Noades proposed to leave their club homeless for the first time since 1904. On hearing of his plan they paraded a coffin in the street scrawled with the words: 'Brentford FC RIP'. In the end, his plan came to nothing: Lange, who had retained a 25 per cent stake, said he would exercise his veto right on the sale of Griffin Park.

For his other asset, the club, Noades adopted an unusual strategy for an owner: he appointed himself as manager. Twenty years earlier he had earned an FA coaching badge, and now he was in his sixties this was perhaps his last chance in life to fulfil a dream. Over his suit and tie, he stood on the touchline at Griffin Park wearing an oversize black Adidas coat with the England badge on his left breast. In truth, Noades was not a hands-on manager. From Monday to Thursday he would barely show his face at the training ground, ceding responsibility to first-team coach Ray Lewington, who had managed Fulham and Crystal Palace. While Noades was officially the boss, most players gave far more credence to what Lewington said.

For Noades, the beauty of being both owner and manager was that he was able to sign a player quicker than anyone else. By the time a rival club had scheduled a meeting between chairman and manger, Noades had snagged his man. 'While they were still poncing about,' he said, 'I'd bought him.'[28] Noades spent £1 million on players, most of it going on

---

28 Ron Noades quoted on www.footballpink.net, 8 January 2021.

Hermann Hreidarsson, from Crystal Palace. Hreidarsson was like a lower-league Franz Beckenbauer, one of the best players Brentford had had in years, perhaps decades, and by the first months of 1999 Brentford were pushing for promotion.

While Noades was living out his dream, Chanchal Saroya's son Nevin was making progress with his. He had been accepted on Brentford's Youth Training Scheme (YTS) along with another Asian teenager, Neerav Patel from Bedfont, and both had spent the last couple of years learning about professional football at Griffin Park. They cleaned the boots of first-team players, laid out their kit on match days and swept the floor. As they matured, the YTS footballers played in a youth league, where games could be eventful: in a 1–0 loss to Southampton in 1997 Brentford's goalkeeper Jason Surban was sent off for handball, Patel for dissent, and Nevin Saroya found himself playing in goal. The following season, with only ten first-team matches left, Brentford were third in the fourth division when 18-year-old Saroya was selected as the designated YTS player to accompany the team to an away game at Hartlepool United.

With Noades and Lewington on the touchline, Brentford fashioned most of their goals through the centre of the pitch, using pace and vertical passing to cut through the retreating opposition defence. For a fourth-tier team they were skilful, and in Martin Rowlands they had uncovered a budding playmaker. The attacks were often rounded off by Lloyd Owusu, who by now had 16 league goals. On the eve of the match at Hartlepool the team travelled by bus to the north-east. Saroya was a little nervous to spend 48 hours with senior players. He knew he would not even get on the substitutes' bench but would live the experience of a Football League game. His chores would involve packing up the sweat-stained shirts and muddy socks and boots of players. On a damp night the next day, in front of a crowd of 2,719, there was so much fog spectators could barely see the far side of the pitch. Brentford beat Hartlepool 1–0 with a goal before half-time by Owusu, cranking up their promotion push.

The mood was buoyant as players piled into the dressing room, and chucked their dirty kit onto the floor for Saroya to collect and take back to London. Mission accomplished, the winning team showered, dressed and settled down on the team bus for the long journey home. As the bus headed south, the chatter among players turned to how the club's winning streak was doing wonders for their bank balances; midfielder Charlie Oatway chirped up that Saroya should also get a £150 win bonus, like the rest of the team. Noades agreed.[29] Brentford were promoted as champions, and Noades was named the Division Three manager of the year by his peers.[30]

Not long afterwards, Noades signed Saroya on professional terms, and he became the first Asian to play for Brentford. (Patel was not offered a contract.) But football has always been a tough business, and for every teenage hopeful that makes a career as a player at least a dozen more do not. Saroya was at Brentford for

---

29 Author interview with Nevin Saroya.
30 The League Managers' Association; in winning the accolade Noades followed managers including Jimmy Armfield, Gerry Francis and Harry Redknapp.

a couple of seasons as a squad player, coming on as a substitute in one game, before his career petered out. Brentford's connection with the huge Asian population on its doorstep in the 1990s was still decades away, and it remained extremely rare to see Asian players on the pitch or Asian supporters in the stands at Griffin Park.

After he was released by Brentford, Saroya used his talent to get a job on the set of a football-themed movie, *Mean Machine*, starring Jason Statham and Vinnie Jones, before launching a successful career as a coach for the PFA, the players' trade union.

Nothing seemed to please Ron Noades more than an astute piece of business. A few weeks into his second season as Brentford manager, he traded Hreidarsson to Wimbledon for £2.5 million, more than three times the price he'd signed him for. A 300 per cent return on an investment in barely a year, it was enough to make even the hedge-fund managers in Mayfair jealous.

However, without their talisman defender, Brentford lost their way and narrowly avoided relegation back to the fourth division. In November 2000, after being knocked out of the FA Cup by non-league Kingstonian, Noades resigned as manager. The fun of the promotion year when fans had worn wigs to mimic his white hair was long gone. Now, some directed abuse at him as defeats piled up and his unsentimental approach to ownership was laid bare by his plans to relocate Brentford's home games to Surrey.

In a photo of him at the time with his wife Novella standing in front of his indoor swimming pool, Noades was approaching retirement age and looked worn out. He wanted to get out of the game and switch his underperforming investment into his golf courses, whose greens fees brought in reliable income. After 25 years, he had had enough of football.[31]

Two fan groups had mobilised during this period, first as a reaction to Webb's worrisome ownership, and then the plans by Noades to sell Griffin Park. Supporters, some of whom were old enough to remember Jack Dunnett's attempts to merge Brentford with QPR, wanted to take back control of the club from owners they considered did not have the club's best interests at heart.

With no more appetite to run Brentford himself, Noades agreed to let one of the groups, Bees United, manage the club on a temporary basis while it tried to put together a takeover package worth north of £3 million to buy him out. Bees United were passionate, enterprising – and broke. They rattled buckets on match days to collect change and banknotes. Members paid a monthly standing order to the not-for-profit organisation. Five of them raised extra cash with a 286-mile walk to a match at Hartlepool. Quiz nights and a monthly jazz night were arranged in the bar at Griffin Park. In a scheme to raise extra revenue, they leased the Princess Royal, one of the four pubs on the corners of Griffin Park.[32]

---

31 Author interview with Greg Dyke.
32 According to an internal club document seen by author, the five-year lease agreement with Fuller's ended up losing the club as much as £5,000 per month.

Despite their efforts, Bees United were unable to even cover the club's annual interest overdraft charge of £290,000. One of the few avenues they had for progress was through a partnership with a property developer that would allow them to pay off the rising debt and move into a new stadium in or around Brentford. Over the previous 30 years the club had looked at numerous sites to build a new ground. Two of the most recent ones they had focused on were by the Western International Market in Heston, near Heathrow Airport, and another in Feltham. With his plan to sell Griffin Park and groundshare blocked, Noades had given up on pushing to relocate. Bees United, however, kept on looking for a stadium site.

The Heston and Feltham sites were not in Brentford and were not particularly popular with fans. However, near Kew Bridge, lay a three-hectare triangle of land that was a couple of hundred metres from the riverside pub where the club was founded in 1889. The land was talked about in hushed tones by Bees United leaders over pints of beer at the Griffin pub, with the proviso: 'Don't tell Ron Noades.'

The site, abutting Lionel Road, was once owned by the Rothschild family. Lionel Road was named after Lionel Rothschild, whose wife Charlotte had once turned her nose up at the drunkenness and poverty in Brentford; and whose son became a club patron. Now the triangle was a wasteland hemmed in between railway lines and owned by the publicly funded Strategic Rail Authority. Most motorists who passed by the fenced-off land in taking the slip road to the M4 flyover had no idea what lay inside. On the plot of wasteland, it turned out, was a hotchpotch of half a dozen or so small businesses operating out of dilapidated warehouses, garages and portacabins. They included a classic car repair service, a recycling business, and a makeshift studio producing pornographic movies.[33]

The plan was that one day, once Brentford had finally got out of their perennial financial crisis, the team would play here in a brand-new stadium and could start to focus on not simply surviving but climbing up the Football League.

---

33 Author interview with Bees United board member Chris Gammon.

Chapter 6

2000s: Griffin Park

Tony Blair's Labour government was enthusiastic about regenerating semi-abandoned parts of London like the site of a former gasworks on the Greenwich peninsula, a brownfield site in a crook of the Thames whose soil was polluted with arsenic, mercury and unexploded wartime bombs.[1] The project to build a Millennium Dome there to mark the new century, inherited from the Conservatives, left Labour charged with what to put inside the vast building. They decided to make it a celebration of modern Britain: Cool Britannia.

The dome itself was ridiculed as an expensive and pointless project by some who accused the government of being preoccupied with marketing. While the launch of the dome was underwhelming, the development of the Greenwich peninsula

---

1 Tom Bower, *Broken Vows: Tony Blair, the Tragedy of Power*.

eventually became, in a roundabout way, an example of a successful public–private initiative, one of the pillars of Blair's so called 'third way' between the traditional left and right of British politics. After the Jubilee Line was extended to this once abandoned terrain, apartment blocks, schools, shops and a cable car followed. The dome was rebranded as the O2 Arena in a lucrative naming rights deal and went on to become one of the world's most popular venues for music and sports events, one year surpassing New York's Madison Square Garden in ticket sales.

At around the same time as the Greenwich peninsula got a makeover, Brentford was earmarked to receive regeneration funding. Hounslow Council worked on plans to attract private developers to redevelop the High Street. Instead of a Greggs, a windowless internet café and a motley selection of takeaways, there would be fashion boutiques and modern flats set around a Mediterranean-style piazza with a fountain. But there was still not much appetite from developers. As other parts of London gentrified, Brentford resisted becoming bourgeois. The council plans stayed on the drawing board. Developers did begin to build a few riverside apartment blocks in Brentford near Kew Bridge, complete with concierge, gym and underground car park, but estate agents used a sleight of hand when marketing these flats. To make potential buyers believe the properties were in a smarter part of town, the name Brentford was left out of the promotional literature. One block was given the name: Kew View.

If the private sector shunned unfashionable areas, Blair planned to empower communities to improve public services themselves. One example was civic action by the people of Wythenshawe. A non-profit trust formed by residents in the sprawling southern Manchester suburb had borrowed £10 million to redevelop a leisure centre.[2] Bees United, the fan group operating as a not-for-profit trust, felt it could leverage Labour's approval for community initiatives to move forward with what they hoped would become the Brentford Community Stadium.

Some of the Bees United trustees, including chairman Brian Burgess, had experience of managing social enterprise projects. Burgess, who was brought up in Hounslow – a Brentford fan since 1962 – had a background in engineering and construction and, during Blair's years as prime minister, had worked on community projects. He bounced around ideas with MPs and local authorities about how to share the costs of building the stadium. Labour-controlled Hounslow Council floated the prospect of a public sports centre being built on the stadium complex near Kew Bridge.[3] The National Health Service, meanwhile, was interested in incorporating a doctor's surgery. As they courted the public sector, Burgess and his peers sought out lawyers, PR consultants, business managers and others to help move the club forward, without being paid for their expertise. In student digs in Layton Road, around the corner from Griffin Park, a young architect fresh out of university used computer software to try to fit a football stadium into

---

2 *Guardian*, 1 February 2005
3 To replace Brentford Fountain Leisure Centre.

the triangle of industrial wasteland identified by Bees United.[4] For his postgraduate degree, he had worked on a speculative plan for an Arsenal stadium near King's Cross. Most modern stadiums like the one that would become the Emirates were shaped like a bowl. It was impossible to fit such a design into a triangle, so he worked on an alternative.

As weeks and months went by, Ron Noades had found no interested parties willing to buy Brentford, bar Bees United. But the fan group was not going to find £3 million anytime soon, so he wanted his money back and he agreed to sit down to negotiate his exit strategy with the group's leaders. The meeting took place overlooking his golf course in Godstone, Surrey, in the spring of 2003. For all his plotting to sell Griffin Park, the relationship between Noades and Bees United was perfectly good. They agreed to a ten-point deal which his secretary typed out on a sheet of A4 paper. The most salient point was, of course, about money. If supporters could raise £1 million towards buying the club, he would match it with an interest-free loan until they could find more cash. It was a reasonable deal on the part of Noades that gave Bees United leaders some time to come up with the necessary money for him to pay off the club's debt and relinquish his shares without any burden on his personal finances. He gave them two years to raise the first million.[5]

---

4 Matt Dolman.
5 At around the same time, to help cash-strapped Bees United, Barclays bank agreed to convert Brentford's overdraft into a £2 million, 15-year-term loan, and Hounslow Council offered a £500,000 bridge loan.

Supporters pursued endless avenues to raise the money. They continued speaking to property developers. They reached out to lenders. They contacted wealthy fans. Greg Dyke, the Director-General of the BBC, was sounded out by a Bees United member about helping while queuing for hamburgers for his sons at half-time at Griffin Park. No longer part of Manchester United's board, he responded to a follow-up letter asking if he wanted to get involved with Brentford, with a short missive of his own on a BBC letterhead: 'It depends on what you mean by "getting involved".'[6] To the band of supporters, anxious for any kind of positive news, that sounded promising. Dyke was willing to invest some of his time in Brentford, if not a large portion his wealth.

What fans were asking prospective investors was, they eventually realised, an unattractive proposition. Nobody seemed to see the benefit of investing in a club with a widening overdraft, ageing fanbase and a hundred-year-old stadium. Brentford was a club with little or no potential and a golden age that dated back 60 years to not long after the end of the Second World War. A couple of months before the deadline set by Noades expired on the final day of May in 2005, Bees United's tireless volunteers were nowhere nearer to coming up with one million pounds. It was at this point that they arranged an interview with David Conn, a journalist then writing for the *Independent*. Brentford was not the sexiest of stories for national newspaper journalists. Not far away, Chelsea were on their way to a second straight Premier League title under new owner Roman

---

6 Author interview, Dyke.

Abramovich; Fulham were in their fourth consecutive season in the top division; and QPR were in the Championship. Yet Conn was passionate about football's role in the community, and, in his article, he praised the voluntary work of Brentford fans trying to save their club. Bees United, he wrote, were desperately seeking a few wealthy supporters to pitch in.

The time to the 31 May deadline ticked down. Not long after it had lapsed, Noades ratcheted up the pressure on Bees United: his accountant rang Brian Burgess, the chairman, to put the club on notice. Barclays Bank was, the accountant said, refusing to extend the overdraft facility unless Noades provided more collateral, something he was not prepared to do. He would not be using his golf courses or Purley mansion for that purpose. Brentford would not have enough money to pay player wages that month, the accountant said, and the club would have to go into administration.

At this perilous time Brentford's manager was 39-year-old Martin Allen. Allen had taken over just over a year earlier with the club in the relegation zone. It was his first appointment as head coach of one of the 92 league clubs and he treated his new job as though he were managing Manchester United – and Brentford fans loved him for it.

On his first day he arrived in Osterley from his home in Berkshire before dawn. When he found a pile of dirty unbranded training shirts on the floor at the training ground in Osterley, he ordered the club to buy a new set and went about hiring a kit man. The little things were important. He distributed a booklet to players – *Guidelines for Success!* – that instructed them how to behave when representing Brentford Football Club. Drinking alcohol at Griffin Park was banned for players, and any of them found boozing before an away game would be sent home immediately, at their own expense. Any player arriving for a match with their top button undone would receive a £20 fine. Any player showing disrespect to the facilities at Griffin Park or club staff would be fined the same amount. (If Allen himself did not wear a club tie at a game, he promised to fine himself £20.)[7]

When Allen met England manager Sven-Göran Eriksson at a BBC event he invited him to come to watch Brentford train.

Eriksson was bemused. 'Who's Brentford? Where are you? What Division are you in?'[8]

Allen walked off as if Eriksson had insulted his family.

When Allen had first arrived at Brentford, there were nine matches left and the club were in danger of being relegated to the bottom division. Before each game at Griffin Park, he stirred up the crowd in the Braemar Road paddock, clenching his fist as he walked purposefully to the dugout. Club tie on, top button done up, he strode through puddles on the clay path by the side of the pitch, seeking to convey an air of supreme confidence. His manner got the crowd going, and they turned up the atmosphere.

Allen would seek any edge to channel positive energy into the club. Whenever he was struck by a moment of inspiration,

---

7 *Irish Independent*, 3 December 2004.
8 The exchange took place at the *BBC Sports Personality of the Year Award, Independent*, 22 January 2006.

he rang Peter Gilham and dictated a message to post on the club website, or in the programme notes for the next match. On the way to away games, when the team bus drove past Brentford fans walking to the stadium, Allen instructed the driver to stop by the side of the road and sweep them up to join the players on board for the last part of their journey. In what was described as 'The Great Escape', Allen's Brentford team lost only one of their last nine games.

The following January, Brentford travelled to the northeast for an FA Cup fourth-round replay at Hartlepool. Besides selling a player, a cup run was one of the few ways of easing Brentford's financial woes. Allen went up north with the team the day before the game. Their hotel was overlooking the River Skerne near Darlington. As players joked over how much money they would swim the 20 yards from one bank to the other for, Allen peeled off his clothes, jumped in the water and swam across the river past empty Coke cans and crisp packets. He emerged slathered in mud and jogged back to the team hotel, where he joined the queue at reception for his room key, behind a group of middle-aged American tourists. The next day, Allen decided there would be no pre-match team talk. He had already channelled his message to them by swimming across the river.[9] Brentford won 1–0, earning a fifth-round tie against Southampton. That season, operating on a constricted budget and with barely £5,000 in the bank, Allen took them to the play-offs.

---

9 *Push Up Brentford!* film interview with Martin Allen.

At the start of October 2005, not long after the call from the accountant of Noades informing him the club would have to go into administration, Brian Burgess went onto the pitch before a league game against Rotherham to make an announcement to the crowd of 5,900 on behalf of Bees United. When he began speaking, Allen had yet to make his generalissimo-style pre-match entrance.

Burgess told the crowd, almost none of whom knew about the administration threat, that there was some good news. Two supporters, he said, had agreed to each loan £100,000 interest free to avoid the club going into administration.[10] Instead of cheering the news, supporters were stunned by how serious the financial situation was. Sure, they had seen Bees United volunteers collecting spare change in buckets outside the ground, but few had any idea that the club was teetering on the edge of insolvency.

As the game got underway, supporters did not respond in the same way as usual to Allen's efforts to rouse them. The team went behind to an eighth-minute goal. Allen blamed Burgess for killing the atmosphere.[11] The announcement had punctured the positivity he'd worked hard to introduce. On Monday morning, creditors jammed the phone lines at the club's offices seeking money they were owed. A few days later the club fielded a call from a man called Matthew Benham, who asked if he could talk to someone about how he could help.

---

10 At first anonymous, later they were revealed to be Greg Dyke and Eddie Rogers, another club director.
11 Brentford rallied to win 2–1.

Benham had read Conn's article in the *Independent* the previous winter and was aware of the club's financial troubles. He decided he might be able to assist, so he met a few of the club's directors, among them Bees United's delegates, in the Griffin Park boardroom to explain who he was.[12] He said he had been a teenage devotee of Brentford, although his passion had lapsed somewhat. His visits to Griffin Park had dwindled to one or two per year because he had a demanding job, a young family, and other matters to attend to. Now in his early thirties, he had grown wealthy and was prepared to help the club of his childhood.

After the meeting, the club directors went away and did some due diligence on him, to check that he was not a charlatan.

Matthew Benham had been brought up amid the grounds of Eton College, where both his parents were teachers. In black tailcoats, wing collars, black pinstriped trousers and black brogues, Etonians dressed like they lived in another epoch. Some boys wore cufflinks on their white shirts, like the young Boris Johnson. According to a former pupil, attending the school was a kind of family heirloom passed down to the descendants of the Edwardian upper classes.[13]

The Benham family lived in a cottage in a quiet street, where several teachers leased homes from the school. The road was set among school football pitches and a nine-hole golf course.

---

12 Bees United, *Bees, Battles, Buckets and Ballot Boxes: How Brentford Fans Paved the Way from Griffin Park to Lionel Road.*
13 Christopher de Bellaigue, www.Economist.com, 16 August 2016.

At the end of each summer, Mr and Mrs Benham organised a fair at which Etonians could fool around on a Saturday afternoon while raising money for charity. One of the stalls provided the chance for locals to hold an impromptu debate with a tailcoated toff. One year, the annual fundraiser in September collected £9,000 (about £25,000 today).

To the south, on the other side of Eton and the River Thames, stood Windsor Castle; to the north, on the other side of the M4, sat Slough. Benham's parents sent their son to Slough Grammar School, where the uniform was less elaborate: raspberry blazers, grey V-neck jumpers and striped ties. A school photo from 1981 shows a diverse school with a sizeable number of Asian pupils and a clutch of shaggy-haired heavy metal fans.

Benham became interested in football and, aged 11, his father – who preferred cricket – took him to his first Brentford game at Griffin Park which, 17 miles east of Eton, happened to be the nearest league ground. With a group of friends from Slough, Benham became further drawn into supporting the Bees over the next few years. When they were having a moment, with Stan Bowles in midfield, he followed them around the country, from Plymouth to Carlisle. Aged 14 he bunked off school on a Wednesday afternoon in December and took the train to watch Brentford play in a fourth-round Milk Cup – then the name for the League Cup – game at Nottingham Forest. Two weeks earlier Brentford had knocked out John Toshack's Swansea 2–1 in a replay at the Vetch Field, their first victory over a first division team in 33 years. Benham was one of 2,000 fans to travel to Nottingham to see if they could down Brian Clough's two-time European champions. A special chartered train left from Ealing Broadway. In the media, all the talk was of the return of Bowles to Forest and whether he could put one over Clough. Brentford lost 2–0.

In his last year at Slough Grammar School Benham won a place at Oxford University's Wadham College to read physics. Wadham had a reputation for nurturing left-leaning state school students who were politically opposed to the then leader of the debating society, a messy-haired old Etonian.

On graduating, Benham went to work in the City of London. Investment banks had recently begun headhunting maths and physics graduates to help them predict what would happen in financial markets. One New York-based hedge fund employed quantitative analysts – or 'quants' – to make billions of dollars of profit each year; the work of the quants was so valuable they had to sign a 30-page non-disclosure agreement. In the City, investment banks wanted a piece of the action, and went in search of the sharpest brains to predict the most profitable time to buy and sell.

Benham initially found himself on a trading desk at Yamaichi Securities, a Japanese investment firm that had traded stocks since 1897 but was expanding into derivatives.[14] Derivatives trading involved a bewildering array of futures, options and swaps linked to, for example, stocks. In 1973 the economists Fischer Black and Myron Scholes had helped cut through the complexity by creating a formula to estimate when to buy

---

14 James Tippett, *The Expected Goals Philosophy: A Game-Changing Way of Analysing Football.*

and sell derivatives based on stock prices, market volatility and other data. In an era when computers were scarce, the Black–Scholes model became a baseline for trading derivatives, although two decades later many traders in the City were not smart or perceptive enough to use mathematical modelling to make decisions.

In the summer of 1990, not long after Benham starting his working life at Yamaichi, he got his first taste of the old-fashioned way of doing things. Market prices had fallen for six consecutive days as the Gulf War loomed, only to bounce back during the US aerial attack, Operation Desert Storm – at which point Benham heard an older trader tell their boss he thought the price spike would be short lived. This, the trader said, was based on 'his gut feeling'. Even as a 22-year-old rookie in the job, Benham considered this way of making decisions to be complete nonsense.[15]

Employing a more scientific approach, Benham worked out the Expected Value of a stock based on years of historical data about relevant metrics such as market volatility. Put simply, the Expected Value was the underlying value of a stock. When the Expected Value of a stock was higher than the market price, Benham would buy; when it was lower, he would sell. Benham became a star derivatives trader and went on to work for Deutsche Bank and Bank of America, which rewarded the highest fliers with generous bonuses. By the age of 30 he lived in a gated mansion in a tree-lined East Finchley cul-de-sac,

---

15 Matthew Benham interview with *Tipsbladet*, 26 September 2014.

where some houses sold for more than £2.5 million. It was then when Benham made a somewhat unorthodox career move into the gambling industry.

When they first met him, the Bees United directors did not delve too deeply into Benham's new business – a start-up company called Smartodds that worked out the form of football teams as part of a betting strategy; it was a similar approach to the one he had employed in the City, although instead of weighing the underlying value of a stock, he calculated the underlying strength of a football team. For now, Bees United wanted only to confirm he was a genuine Brentford fan, and that he had the money he said he had. They spoke to one of their members from Slough, who as a schoolboy in the 1980s had gone to games with Benham. He confirmed Benham had indeed been a Brentford nut as a teenager. Meanwhile, Benham gave the directors the contact details of his Swiss bankers, who confirmed that his wealth stood at millions of pounds. This was enough: Benham ticked both boxes.

Initially, Benham's idea was simple: to save Brentford from administration and possible bankruptcy. He provided a £500,000 loan to help bridge the funding gap necessary to buy out Noades. He did not want to draw attention to himself, so the loan was made through a company called Midas Way Ltd.[16] For a while, to the outside world, and in classic news parlance, Benham was known as a 'mystery investor'. His idea back then

---

16 Brentford FC website, 20 January 2006.

was to 'just to put a bit of money in but not be involved day to day,' he said. 'Just peek behind the scenes.'[17]

Benham's bridge loan, interest free, helped Bees United achieve their goal and so, on a January 2006 morning in the City, the fan group acquired Brentford Football Club.

Noades had contracted an upmarket law firm called Dechert to oversee the sale. The firm was used to dealing with sizeable corporate deals, and their partners moved in the same circles as chief executives and hedge fund managers. They charged hourly fees approaching £1,000. At their offices, near St Paul's Cathedral, a corporate lawyer acting for Noades perhaps felt a little underwhelmed to be overseeing the sale of such a modest going concern, a third-tier football club from Hounslow. Nevertheless, he had prepared documents that stated Noades was relinquishing his 60 per cent stake in Brentford to Bees United, which became responsible for the club's £5.5 million overdraft. If the deal was not very exciting for the lawyer, it was also something of a downer for Noades. For the first time in his life, he had failed to flip a football club: under the deal, Bees United paid £1 for Brentford Football Club and £1 for Griffin Park. That was not good business by any standard. Spinning the club and ground off as two different entities had not achieved anything.

Usually when there is a token payment involved in a business transaction the money does not actually change hands, but the corporate lawyer was a stickler for detail and

---

17 Matthew Benham interview, Bees United website, 27 May 2022.

adamant the £2 payment should be made. The two Bees United representatives present had not come prepared. It was a bit embarrassing. Would they have to go to the bank? Hunting around in their pockets, they each came up with a one pound coin which they rolled across the table. The lawyer put both coins in the pocket of his well-cut suit.[18] It was official: Brentford Football Club and Griffin Park were now owned by supporters. That was the good news. The bad news was that the market value of both of them together added up to no more than the price of a cup of tea.

With Bees United now the majority shareholder, it appointed Greg Dyke – who had now left the BBC – as Brentford chairman. When he had written to the fan group to say he might be interested in getting involved, his idea was not to devote all his time, or money. He could, however, envision a role in which he tapped his network of contacts to help nurse the club he had supported as a boy back to health. A gregarious type, Dyke's contacts spanned media, business, government and sport, and he was equally at ease talking with world leaders as football fans in Griffin Park. Even when the surroundings were more refined than the Braemar Road stand, he liked to throw an F-bomb into conversation to underline his credentials as a straight talker.

Dyke set up a meeting in the office of London mayor Ken Livingstone, an old friend of his and a fellow straight talker. Bees United were trying to secure an option to buy the triangle of

---

18 Author interview with Chris Gammon; the two representatives were Gammon and Bruce Powell.

land by Lionel Road that was now in the hands of Chancerygate, a private developer which planned to move on the motley assortment of businesses in rusting premises, tidy up the area and build some smarter warehouses with higher rental value. Bees United leaders pitched their community stadium plan to Livingstone. The socialist known as Red Ken liked the sound of what the supporters were trying to do. When they had finished their half-hour presentation, he said: 'What do you need from me?'

They asked him if he could raise the prospect with the developer of public authorities making a compulsory purchase order on the triangle of land. Livingstone agreed. After a meeting along the same lines with transport minister Tom Harris, the supporters' lobbying of the Labour Party paid off and the developer gave Bees United an option to buy the land, giving fans time to develop a project to build a stadium there.

The group of supporters were doing everything in their power to advance the interests of the club. Sometimes, they made small gains, other times, they were knocked back. At one point Bees United chairman Brian Burgess suggested to Martin Allen that he might be able to tap the football know-how that Benham was developing at Smartodds to benefit Brentford. 'He's got all these guys on computers watching football and compiling data to make money in the gambling industry,' he told Allen. 'It could be really useful.'

Allen did not appear remotely interested.[19] Soon after the disappointment of a second play-off defeat in two years, this

---

19 Author interview with Brian Burgess.

time to Swansea, Allen resigned when his request for a bigger transfer budget was rejected; he left behind a trove of fond memories and colourful anecdotes.

The Smartodds office was on scruffy Highgate Road in north London, above a pub which at one point turned into a hipster bar with a magenta-baize pool table and clients wearing beanie hats. The office was in a former warehouse building, shared with a couple of dozen businesses, including a television production company and an architectural firm that designed urban buildings.

Benham had rented a small space in the building, not far from his home, in 2004. There was room for about a dozen desks. To the outside world, it was not immediately apparent what Benham or the business did. When he founded the venture that year, he described himself on the company formation papers as 'a strategist'. The space he leased was behind a grey steel door with a spyhole that allowed staff to screen whoever came calling.

Some of the first hires were quants, who helped Benham develop a proprietary model to predict the outcome of football matches by working out the true form of the two teams playing each other and deciding whether bookmakers were miscalculating their odds. Very often the bookies were wrong: in those early days the Smartodds model had an average profit margin on each game of as much as six per cent, according to a source familiar with the professional gambling sector.[20] In other words, for every £100 bet, gamblers using the model would

---

20 Author interview with source.

make an average profit of £6. However, to make big returns you had to get a lot of money down.

Ideally, up to £1 million.

The concept of a small group of boffins using mathematics to bet huge amounts of money on sports results was not completely new: there was a precedent with almost mythical status, known as the Computer Group, which had based itself in Las Vegas.

In 1970s Las Vegas, sports betting remained largely a peripheral business, sometimes conducted furtively on side streets to skirt a state sports-betting tax of ten per cent. Or, in back streets, bookies operated on sawdust-floor shops with a chalkboard. The smattering of American professional gamblers tried to get an edge by cultivating sources around players for inside information about their injuries, partying habits and relationship break-ups. They scoured regional newspapers for nuggets of information. In time, one paid the guards at Las Vegas Airport to collect the early edition papers left on aeroplane seats so his team could get an early look at the sports pages.[21]

Then the Nevada state betting levy was lowered to 2 per cent and sports betting became part of the glitzy Vegas strip, where showgirls in white hotpants invited you to come in and test your appetite for risk.[22] The Stardust resort, which had imported the cast of a Parisian cabaret show to entertain clients, was among the first entertainment complexes to offer customers

---

21 Billy Walters interview, YouTube, 10 February 2023.
22 The tax was soon cut again, to 0.25 per cent.

the chance to bet on sports. A 600-capacity theatre was fitted with upholstered seats – some with their own desks and lamps – and a 48-square-foot television screen showing horse racing and NFL matches.

As wives staying at the resort bronzed on sun loungers by a swimming pool and ordered cocktails from waiters, their husbands gambled on sports. In Las Vegas, the underdog – traditionally known as 'the chalk' – was given a points advantage. The San Francisco 49ers might, for example, be a seven-point favourite (+7) against the Philadelphia Eagles (-7).

While national television sportscasters legally could not mention Las Vegas betting prices on air, they were printed by newspapers across the US, piquing the interest of a mathematician living and working in Pittsburgh. Michael Kent's day job was to develop nuclear submarine technology for a US Navy contractor. In his spare time he began to work on a model to predict college football scores. When he had a break in his work schedule, he dropped by the library to note down years of results from anthologies. In the evening, using a computer from work, he incorporated variables like home and away form, scoring patterns and travel distance to games into a mathematical model. After seven years of graft he came up with a power rating that calibrated each team's form and chance of winning their next game. He stress-tested his work repeatedly. In 1982 Kent was convinced his system was more accurate than the qualitative judgement calls of bookmakers in setting odds, so he moved to Las Vegas to seek his fortune.

Because his margins over the take of bookmakers were generally relatively thin – just a couple of percentage points – Kent needed to get enough money down on matches to reap juicy returns. But, as a shy academic type, he did not like the idea of walking through the dimly lit back streets of Las Vegas carrying a briefcase full of cash. Instead, he teamed up with a hustler with more swagger: Billy Walters, a hard-living gambler from Kentucky who once lost $1 million in a single evening playing blackjack. When they first met, Walters' impression of Kent was that he was 'a complete square'.[23] They decided to team up.

Taking care of the logistics of the business, Walters assembled a network of 30 runners in Las Vegas to put down bets of as much as $50,000. By then, most other casinos had joined the Stardust in offering sports betting. If Kent's model showed odds were 1.5 percentage points or more out of sync from his model, Walters would activate his army of runners carrying wads of banknotes. In an era before mobile telephones were commonplace, they received their instructions on how much to bet, and at what price, on Nextel pagers.

Kent updated his power ratings each day. The key to the ratings was they did not focus on NFL teams' season-to-date record, which could be misleading, but measured their performances based on a series of other underlying metrics. Their syndicate was so successful that, according to Walters, they were betting as much as $10 million over the course of

---

23 Billy Walters, *Gambler: Secrets from a Life at Risk.*

a weekend. Besides American football, Kent built models for the NBA, golf, baseball, tennis and more. Walters, meantime, hired more runners, some of them laying bets on unregulated bookmakers in other parts of the US. The sprawling syndicate eventually got its own name: the Computer Group.

When the group's bets rained down, bookmakers would shift their prices to protect themselves against losses. Sometimes, to confuse the bookies, Walters employed what was known as a head fake, placing an opening bet to move the market only to put down a much bigger bet – as much as double – on the other side of the betting line.

Kent and Walters worked every day of the year, including Christmas Day. When autumn and the NFL season began, Walters got up at 4.30 a.m. and did not finish work until he had settled the day's accounting, and Kent had updated the power rating of each team that had played that day.[24] With games starting almost every hour, and Walters busy managing his army of runners, there was no way either of them had time to watch them all.

In the UK the concept of using mathematical modelling to make money from football betting had existed, at least in primitive form, for the best part of a century. After the pools exploded in popularity in the 1930s, a cottage industry developed in Britain encouraging syndicates to use betting systems in return for a few pence.

---

24 Walters, ibid.

In mid-1950s there was a hard-backed tome, *100 Famous Football Systems*, which for £1 (about £22 today) offered some interesting tips to predict scores that, while apparently not backed with much statistical rigour at the time, made some sort of sense. The advice included studying teams' goal differences to better evaluate form, and factoring in the distance they had to cover to travel to away games. The further teams had to travel, the book's authors wrote, the more likely performance would be affected.

Some of the tips were more questionable. There was a strategy to categorise teams according to the number of goals they scored in each half – those that were stronger in the second half ('stayers') should be backed to win at home over those who weakened ('non-stayers'). Other ideas were plain daft: pick teams to tie if they have a lower than average number of draws for the season.

Often, so-called experts would leave readers hanging with advice, promising insight that was, at best, pretty sketchy. That stood to reason: after all, if they knew the secrets to winning a huge pile of cash, why would they share them publicly?

But the lure of a big win pulled in many Britons. Horace Batchelor advertised a tips-by-post service on the radio, selling his guidance for £1 a time in the 1950s and 1960s. Customers were asked to send mail orders to his home in Keynsham, Somerset, and the money came pouring in, one pound at a time. To make sure they wrote down the address correctly, on his radio broadcasts, he always spelt out K-e-y-n-s-h-a-m.

Batchelor claimed he had helped punters win the pools more than one thousand times but, beyond a talent for marketing, the efficacy of his system was dubious. He left a will of £148,000 when he died in 1977, about £830,000 in today's money, but the pools had not endowed his family with much wealth other than the property they owned. Soon after his death, Elsie – his partner of 40 years – was confined to two rooms of their decaying 18-room Georgian mansion on a £15 a week pension and said she could not afford to pay for repairs.[25]

Unlike the pools tipsters who had gone before him, Benham and his quants were working on a more sophisticated plan when it came to predicting football results that relied on probability theories which were hard for the layman to understand. To work as a Smartodds quant the minimum requirement was a master's degree in physics, maths, computer science or engineering. If you had a doctorate in statistics, so much the better.

By 2011 there were 18 quants in the Highgate Road office, and, to some extent, they were the rock stars of the business. They were at the cutting edge of finding value in the football betting market. Among them was Stuart Coles, the co-author of the 1997 bookmaker-beating paper that had made a minor ripple when it was featured on the BBC's *Tomorrow's World*. Another was Phil Giles, who had graduated with a first-class degree in mathematics and statistics from Newcastle University.[26] Born

---

25 *Western Daily Press*, 19 January 1977 and 4 March 1977.
26 Giles also has a Ph.D in statistics from Newcastle University.

and raised a Geordie, Giles was also a football nut: for much of his life he had had a season ticket at St James' Park.

Because they were competing for graduates like Giles, who were in demand among investment banks, the perks offered by Smartodds were lavish: there was an in-house chef and masseuse, 30 days of paid holiday, private medical cover and a discretionary annual bonus. In return, the quants were expected to work hard for the cause.

As with financial markets, the global betting market never really closed, and so neither did the Smartodds office: it was staffed 24 hours per day. Staff were arranged in three groups: the quants, who built a power rating of teams like the Computer Group in Las Vegas to measure form; the analysts, who watched matches and provided scouting reports on goalscoring chances; and the traders, who placed bets. When a visitor arrived in 2008, Benham was seated in a glass cubicle in the middle of an open-plan office.[27]

Over the previous decade, Benham had become certain that goals in football were based on random events: the ball might spin off a player's shin and drop in front of a striker, or deflect off a defender's thigh and wrong-foot the goalkeeper. Therefore, match results, and even a team's position in the league after half the season, were not a true reflection of their underlying form. In Benham's view, rating a team's goalscoring opportunities was a more effective way to measure their strength.

At Smartodds his staff ranked the quality of each goalscoring chance created and conceded based on the probability of scoring

---

27 Christoph Biermann, *Football Hackers: The Science and Art of a Data Revolution*.

from the same position in thousands of matches. They then built what they called the 'Justice Table', which showed where teams deserved to be in the table. This alternative standing formed the basis of the Smartodds betting strategy. If, for example, they found the bookmakers' odds of a Tottenham win at Chelsea had failed to factor in Spurs' underlying form, Smartodds would recommend a bet on them to win.

The working week at Smartodds began on Monday and reached a crescendo around 2 p.m. on Saturday, when Premier League managers announced their starting eleven. At this moment betting markets were at their most liquid, and the work of the quants was parlayed into some monster bets.

Although Smartodds described itself on its website as a consultancy that advised professional gamblers on sports-betting strategies, one of its biggest clients was, in fact, Benham himself. Staff also had stakes of varying sizes in a company syndicate. There was a seniority system, based on 'moons', that defined how much money employees would have riding on bets: junior staff had one moon; middle management two moons; and senior bosses three moons. (Apparently, the only reason Smartodds used moons as a marker was because another syndicate used stars.[28]) Time and again, staff identified inefficiencies in the football betting market; so successful were they that by 2012, according to Coles, Smartodds clients were betting £25 million per week.[29]

---

28 Tony Bloom's Starlizard syndicate.
29 Stuart Coles, University of Padua lecture, 15 June 2012, YouTube.

The only market where it was possible to stake amounts of that magnitude was on the other side of the world. In Asia, you could bet £1 million on a single game, and the market would barely notice because of the large volume of bets. Just before 3 p.m. on Saturday, late evening in Asia, the market was at its most frothy. Gamblers from Bangkok to Kuala Lumpur and Manila were placing bets on games in Europe.

Betting markets anywhere else were considered too small to be worth the attention of Smartodds. In Britain, for example, bookmakers protected their margins aggressively and would limit bets from customer accounts that consistently won – or close them down altogether. It was pretty much impossible to get rich by gambling with British bookies. One hot-shot gambler who used maths to model scores said he had opened 200 accounts at Paddy Power: each lasted an average of just four days before it was shut down.[30]

In theory, the internet made it easier than ever for gamblers to bet – certainly more so than in the 1980s and early 1990s, when pagers or fax machines were part of the equipment used by serious gamblers. Yet even in the new millennium some professional syndicates preferred not to open online accounts directly with bookmakers, instead placing bets through agents in Asia who mixed them in with wagers of casual gamblers. In this way, the bookies would not be able to identify what was known in the business as 'the smart money'.

---

30 Billy Walters' account of his dealings with British bookmakers in his autobiography, *Gambler: Secrets from a Life at Risk*.

Exploiting the inefficiencies of Asian betting markets with the help of his Smartodds quants, Benham was making millions of pounds in winnings, which – thanks to the peculiarities of British law – were untaxed. This exemption dated back to a 1925 ruling on a case brought by a tax inspector against a man called Mr Green, who made a living from betting on horse racing. Judge Rowlatt, ruling on the case, found that, even if skilful, Green could not be considered to have a business in the same way as a bookmaker did. The judge said that even if he was smart, he was effectively a chancer whose success was based partly on luck. Green was, Judge Rowlatt considered, no different from a poker player. The case is still cited today as a legal precedent in an official UK tax manual about gambling and, while not much is known about him, Mr Green has become something of an icon.[31]

Not that Benham was absolved from all taxation. Smartodds Ltd., the consultancy based on quant analysis, paid tax on any profits.

To place bets in Asia, Benham and the Smartodds syndicate used a separate trading arm, and from this they were legally able to reap their winnings tax free. The fees Benham paid his own company for betting advice began at around £800,000 per annum, but one year rose to more than £4 million, an indication of how much money he was making.[32] In fact, he barely knew what to do with it all, so he began giving it to charity.

---

31 *HMRC Business Income Manual*, paragraph 22017.
32 Smartodds accounts, Companies House.

First organised in 1988, Comic Relief was an eight-hour telethon on the BBC fronted by Lenny Henry and Griff Rhys Jones and featuring Harry Enfield, best known for a sketch about a gobby Cockney wide boy who repeatedly shouted, 'Loadsa Money.' In the first year the telethon raised £15 million towards under-privileged people in Africa and the UK. Over time, the telethon would become a biennial event that brought in growing contributions, and for the 2003 edition raised almost £62 million. Some of the biggest contributors were anonymous, among them Benham. Only a small number of BBC staff knew who they were. As a way of making up for not paying any tax on his winnings, Benham contributed several million pounds, swelling the tally of charitable donations.[33] In 2009, Benham said he continued to make 'many large charitable donations', adding that he did not consider the money that he was sinking into Brentford to be purely an act of philanthropy.[34]

Initially, Benham was too busy to dedicate much time to Brentford – he did not join the board. For a couple of years he continued an arm's length relationship with the club. He focused on building his business and, rather than turning up for meetings, he sometimes mandated Smartodds chief executive Phil Whall and finance director Cliff Crown as his envoys in dealing with club affairs.

---

33 Author interview with Greg Dyke.
34 Bees United website, 5 August 2009.

Bees United's £2 acquisition of the club and stadium changed little. Brentford were still broke, living hand-to-mouth and relying on handouts from board members. Greg Dyke coined a name for the group of four middle-aged men who had to delve into their savings on an ad hoc basis to bail out Brentford: 'Don't Tell the Wives Club'.

One of the quartet, Alan Bird, a semi-retired business manager who had followed the club as a supporter since 1947, was not actually so secretive. When asked by his wife if they would ever get back the £250,000 he had advanced, he told her, 'Almost certainly not.'[35] Bird, who had worked for Saudi companies flush with money thanks to bountiful oil supplies, found himself dealing with a different reality at Brentford, where funds had run dry long ago.

Bird arrived at his first Brentford board meeting at Griffin Park in November 2007. Within ten minutes of the meeting opening he was asked to chip in £10,000 to help cover that month's player wages.

Benham was asked for money too. Smartodds was doing well and over three years he advanced another £4 million in interest free loans to Brentford, on top of his original bridge loan.

By the time Smartodds was in its fifth year, Benham had a little more time on his hands, and he wanted to make sure all the cash he was lending the club was being put to good use and that, one day, he might even be paid back. He began to analyse

---

35 Author email exchange with Alan Bird.

the way Brentford was run, asking Crown to have a look at the club's accounts for him.

Cliff Crown, an Arsenal fan, had a scout around and came back with an objective perspective: Bees United were honest and committed, but Brentford were not being run as efficiently as they might be. They were being run more like a voluntary organisation than a business. Benham soon found himself being absorbed into how to change this. He was intrigued by the challenge of turning their fortunes around and felt he could make a difference. Benham asked Crown to find a director to oversee the club's finances. Crown decided after thinking it through that it was a role he would like to do himself.

After making a business plan, Benham proposed a deal with Bees United to pay £1 million for five consecutive years in return for a 35 per cent stake, with an option to take over the club as majority shareholder after that period. The fan group saw no objections. They liked Benham – he was both a genuine fan and generous with his money. Besides, nobody else was beating down the door to take over the club.

In a letter to the fan group, Benham outlined the key principles he wanted to introduce with a view to the club returning to the Championship for the first time in two decades. He proposed, among other things, to turn them into a slicker business.

There was an awful lot of work to do.

Part Two

Rise

Chapter 7

2010: Jersey Road, Osterley

Four miles from Heathrow Airport lies the commuter suburb of Osterley. Every couple of minutes, aeroplanes rumble and screech as they make the last stage of their descent. From the Great West Road and M4 which envelop Osterley you can hear the swoosh of passing traffic. There are rows of semi-detached houses, some with pebbledash façades and mock Tudor design elements. Off one of these roads there was a slither of well-tended green land just big enough to fit five football pitches. Next to the nearest pitch was what looked like a cricket pavilion with a small clock tower, and three large portacabins by a few smaller ones. From satellite imagery above, they looked like they might be for storage, lock-up garages, or perhaps greenhouses for gardeners. The adjoining land was barren and little used, apart from a couple of school football pitches.

In the summer of 2010, when one visitor arrived at the semi-deserted training ground, there was no gate and part of the sign outside had come apart. The part of the sign that remained, read: 'ntford Football Club'.

With the Brentford club crest featuring two bees, a beehive and the three-sword emblem of Middlesex stitched into a cotton–polyester mix, Brentford players trained in £10 Fruit of the Loom sweatshirts. After being washed and tumble-dried a few times, the sweatshirts were more like t-shirts, according to one player.[1] In terms of catering, there was no hot food available in the pavilion when players arrived; kit man Dave Carter volunteered to make sausage, eggs and beans. As well as washing the kit, Carter also tended the training pitches. Now he added a third role: breakfast chef. The smell of fried sausages drifted into the weights room, and the odour of sweat entered the dining area. At the end of each week, the players would each tip Carter a few pounds for cooking them breakfast.

Carter's humour disguised deep affection for the club. He had got the job as kit man from Martin Allen while hanging around the training ground. Once, when a fan based in the United States stopped by one day to see the players, Carter looked back at him as if he was mad. 'Have you come all the way from America just to see bloody Brentford?'[2]

Amid the suburban sprawl, the training ground was in one corner of a 47-acre patch of mostly scrubland abutting

---

1 Richard Lee, *Graduation: Life Lessons of a Professional Footballer*.
2 Post by supporter on www.Griffinpark.org, 2011. When Dave Carter died of cancer in 2011 players paid tribute to him by wearing black armbands in an away game at Exeter.

the fringes of Osterley Park. When the area was a rural idyll, centuries before the construction of the Great West Road and Heathrow Airport, much of the land was owned by Thomas Gresham, who helped to cement the City as one of the world's financial centres. Gresham, whose father was Henry VIII's financier, was a loan-maker to four separate kings and queens and was so influential that Elizabeth I went to visit him at Osterley.[3]

The tranche of land on which Brentford's training ground lies has been managed since 1512 by a group called the Worshipful Company of Mercers, once a powerful guild for merchants trading in wool, silk and velvet. Today, the former guild is a charity better known as the Mercers' Company, which channels the annual income derived from Brentford's lease – about £25,000 in 2010 – to St Paul's School, the Barnes-based private school with which it has links dating back five centuries.[4]

Mercers' – motto *Honor Deo* (Honour to God) – has a chapel in the City of London, five acres of land around Covent Garden, and former leaders including Dick Whittington, the London mayor best known for a fairytale in which he came to the capital to seek his fortune with a cat. Even today, Mercers' remain somewhat archaic: when Brentford arranged a lease agreement for the training ground in 2006, they signed a deal with the

---

3 Simon Jenkins, *A Short History of London: The Creation of a World Capital.*
4 Author interview with Mercers' in-house historian Jane Ruddell. The land on which Brentford's training ground stands today was bequeathed to the Mercers around 1510 by John Collett, dean of St Paul's Cathedral and founder of St Paul's School.

fantastically named 'Wardens and Commonalty of the Mystery of Mercers'.[5]

Still, never mind the history, at £2,000 a month the rent was cheap.

Like in a family business where everyone helps, Brentford's small number of staff has multitasked for decades, often in return for little or no money. Some have become part of the fabric of the club. Eric White, an insurance broker from Greenford, was match-day press officer for 40 years until his death, aged 71, in 1996. He also edited the match programme, in which a small ad for his insurance business appeared, and edited the history *100 Years of Brentford*.

In the modern era, none has been more faithful than Peter Gilham. Apart from programme editor, his myriad roles over half a century have included on-pitch announcer, press officer, marketing director, commercial lead, and player-welfare manager. As noted, as match-day disc jockey in 1968 he was responsible for making 'Hey Jude' the club's anthem – partly because he had a friend called Judy, a teacher from Ealing. Gilham had combined some of these jobs with employment in the BBC accounts department before coming to work at Brentford full-time. Eventually, Gilham inherited an unofficial honorary title from White: 'Mr Brentford'.

When Matthew Benham started putting more of his money into Brentford, the manager was Andy Scott. Scott became

---

5 Companies House filing, April 2006. 'Mystery' is a term from the Middle Ages that loosely translates as 'guild'.

the fourth manager in a turbulent 18-month period following Martin Allen's departure, during which time the club was relegated to the fourth tier, League Two. He guided them back to the third tier (League One) in 2009. Both Scott and his assistant Terry Bullivant had played at Brentford and knew the club inside out; it had barely changed over the years. With fewer staff and resources than most London clubs, Brentford were relatively slow to embrace performance analysis that had begun in the Premier League and was filtering down to the Football League, but over the summer chief executive Andrew Mills decided to send Scott and Bullivant a paperback copy of *Moneyball*.[6]

In the book, author Michael Lewis writes about how Oakland A's general manager Billy Beane, with one of the lowest payrolls in baseball, used overlooked on-base statistics to grade players. Long before the movie version starring Brad Pitt, *Moneyball* had become a seminal book about how a smaller sports team could find an edge against bigger rivals. Scott enjoyed reading *Moneyball* while on holiday in Florida: it was inspiring, he told Mills.

Bullivant managed only the first chapter of the paperback. With Brentford's budget squeezed to the last few pounds, it was perhaps hard to see past the end of the week, let alone into the future of football data analytics.

Under old-fashioned British football norms, whether Brentford embraced new thinking was up to Scott. The

---

6 Author interview with Andrew Mills.

manager was all-powerful when it came to strategy: he only lost his power when the board was spooked by a poor run of results. Benham felt this archetypal way of operating a club was not innovative enough. 'The general culture and environment across the entire club wasn't as receptive to new ways of thinking,' Benham said later.[7] 'Basically, the actual owner, his job is to keep his mouth shut and write the cheques.'

Club chairmen – even those who were the most successful of businessmen – were poo-pooed by managers and fans for interfering in the business of football. At Derby County in the 1970s Brian Clough became embroiled in a personal feud with Sam Longson, the owner of a road haulage business. When one chairman began talking to him about tactics, Clough said he responded: 'How can you talk to me about something that you know *nowt* about?'[8]

Yet even before he had a majority stake in the club, Benham had begun to take an interest in calling the shots. At the very least, he had the right to hire and fire the manager. The way he saw it, it was his money on the line.

Benham was still working out how to navigate the shareholder–manager relationship when, in the early summer of 2010, Scott visited the Smartodds office with Mills and Bird, the semi-retired business manager, and asked for extra funds to sign new players for the upcoming League One campaign. The money would cover fees, signing-on bonuses and wages.

---

7 Benham interview, Bees United, ibid.
8 Brian Clough interview, Sky Sports, 2002. He did not identify the chairman.

Brentford had recently finished ninth in their first season back in the division.

Benham asked him how much he wanted. Scott, picking a number, said £3 million. This was 50 per cent more than the previous season's budget but, according to Scott, was necessary to stand a chance of again finishing near the play-offs.

'Where would that get us in the table?' Bird asked.

'Around ninth,' Scott said.[9]

Polite, charming and smartly dressed, Scott had credit in the bank both as a former Brentford winger and now as manager – he had just had a promising first season in League One. After meeting him for an informal interview in Costa Coffee in Croydon that summer, goalkeeper Richard Lee was impressed. 'He was considered a bright young manager, who had a big future ahead of him,' Lee said.[10]

Benham said he would think over Scott's budget proposal. He called him back to his office a few days later and agreed to release a little extra than what the manager had asked for, granting him £3.5 million. That felt like a fortune for Brentford: a couple of seasons earlier the club was so short of funds that they were paying players as little as £120 per week and Scott had been too embarrassed to negotiate terms himself.[11]

Scott went on a spree over the next eight months, signing more than a dozen players for modest fees, free transfers or on loan deals. Nicky Forster, who had played at the club as a

---

9   Bird email exchange, ibid.
10 Lee, ibid.
11 Andrew Mills interview, ibid. Mills said Scott asked him to negotiate terms.

young striker, returned after a 13-year absence at the age of 36. Lee, the goalkeeper, also signed on. Some of the recruits came from Championship clubs, including Gary Alexander and Lewis Grabban, from Millwall, and Robbie Neilson and Jeffrey Schlupp, from Leicester City.

Benham travelled to some away matches to check on how his money was being spent, sometimes sitting in the directors' box with Bees United representatives. It was more common to see him in jeans and hoodie than a suit and tie. At Brentford this kind of attire would have seen him fined as a player or a manager under Martin Allen's *Guidelines for Success!* handbook, but Benham was not a rule-breaker in the boardroom: as soon as he became chairman, Greg Dyke removed the requirement for directors and guests to wear ties. The boardroom dress code became smart casual.

Nevertheless, Benham's attire was frowned on by stuffier directors at other clubs. When he turned up at Birmingham City's boardroom for a League Cup game, one or two of the home directors sniffed at the scruffy representative from Brentford. They felt he looked like an ordinary fan.[12]

In previous seasons, Scott had coached the direct style of football Brentford had long played, using the wings more than the centre of the field to launch attacks. However, he was trying to introduce a more attractive blend of passing football. But when results went against them, Scott quickly reverted to the old tactics. At the start of the season, they won just two of

---

12 Author interview with Greg Dyke.

their first 11 league games. Among the losses was a 1–0 defeat to Brighton, a reverse that might have hurt Benham a little more. That was because Brighton were by now owned by a man called Tony Bloom, who had become Benham's nemesis – and Bloom's team were flying.

A decade earlier, Bloom and Benham had set out on the path to make serious money through football betting but, after a few years working together, they had a dispute over the use of a proprietary betting model that was so acrimonious that it resulted in Bloom starting legal proceedings, according to a person familiar with what happened. Neither has discussed the episode publicly, although what is clear is that they went from being colleagues to rivals.

Like Brentford, Brighton had spent years in the doldrums. They were forced to sell the Goldstone Ground, their home for 95 years, to pay creditors, and for two years they played at Gillingham's stadium – a three-hour round trip by car. They eventually returned to Brighton, using an athletics arena with uncovered temporary stands for matches, and sharing a training ground, complete with dodgy showers, with University of Sussex students. But as they did the double in the league over Brentford that 2010–2011 season, Brighton lost only seven of 46 games. They played a version of tiki-taka, a term first used by an exuberant television commentator delighted by the pinball-style short passing of the World Cup-winning Spanish national team. Iñigo Calderón, a full-back who had arrived at Brighton from Deportivo Alavés in northern Spain, said the way he was playing was normal in his country – but in League One it was outstanding. Supporters told him the team were playing the best football they could remember. Opposing players were flummoxed about how to handle the rapid passing style. They were not used to this type of football and Calderón saw some looking over to their manager in the middle of matches as if to ask, 'What do we do?'[13]

While Benham was new to professional football, Bloom had some inside knowledge of the business thanks to family connections. Bloom was educated at Lancing College, a private school near Brighton set among fields and dominated by the soaring spires of a gothic church, where students attended services in the morning, and tumbled out onto the grass to play football in the afternoon. By the time he sat his final-year A level exams, his talents were clear: he took maths, further maths, statistics and economics. At Manchester University he studied maths, before taking a traditional route for graduates: a stint at accountancy firm Ernst & Young.

Bloom's grandfather Harry was a hotelier and car dealer who liked to have a bet playing cards, owned greyhounds, and loved football. Raised in the East End of London, he had moved to the South Coast, where he would become vice-chairman of Brighton & Hove Albion in the 1970s. Harry was a vivacious man and dapper dresser. He wore a trilby hat and red braces under his mohair overcoat.

In the school holidays, Tony Bloom once went greyhound racing at Hove, taking £2,000 of his older brother Darren's

---

13 Author interview with Iñigo Calderón.

money and returning with a 50 per cent return. In his twenties, before joining Victor Chandler, he left his office job to play on the poker circuit from Sydney to Las Vegas. To another player he came across at the time he was straightforward and easy to talk to, if a little serious. He did not come to party; he came to make money. He was cool under pressure, earning the nickname 'Lizard'.

When he was 27, Bloom had relocated to Bangkok to set up an office for Victor Chandler, the self-proclaimed gentleman bookmaker who wore classic British clothes such as velvet-collared overcoats. His natural habitat was the Cheltenham Festival, the March meeting set among the rolling hills of the Cotswolds. The capital of Thailand was nothing like the countryside capers of English horse racing: it was a sweaty metropolis with an anything–goes nightlife. In a concoction of hedonism and danger, Bangkok mixed Western consumerism with Thai vices. To Bangkok, Chandler brought Bloom and three other young men who were 'all nice boys who hadn't been away from home that often and were all good to their mothers'.[14]

For Bloom, arriving in Bangkok – with all the financial opportunity that the Asian football betting market presented – must have been as exciting as when (as a schoolboy) he saw the flashing fruit machines in an arcade off Brighton's seafront for the first time. For a start, using relatively simple maths, it was possible to reduce your risk to virtually zero. Because

---

14 Jamie Reid, *Victor Chandler: Put Your Life On It: Staying at the Top in the Cut-Throat World of Gambling.*

of the difference in market pricing between Asia and Europe you could use arbitrage to make a profit: this was, one British gambler said, like finding piles of money in the street.

For sharp minds, there was plenty more opportunity in the East. Betting was deeply embedded in the culture: thousands of years before the roulette wheel was invented in France and gentlemen in tuxedos made a beeline for Monte Carlo's casinos, rural gamblers in China were staking money on predicting the number of items that would remain after the village croupier's random removal of sticks, buttons or coins. In more modern times, social gambling in China was seen as a joyful and harmless form of entertainment to mark weddings, birthdays and the New Year. But there was also a dark side whereby family men ruined finances and relationships because they could not stop; one estimate put the prevalence of gambling addiction in China at between 2.5 per cent and 4 per cent of adults – far higher than in the UK.[15]

When regular live television coverage began to take off in the 1980s, the Asian people's craze for gambling found a new outlet: betting on European football became a favoured predilection for a generation, particularly for young men. All strata of society could place their bets: street-corner agents took cash bets of as little as $50 on behalf of bookmakers. Trading houses, meanwhile, accepted telephone bets on credit of as

15 'Gambling Addiction in China: a survey of Chinese Psychiatrists' by Xiuqin Huang, Du Shijun and Sanju George; an academic study published in 2014. A Public Health England report published in 2021 put the percentage of 'problem gamblers' at 0.5 per cent of the UK population.

much as $50,000. In Bangkok, and four other Asian cities, could be found football betting's equivalent of the stock exchanges of New York, London, Frankfurt, Tokyo and Hong Kong. These clearing houses would, for a single football game, take wagers of as much as $1 million.

One of the biggest betting centres was in Johor Bahru.[16] Known as JB, Malaysia's second city was a border town that had seen a boom in tourism, retail and finance in recent years thanks to cheap rent and good transport links: it had an airport and was connected to Singapore via a half-mile causeway. Seen from the sky, the skyscrapers jutting out the waters of the Johor Strait on the southernmost tip of the city could pass for a mini version of downtown Manhattan.

Because of the time difference, at 10 p.m. or 11 p.m. on a Saturday the English first division games of Manchester United and Liverpool were shown at karaoke bars from Hong Kong to Singapore and Kuala Lumpur. During tournaments like the FIFA World Cup and UEFA European Championship the city moved even more money: tens of millions of dollars in football bets.

While the financial flows at these times were impressive, the football bourse in Johor Bahru was nowhere near as grand as the New York stock exchange, with its grand *beaux-arts* façade off Wall Street. To get into the trading room in JB in 2001 you had to walk through a restaurant. Inside, there were a few rows of desks with computers and TV screens showing

---

16 The other hubs were in Hong Kong, Taiwan and Indonesia.

half a dozen football matches. There was the hum of activity. As bets came in by phone, trading-room operatives seeking clearance from the head trader shouted out larger wagers of more than $500,000. The most common bet was known as the Asian handicap – *Hang Cheng* in Chinese. Under this system, the bookmaker could give the underdog a head-start of up to three goals when, for example, Manchester United were playing at home. Gamblers had to factor this handicap in when gambling on the result. Another popular wager was predicting the number of goals in a game: usually, the marker was set at 2.5 goals and bets were taken on whether the number would be higher or lower.[17]

The sprawling network of bets was informal and hard to navigate. In the 1990s, perhaps only a dozen people in Europe were betting on markets in the Far East. You not only had to find the right person to bet with, both parties also had to trust each other. There was a system of vouching that, according to one observer, was like 'joining a country club or a fraternity'.[18]

Chandler had got his entrée through a man he codenamed 'Swordfish'.[19] They were introduced at Les Ambassadeurs, a members-only club with a casino in London's Mayfair. Swordfish invited him to his apartment for lunch. A Scottish Premiership football game was on television. There and then, his host asked Chandler to lay him odds on the result. Swordfish

---

17 This is known as an 'over-under' bet.
18 Brett Forrest, *The Big Fix: The Hunt for the Match-Fixers Bringing Down Football*.
19 Reid, ibid.

bet £20,000 – and lost. Weeks later, Swordfish invited Chandler to Singapore and asked him to lay odds on a horse race. He bet £20,000 – and lost again. After both men had gained each other's confidence, Swordfish 'went absolutely potty', according to Chandler, betting on so much sport that he could hardly keep pace. He arranged for three of his staff to field Swordfish's calls that came at any hour of the day or night.

Chandler went to Asia to find more clients who didn't mind parting with a small fortune. For his authorised biography, he recounted travelling by car through Malaysian paddy fields to a simple one-storey building with a fleet of Rolls-Royces and Jaguars parked outside. Inside, a group of high rollers were divvying up their weekly takings by stuffing cash into empty duty-free Marlboro boxes. [20]

Because betting accounts were mostly settled with cash it was impossible to calculate how much money was swirling around in the Asian betting markets each year: back-of-the-envelope estimates started at $100 billion and would go as far as $1 trillion.[21] But there was no question this was, by a considerable distance, the biggest gambling market in the world: a Briton visiting a basement trading room in Bangkok was stunned by the bets streaming through on a computer terminal. The $50,000 wagers, considered hefty in the UK, were the equivalent of tadpoles swimming among koi carp.[22]

---

20 Reid, ibid.
21 Asia Gaming Brief website, 29 June 2021. Transparency International put the value at $500 billion per year; *Josimar*, a football magazine, estimated in an article it was worth $1 trillion, 12 September 2021.
22 Author interview with a professional gambler.

Using his talent for numbers, from Bangkok Bloom helped to set the odds for Victor Chandler's growing client base of Asian punters. However, within a few months, an incident occurred in a nightclub that sent the plans off course. An inebriated policeman in military fatigues who knew Chandler and his staff, playfully grabbed Bloom's hair, pushed his head down and thrust a pistol in his mouth: 'You better stop tipping me losers – or else.' The policeman was acting 'like it's all a big joke', according to Chandler, who nevertheless was spooked enough to shut down his office within 48 hours and sent Bloom and his colleagues back to Europe.[23]

By the time the 1998 World Cup final came around, Bloom was working out of Chandler's offices back in Europe, but still with an eye on Asia. The World Cup final, by some distance, moves the most betting money of any match during the football calendar. Much of casual gamblers' money is bet on the favourite. That year, the final was between Brazil and France in Paris. Brazil: the country of Pelé, canary yellow shirts, and a record four World Cups. They were the obvious choice to win. The final was on home turf, but France had never reached the final, let alone won the tournament. This was the kind of lazy thinking that Bloom had learned to exploit. The combined bets of punters who based their wagers on sentiment rather than data had a name in the gambling world: 'the mug money'.

At the time, the amount of publicly available match data was close to zero – apart from goals, and red and yellow cards – so

---

23 Reid, ibid.

Bloom began to compile his own statistics, with the help of Mark Dixon, the former Lancaster University researcher. In the days leading up to the World Cup final, and using comparatively basic maths, Bloom weighed the strength of the Brazil and France teams using metrics including the benefit of home advantage and attacking and defensive prowess. According to Chandler's authorised biography, Bloom's 'statistical analysis of a team's form, fitness and record was simply greater than anything the Asian bookies could muster'. Based on his analysis, Bloom predicted Brazil would lose.

Bookmakers often bet themselves with other operators, sometimes as a hedge or insurance policy against losses; Chandler took Bloom's advice, wagering £3 million on France and accepting, among the money for Brazil, a big bet of £1 million.[24]

On an overcast day crowds of Brazilians headed to Copacabana beach by bus to watch the final on a big screen. Brazilians were used to winning, and they were exuberant despite the weather. They had won the World Cup in 1958, 1962, 1970 and, most recently, in 1994, making them the defending champions. They wore t-shirts and caps with the slogan 'On the way to No. 5'. While thousands of them were on the way to Copacabana, news filtered through that Ronaldo was not on the teamsheet. Something was not right. Then, radio stations reported *O Fenômeno* – the Phenomenon – was back on the list. He took to the pitch looking pale. On the

---

24 Reid, ibid.

morning of the game, it emerged he had suffered a convulsive fit in his hotel room.

Wearing their canary yellow shirts, Ronaldo and his teammates were no match for the French. France won 3–0. Up to a million people flooded onto the Champs-Élysées to celebrate. About half the £20 million Victor Chandler earned from the World Cup came from the final.[25] Probably by some distance, Bloom could have claimed the accolade of employee of the month.

A couple of years later, Bloom left to set up Premier Bet, an online bookmaker based in London with a plan to take Asian handicap betting global and lure some of the devil-may-care high rollers who gambled in the Far East. Rather than bets of, say, £25 or £50, which were common in the UK, Bloom intended to attract gamblers willing to bet tens of thousands of pounds online.[26] He rented an office at 32 Cornhill, around the corner from the Bank of England, and hired about a dozen staff, some of them from Victor Chandler, others from Zetters, a football pools business that had diversified into sports spread betting. He also welcomed Matthew Benham, who applied for a job as a trader.

Bloom worked on a proprietary model like the one Benham would emulate at Smartodds to rank the form of football teams and make sure the odds that Premier Bet offered were based on solid research. Benham was, by some accounts, the star

25 Reid, ibid.
26 Author interview with Thomas Taule, Premier Bet Ltd director.

employee because of his understanding of quantitative analytics and experience as a trader, not to mention his knowledge of football.

As a sideline, Bloom organised a syndicate with staff, including Benham, that bet in the Asian market. Soon enough, Bloom found that the syndicate was a much better vehicle to make money than the online bookmaker. After three years in business Premier Bet had paltry profit on a modest annual revenue of £25 million. It was almost nothing when compared to the size of betting money swirling around in Asia.

Many of Premier Bet's 36,000 registered users were only occasional European bettors, who might have signed up to a few other websites that were luring in customers with free initial bets. These users were not loyal to Premier Bet, nor were they particularly big gamblers. What Bloom had helped Victor Chandler earn during the 1998 World Cup took him a year to match at Premier Bet. And that was before covering overheads: office rent, the payroll of traders, website designers and software programmers.

The staff syndicate, meanwhile, had few costs and had huge upside. Frustratingly, Bloom found managing Premier Bet distracted him from what he liked best: gambling.[27]

At around this time, Bloom had the bitter falling-out with Benham. Both men were intelligent and highly driven but could not find a way to meld their talents, a rift developing between them in the autumn of 2003 over the use of the syndicate's

---

27 Taule interview, ibid.

betting model. A lawsuit issued by Bloom was eventually settled out of court, without details emerging.

The following year, Benham went to a lawyer's office in Hammersmith to sign the documents to open his own syndicate called Smartodds. Bloom subsequently sold Premier Bet to a conglomerate called Interactive Gaming, which bundled the website with more than a dozen other gambling sites. Bloom shrugged off the £1.2 million he received for his company from the sale as 'chicken feed'.[28] He then founded a company to professionalise his original syndicate, deriving its name Starlizard from his poker moniker. Benham and Bloom were now focused on the business of beating the bookmakers in Asia, separately.

Brentford were finding it harder to navigate League One than Brighton. On a regular basis, and with results going against them, Andy Scott was called in to explain strategy to Benham and the rest of the board. By now, Benham had begun sounding out Mark Warburton who, like him, had worked in finance.

They met when Warburton, working as a youth-team coach at Watford, was involved with a tournament for teenage players called NextGen that featured Champions League teams such as Sporting Lisbon, Ajax and Inter Milan. At one point Warburton asked Benham about investing in Watford. Benham declined, but they kept in touch and talked about the game. Once, apparently following a suggestion by his confidant,

---

28 Michael Atherton, *Gambling: A Story of Triumph and Disaster.*

Benham offered Scott the opportunity to shadow training sessions of Champions League teams. Scott took umbrage at that invitation.

Sometimes when Benham made suggestions or questioned the way football managers worked, he found that they bristled. They took it as a criticism, but Benham did not see it that way. He was merely trying to help the cause by challenging perceived wisdoms. 'It is natural for me, and in the scientific world I come from, that people constantly ask themselves whether they can do things even better,' Benham said.[29]

In February 2011 Brentford were plummeting towards the relegation zone. Scott would later admit that some of the players he'd brought in had damaged the team spirit. According to one, churning the squad so much had alienated some players.[30] Benham, with an eye on the success that Bloom was enjoying with Brighton, was unhappy that, with a bigger budget, Brentford were doing worse than the previous season. The extra £1.5 million he'd contributed had effectively achieved no quantifiable return. At one point he phoned Alan Bird, the business manager, to complain. Benham said all Scott was doing was signing loan players on short-term deals, and when they did not work out sending them back to recruit others who were even worse.[31]

After beating Dagenham & Redbridge at Griffin Park on New Year's Day, Brentford had managed only one more point from six other fixtures in January. Benham did not go to all the

29 Matthew Benham interview, *Tipsbladet*, 6 October 2014.
30 Lee, ibid.
31 Bird email, ibid.

games, sometimes listening on the radio to the commentary. On a Tuesday night in February, he tuned in to hear the account of a 4–1 loss in the return fixture at Dagenham & Redbridge. After the final whistle he called a Bees United director: it seemed his patience with Scott had run out.

At a meeting months earlier, Benham had laid down a ground rule. 'You won't ever get bad news from me,' Benham had told Scott. He pointed to Andrew Mills, the chief executive. 'You'll get it from him.'[32]

Later that night the decision to fire Scott and break Brentford's decades-old management structure crystallised in Benham's mind. At around 1 a.m. he called Mark Warburton at his home in Enfield to offer him a job as the first sporting director in Brentford's history.

Warburton was used to being woken from his slumber. As the head of the Royal Bank of Scotland (RBS) foreign exchange desk in the City of London, Warburton was regularly roused by night-time calls from Tokyo asking him to sanction trades worth millions of yen. He usually went back to sleep before his 4.42 a.m. alarm call that signalled the start of his working day. But, after taking Benham's call, Warburton could not sleep. This was the breakthrough moment in professional football that he had been waiting for, and it was somewhat unexpected. He spent the rest of that night googling the Brentford squad to learn basic information such as their names and positions on the pitch.

---

32 Mills interview, ibid.

In the early hours, Benham also called Mills to prime him. 'It feels like we have got to the end of the path,' Benham said. Mills asked him to sleep on it before deciding. A few hours later, at around 7 a.m., Benham called back to confirm he had made up his mind.

Mills phoned Scott and Bullivant and asked them both to come to a meeting at the Petersham Hotel by Richmond Park an hour or so later. There, he told them they had lost their jobs. They took it badly, and angry words were exchanged.[33]

Mills, feeling a little shaken, then went to Osterley to inform players before training. He then took a third call that morning from Benham, who said there was someone whom he would like him to meet. Mills declined; he felt it would be disrespectful to hold such a meeting so soon after Scott's dismissal.

Within days, veteran striker Nicky Forster was named as caretaker manager and Warburton was appointed sporting director. Also variously known as director of football or technical director, sporting directors had been around in continental Europe for years. They could be a conduit between the board and coach, and oversee long-term recruitment. In theory, if the coach was fired, the club would not have to start planning from scratch. In practice, some of the first sporting directors in England were jettisoned as quickly by owners as the managers they might have been expected to outlast, such was the panic arising from the threat of relegation.[34]

---

33 Mills interview, ibid.
34 One of the first in the Premier League, Damien Comolli, lasted barely a year at Liverpool.

Warburton had been released by Leicester City as a trainee, leaving behind a career in professional football with a large dose of regret. Instead, he pursued a career in finance. Every weekday morning, Warburton would take the 5.12 a.m. train from Enfield to Liverpool Street and start work before 6 a.m. In his twenties, he had played for non-league Enfield as a defender who, according to a former school friend, was 'a bit error prone'. By the age of 42, Warburton had paid off his mortgage and had enough savings in the bank to consider a career change. He still itched for football. He told his wife it was now or never.

He took a sabbatical from work, spending a year visiting football academies in Portugal, Spain and the Netherlands. He asked questions about the gym programme at Sporting Lisbon to see why players like Cristiano Ronaldo looked 'like cruiserweight boxers', and enquired about the discipline at Barcelona's famed La Masia academy. When he returned to England he got a job in football, on a salary of about £20,000, less than 10 per cent of his basic pay at RBS. He became under-13 academy coach at Watford and started out on the road to break the glass ceiling that reckoned, 'If you haven't played the game, you don't know the game.'[35]

Within weeks of joining Brentford, Warburton became a popular figure: he was enthusiastic, clever and easy to get on with. He worked just as hard as he had in the City. He turned up for work before dawn at Brentford's still-deserted training ground in Osterley in a customised black Range Rover, and sometimes could still be found there 12 hours later.

---

35 Author interview with Mark Warburton, *Bloomberg News*, 23 October 2015.

Warburton made a series of changes, based on what he had learned from across European football. On the way to training, players were instructed to sip a bottle of water in the car to improve their performance when they arrived. They gave daily urine samples to test their levels of hydration. (Presumably, these daily tests also deterred the beer-drinking culture of the old days.) Gym work was introduced, and the tempo of training increased. At the training ground, a £60,000 kitchen was installed. The greasy-spoon style breakfast was replaced with healthier fare. And, finally, performance analysis staff were hired.

When I visited the training ground on a windy day a couple of years later, a sports science graduate in his early twenties was looking bored while filming an aerial video of a training session to track player movement. The overhead camera on a pole he was holding rocked in the breeze. His job was just to hold it and then review the movements of players on the training field. This work was like panning large tracts of wasteland for tiny nuggets of golden insight that could make a marginal performance difference.

At most clubs, performance staff typically had sports science degrees, and were seen as junior staff, operating behind the scenes and out of sight. If a potential nugget of information was found, maybe a much higher percentage of goals was being conceded by the goalkeeper from in-swinging corners than out-swinging corners, the data would be cleaned, checked and polished before being presented to the manager. He could consider how to use the data to work on defending in-swinging corners – or he could completely ignore it.

At Brentford, the new performance analysis unit was more than a decade behind the curve.

Chapter 8

2000: Bolton, north–west England

It was a habit of Alex Ferguson's after each Premier League game to share a glass of red wine with his opposite number. The Manchester United manager particularly liked a drop of Tignanello, a Chianti that could cost as much as £400 for a bottle. (Ferguson's wine cellar would later become worth several million pounds.) As he walked through the warren of rooms under the stands of Bolton's Reebok Stadium looking for Sam Allardyce, he peered into a narrow windowless room with whitewashed walls. The door was ajar. Inside, he saw three young men sitting in a row, eyes fixed on some of the ten screens in the room. One of them turned around to inform Ferguson that Allardyce's room was around the corner.[1]

---

1 Author interview with former Bolton analyst Ed Sulley.

To Ferguson, the warren crowded with monitors and laptops must have looked a little like a television studio, or a police surveillance unit. In fact, the three men in their early twenties were part of the first wave of the Premier League's performance analysts. Three of their ten screens showed the views from cameras trained on the pitch that they could move by remote control.[2] During the match, the trio, seeking an edge, talked into the earpiece of Allardyce, sitting in the stands, as he chewed gum ferociously. At half-time, the performance analysts listened into his team talk via a microphone he was hooked up with. As Ferguson peeked into their room, they were compiling their analysis of the match for a Monday morning debrief.

A couple of years earlier on the eve of the new millennium, there was only one computer at Bolton's stadium – it sat in the secretary's office. Ahead of the first day of the new century, UK businesses were required to report they'd taken action to prevent what had become known as the impending Y2K meltdown. At Bolton, there was little danger of that. Most of the football knowledge at the time was not on hard drives, but in the heads of coaching staff.

So who were the three men in the Bolton bunker? Some of the old timers at Bolton poked fun at these earnest young men. One was just out of university, another had worked as an estate agent, and the third had been seconded from Prozone, a start-up in Leeds which had recently begun collecting match data for

---

2 This practice was subsequently banned for much of the next decade by the Premier League. Today, the league provides live player tracking to each of the division's 20 clubs.

clubs to analyse. Prozone seconded analysts to a few clubs to advise them what to do with all the numbers. Bolton's Prozone man, who was always typing numbers into his laptop, became known as 'Fingers'.[3]

Even before *Moneyball* was added to the lexicon of football, Bolton were something of an outlier in seeking to use data to obtain an edge. There were few other data evangelists in the game. Around that time, when I was working as a journalist in Madrid, I asked a respected football commentator about how important statistics in football might become one day.

Tall and slim with slicked-black curly hair, Jorge Valdano had excellent diction and an imperious air when waving off journalists' questions when he was sporting director of Real Madrid. He wrote poetry in his spare time and penned books about leadership. He had been part of Argentina's 1986 World Cup-winning team. He seemed to know a lot about football. Hell, he had played with Diego Maradona.

For the previous seven years Real Madrid had signed some of the best-known players in the world – so-called *Galacticos* like Luís Figo, Zinedine Zidane and David Beckham – to supercharge the club's revenue in the same way Hollywood studios hired the most famous actors to make blockbuster movies. This allowed them to overtake Manchester United as the world's biggest club by revenue.

Valdano patted me on the back and said that analytics would only ever be a peripheral part of football. The use of data to gain

---

3 Sulley interview, ibid.

an edge was hit-and-miss – and there were more misses than hits, he told me. 'Statistics,' he said, 'will not play an important part in the future of football.'

Alex Ferguson, who had recently been knighted by the Queen, and was now known as Sir Alex, appeared only vaguely interested in the potential of data. It was worth looking at but would not change his management style, honed over a quarter of a century. He trusted his reading of the game. After all, he had guided United to eight out of the first 11 Premier League titles. Asked to endorse Prozone – which his assistant Steve McLaren had introduced him to – Ferguson's praise was thin: 'It is of benefit.'[4] United declined to pay Prozone for data and analytics services. Bolton, meanwhile, signed up for the premium service at £100,000.

Samuel Allardyce, a dyslexic who did not pass any secondary school exams, was an unlikely pioneer of analytics and sports science. His first job was on a factory production line making record decks. He became a journeyman pro, a 6 foot 3 inch centre-half with a strong work ethic. Big Sam had begun his career as a player for Bolton. He would get up without complaining after the kind of bone-crunching tackles that would lay out frailer players. Before running out on the pitch for matches, he and his teammates took a nip of whisky to fire them up. At half-time, he drank hot tea with two sugars.

However, Allardyce had learned about new techniques in US sports during a brief interlude from the rough and tumble

---

4 Rory Smith, *Expected Goals: The Story of How Data Conquered Football and Changed the Game Forever.*

Rise

ntford owner Matthew Benham, no fan of suits, drew critical looks in Birmingham City's rdroom for his scruffy clothing. *(Photo by Lars Ronbog/Front ZoneSport/Getty Images)*

y Bloom, who fell out with Benham over gambling, watches Brighton from the terrace at ffin Park with family and friends. *(Simon Dack/Telephoto Images/Alamy Stock Photo)*

People in Shanghai watch Brazil in the 2018 World Cup; Benham and Bloom bet in Asia, where t[he] market was most liquid. *(AFP via Getty images)*

The Griffin pub, used as a changing room by Brentford players in the 1890s, remained a popular place for fans to socialise 120 years later. *(Photo by Colin McPherson/Getty Images)*

rmer BBC Director-General Greg Dyke, a boyhood Brentford fan, became chairman in 2006 as
club teetered on the edge of insolvency. *(Photo by Paul Gilham/Getty Images)*

rcello Trotta, on loan from Fulham, hides his face after missing a penalty that would have won
ntford promotion to the Championship in 2013. *(Photo by Mike Hewitt/Getty Images)*

Former currency trader Mark Warburton impressed Benham when starting out in football and wa hired as sporting director then manager. *(Photo by Ben Hoskins/Stringer/Getty Images)*

Spanish winger Jota, who failed to earn a regular spot for Celta Vigo, was one of many Brentford players recruited based on Smartodds data. *(Photo by Justin Setterfield/Getty Images)*

a contrarian move, Brentford appointed Phil Giles, who had a PhD in statistics but no previous ootball experience, to become sporting director. *(Photo by Phil Shephard-Lewis/Popperfoto via Getty Images)*

f-described football geeks Benham and Rasmus Ankersen celebrate in 2015 as FC Midtjylland se in on their first Danish league title. *(Photo by Lars Ronvog/FrontZoneSport via Getty Images)*

A Brentford fan becomes emotional as the team walks onto the pitch for the team's first Premier League game, against Arsenal in 2021. *(Photo by Eddie Keogh/Getty Images)*

ristian Nørgaard celebrates after scoring in the season-opening game, sealing Brentford's first gue win against Arsenal since 1938. *(Photo by Eddie Keogh/Getty Images)*

alkeeper David Raya was signed partly for his passing skills, an example of how Brentford sought derlying value in the transfer market. *(Photo by Juan Gasparini/MI News/Nur Photo/Alamy Stock Photo)*

Architects squeezed Brentford's new stadium into a triangle of wasteland, a couple of hundred metres from where the club was founded. *(Maurice Savage/Alamy Stock Photo)*

Ivan Toney covers his ears after scoring in a 2–1 win at Manchester City in 2022; at the time he was under investigation for betting on football. *(Photo by Alex Livesey/Getty Images)*

of British football: in 1983 he moved to Seattle, then a tech hub in the making. The weather was hot, some of his new teammates were South American and there were no muddy fields – his employer, the Tampa Bay Rowdies, played indoors on artificial turf. Allardyce moved into a condominium where his neighbours were the broad-shouldered players of the NFL team the Tampa Bay Buccaneers, and he got his first glimpse of the future. The Bucs employed statisticians and analysts to work out the most effective plays, while also monitoring diet and health closely. Instead of tea and whisky, Allardyce gulped down sports drinks.

English football was two decades behind the NFL when it came to sports science but, thanks to his stint in the US, Allardyce was readier than most of his peers to experiment. After leading Bolton back to the Premier League, he found himself with a budget of £15 million at his disposal. Among the club's staff was Mike Forde, who had recently graduated with a degree in sports science and had a job title that was little known in football: performance director.

Allardyce encouraged Forde to search for some of the best ideas in sport and see which of them could be applied at Bolton Wanderers. Forde, a Mancunian, travelled around the UK to pick up tips. As well as learning from England's rugby team, he heard from staff at the BAR–Honda Formula One team in Brackley, near Oxford which used heart monitors for their drivers to track their freshness and reaction speed. When he had finished talking to some of the smartest thinkers in UK sports, he went abroad, visiting baseball's Atlanta Braves, the San Francisco 49ers in the NFL and rugby union's All Blacks. In New Zealand he found a team that worked to create an open culture in which no single player was bigger than the collective.

Every Monday morning, as many as 20 staff met at Bolton's training ground in the so-called 'war room'. There they analysed everything from the data from the weekend's match to alternative training techniques and nutritional advice. Allardyce – not known for modesty – would later describe the war room as the 'Oxford University of football'.[5]

Bolton's staff pored over the Prozone data, picking out what they considered to be key metrics. While some clubs would overlook footballers in their mid-thirties, Allardyce and his colleagues studied the 'distance covered' statistics for players – the amount of miles they ran in a match – and used this as a basis for signing a number of veterans on free transfers, or for modest fees; the Prozone data showed these players were running as much as their younger peers. These ageing recruits included Gary Speed, 34, from Newcastle United. Speed went on to play 121 times for Bolton, becoming the first player, at the age of 37, to appear in 500 Premier League games.

Big Sam endorsed techniques to make the squad fitter to tackle a season that meant some players would have more than 50 games in their legs by May. To aid muscle recovery after matches, players were told to plunge their bodies into a cryotherapy ice fridge whose temperature could be lowered

5 Sam Allardyce, *Big Sam: My Autobiography*.

to minus 150 degrees centigrade. Also introduced was acupuncture, yoga and a fat-burning regime. A protein diet aimed to get players' body fat down to eight per cent; they were ordered to avoid eating carbohydrates from Monday to Thursday. They also were instructed to do extra sprints before daily training had even begun. The players gave all this a nickname: 'the Fat Club'.[6]

Not all of Bolton's ideas were properly thought through, according to midfielder Gareth Farrelly. England's rugby coaches had apparently brought in the protein diet for players during the offseason, but Bolton tried it during the season. Normally footballers might come down with cramp towards the end of a cup match, or during extra-time, but 15 minutes into a Premier League game at Newcastle, Farrelly felt a shooting pain in his leg and collapsed in agony. He blamed the protein diet. 'Bolton,' he complained, 'were a Coca–Cola Light version of the England rugby team.'[7]

When heart monitors were introduced to help to gauge when players were overtraining, Ian Marshall, a veteran striker who lived in Leicester, was given leave to train at home on some days to avoid the 230-mile round trip to training. In return, he too had to wear a heart monitor. On mornings when he felt like taking it easy, he attached the device to his ageing dog Tess and threw a ball around a local park for her to chase. Bolton's medics, when handed the readings, thought they were looking

---

6 Author interview with Gareth Farrelly.
7 Farrelly interview, ibid.

at Marshall's soaring heartbeat. They called in the centre-forward for a meeting to ask how he was feeling.

'The results,' Allardyce said, 'are a bit off.'

Marshall said he felt fine, and the device must be broken; he continued with the ruse for two more weeks before confessing. 'Thankfully,' Marshall said, 'Sam saw the funny side.'[8]

Despite a few early difficulties, Bolton's efforts to take a more scientific approach helped them to outperform richer clubs in the Premier League. In 2005 they finished sixth and qualified for the UEFA Cup, even though 15 Premier League clubs had a more expensive squad. Their use of analytics for the recruitment of players like Gary Speed, and their Prozone-assisted analysis of matches, sparked curiosity among other teams about their methods, which seemed to be highly effective. Soon enough, some of Bolton's performance staff were headhunted by Chelsea and Manchester City, both of whom were aiming to sharpen their game in the Premier League and European competitions.

Mark Warburton's methods as sporting director were drawn from some of Europe's biggest clubs which he had visited during his sabbatical, and one or two of them came from the RBS currency desk. He encouraged players to bulk up their upper body with weight training, a tip he had picked up from Sporting Lisbon. He suggested routines he had seen at Ajax and Barcelona, where a possession game in a restricted grid known as

---

8 Ian Marshall interview, *Bolton News*, 30 March 2015.

a 'Rondo', essentially a football version of 'piggy in the middle', was both a valuable and enjoyable part of practice sessions.

At RBS Warburton had learned the importance of team spirit, geeing up his colleagues when they were down. He helped to invigorate Brentford players as well as they reversed their slide towards the bottom of League One. They lost just three of the next 13 games and began to climb away from the relegation zone, eventually finishing the 2010–11 season in mid-table.

Before the campaign ended, they even had a trip to Wembley after reaching the Johnstone's Paint Trophy final, the competition for lower league teams. It was a nice day out and chance to replenish the cabinet in the Griffin Park boardroom that had not really seen any new silverware since the Second World War, but Brentford lost 1–0 to Carlisle United.

While Warburton enjoyed being sporting director, his real ambition was to be first-team coach. He had his coaching badges, and with the youth team at Watford had enjoyed being out on the pitch and working with players in groups and individually. In the summer of 2011 he and Forster were among the seven candidates shortlisted for the permanent job of Brentford head coach. After several rounds of interviews, Warburton just missed out to Uwe Rösler.

Rösler was best known for a stint as a Manchester City striker in the 1990s, but had started out as a manager in the relative obscurity of the Norwegian league. Nevertheless, he was a familiar face and someone fans and supporters could relate to more easily than a former currency trader. Warburton remained as sporting director and was careful not to interfere, largely staying off the training ground but working with Rösler on player recruitment. When they identified a player who they wanted to sign, they informed Benham, who took the name back to the Smartodds quants.

These quants had a different skill set from most of the first wave of performance analysts in British football. Many of the first performance staff had graduated in sports science from universities such as Sheffield and Liverpool, starting out on salaries of not much more than £20,000. In the noughties, theirs was a hybrid job covering everything from fitness and nutrition to data analytics. And they were just scratching the surface when it came to using data. One of the sports science graduates at Bolton had admitted the volume of data extracted from football was frightening: it was hellish, he said, to find meaning in all those numbers.

The quants Benham employed, however, were the cream of university graduates and the peers of Ph.D students from centres of learning like Cambridge, Harvard and the Massachusetts Institute of Technology. They were supremely bright and could command entry-level salaries upwards of £100,000. For them, making sense of a mass of data was fun. They enjoyed the intellectual stimulus of applying analytics to all those numbers in football. In fact, they enjoyed it so much they took their work home with them and in their spare time played about with maths formulae.

Besides Prozone, ever more data collection companies were catering to football clubs to help them with analytics. They used scouts, some of them students on £10 per hour, to log basic data such as tackles, passes, shots and corners. Smartodds, however, were collecting their own more precise data, including the coordinates on the pitch of key moments in the game. These and other statistics were filtered through algorithms to help rate the form of players and teams. In an unremarkable corner of north London, behind a steel door, Smartodds were going deeper into analytics than most people imagined was possible.

Over the years, as his business expanded, Benham had leased more office space in the same building on Highgate Road. By now staff worked in a cavernous open-plan office. After taking the lift to the entrance, one visitor was stunned to see so much activity as he was let in. Laid out before him was row upon row of staff – more than 200, he estimated – engaged in the minutiae of the process of beating the bookmakers. 'It was like nothing I had ever come across in my life – like an American movie,' he said.[9] It felt a little like he had walked onto the set of *The Sting*, the 1973 bookmaking caper starring Robert Redford and Paul Newman.

Set out before him were three groups. The analysts, or watchers, earned £20 per match to watch games and log the position of each goalscoring chance. The games were from leagues around the world, from the Premier League to the Hungarian league, according to a student who worked as an analyst.[10] Each game was assigned an alternative scoreline based

---

9 Author interview with FC Midtjylland manager Glen Riddersholm describing his visit to Smartodds in 2014.
10 Tippett, ibid.

on the goalscoring chances: this became known as their Expected Goals, or xG. A group of quants took care of the Smartodds algorithm, feeding in the Expected Goals from each game analysed and building the Justice Table. A third group studied whether the bookmakers' odds converged from the so-called Justice Table and whether they recommended placing a bet.[11]

The primary objective of this painstaking process was to help identify when Asian bookmaker odds were wrong but, as Benham became more involved with Brentford, he asked some Smartodds quants to assist with Brentford's player recruitment too. Effectively, they were being employed to do due diligence on how his money was being spent in the transfer market.

When weighing up whether to sign a striker, or not, most English football clubs based their decisions on the past. They would look at his goal tallies in previous seasons. This was a flawed approach: what was more important was predicting his goal tallies in forthcoming seasons. Such forward thinking had been employed by Benham in the City when betting on stock prices, and was common in big business when making strategic decisions. For example, healthcare companies simulated the value of a new drug based on future changes to demographics and health data. Technology companies forecasted market trends to calculate the benefit of making a novel gadget. From Benham's perspective, player transfers merited the same kind of research: it was important to determine how much value a new recruit would bring to Brentford.

---

11 Tippett, ibid.

Among the brainpower being channelled by Smartodds was that of a Ph.D statistics student,[12] who Benham's company was sponsoring to work on a rating system for goalscorers that would be more insightful than the previous season's goals tally. What the student was trying to do was to look into the future. He built a model to rank what he called a striker's 'true goalscoring ability'. To do this, he plugged variables into his algorithm such as his percentage of converted chances, and the quality of his own team and the opponent. Back-testing the model against 20,000 shots by 15 Premier League strikers, he found it was a more accurate predictor of their subsequent season's goal tally than their average goals-per-game ratio – sometimes it was almost bang on target.[13]

The student, who was from Poland, also worked on a system to rank midfielders. This model went deeper than their pass-completion rate, the standard benchmark. A sideways pass between defenders was not actually a good reflection of a player's skill. In fact, a player making too many sideway passes could be negative for team performance. (As anecdotal evidence, there were stories about Eastern European players offered cash bonuses for meeting pass completion targets, gaming the system by hitting unnecessary short passes.)

The student developed a model that used extra variables for each pass, such as time on the ball, proximity to the opposition goal, and whether or not the pass was in a home or away match.

---

12 Lukasz Szczepanski, who was studying at Salford University.
13 Even after moving clubs, the predictive rating for Mark Viduka was out by just 0.02 goals per game.

Effectively, he was rating how difficult each pass was. Using this system, he found that one midfielder's 73 per cent pass-completion rate undersold his skill; the model gave him a rating equivalent to 81 per cent.[14]

Such modelling helped make better decisions. When Benham came back to Rösler and Warburton after his quants had run the numbers on their transfer targets, he returned with a verdict: three stars meant go ahead, two stars meant maybe, and one star meant no.[15]

At around this time, Benham approved the signing of Jonathan Douglas, a midfielder signed from Swindon who would play more than 160 times for Brentford. Meanwhile, Adam Forshaw, another midfielder, arrived on a free transfer from Everton. Two years later, he was transferred to Wigan for £3 million. It was with transactions like these that quants added value to Brentford, not only by improving performance, but also by helping them to make money in the transfer market, partially offsetting Benham's annual financial loss.[16]

Of course, data alone could not win football matches. Results were random events based on millions of unforeseeable factors, from the weather to the bounce of the ball, to team spirit and the individual temperament of each player. Quants only sought to predict what might occur, and none of them could have

---

14 Mikel Arteta, playing for Everton.

15 Tim Street and David Lane, *The Brentford Revolution: The Bees' Rise from the Basement to the Premier League*.

16 The loss, mainly incurred from player wages, at the time stood at around £4 million.

foreseen what would happen to Marcello Trotta on the last Saturday of April in 2013.

Raised in a small town in Campania, southern Italy, Trotta joined the Napoli youth team at the age of 12. In this football crazy part of the world, it was as hard as anywhere to make it as a professional footballer. Everyone wanted to escape low incomes to make it in the game. Pitches were rock hard from the blazing sun and tackles were as hard as they come too. Because there was an unrelenting supply of comparable talent from the area surrounding Naples, the club refused to pay Trotta's travel costs to training. This was a blow to the Trotta family's finances, and his father Angelo was not happy. 'I am not Rockefeller,' he said. He arranged for his son to move abroad to the Manchester City academy, where his expenses were taken care of.[17] After that Trotta switched to Fulham, where he signed professional terms and was sent out on loan to a couple of lower league clubs to gain experience, ending up at Brentford.

Brentford's ten-month campaign had come down to the last day of the season, a home match against Doncaster Rovers. In front of a sell-out 12,300 crowd at Griffin Park, both teams had a chance of promotion; Brentford needed a win, Doncaster a draw.

With the game goalless and entering injury time, Doncaster were heading for promotion. In the 94th minute Brentford were awarded a penalty kick. With the clock ticking down, the whole season had come down to this single kick. Trotta picked up the ball and would not give it to any of his teammates. Kevin

---

17 Italian football website www.ilpallonaro.com, 19 August 2010.

O'Connor, the 31-year-old Brentford captain and designated penalty taker, was among six teammates who went over to discuss what to do, but the 20-year-old Italian – officially a Fulham employee – clung to the ball.

When the other players had dispersed, Trotta put the ball on the penalty spot. If he scored, Brentford would be promoted to the Championship, fulfilling Benham's objective when, four years earlier, he'd laid out his plans for the club. Trotta took six or seven steps backwards. He ran up to strike the ball, hitting it with all his heft. It smashed against the aluminium crossbar with such force that you could hear the clank of the leather hitting the metal from behind the goal. The ball ricocheted into the centre of the penalty box and, in a counterattack, Doncaster scored to make it 1–0, securing promotion. On Twitter, a Fulham supporter wrote: 'Agent Trotta, return to base.'

Three weeks later Brentford missed another chance to win promotion to the Championship, losing 2–1 to Yeovil in the play-off final at Wembley. Perhaps feeling the moment had gone, Rösler resigned three months into the next season and moved up a division by another route: he became manager of Wigan Athletic.

In his day job Benham was used to seeing past random events like Trotta's penalty miss. Every week results would go against the Smartodds model. That was part of the business. The most important thing was to keep an eye on the big picture. You had to be making progress overall, advancing in the right direction. Benham made a show of his commitment to Brentford at the most trying of moments: immediately after the play-off final defeat at Wembley he went to the dressing room to gee up players.[18] He had no plans to withdraw his money from the club because of one arbitrary moment. In fact, he would soon double down on his investment.

18 Street and Lane, ibid.

Chapter 9

2014: Jutland, Denmark

As head coach, Mark Warburton continued to shape a team that was comfortable on the ball and dominated possession – they were what fans, with only a certain degree of hyperbole, called a lower league version of FC Barcelona. There was no Lionel Messi or Andrés Iniesta, but it was certainly good to watch, especially for fans used to more basic fare. Loan signings arrived from Premier League clubs, including playmakers Alex Pritchard, from Tottenham, and George Saville, from Chelsea.

They complemented talent sanctioned by Benham's traffic-light recruitment system that, delving into player data from some of Europe's smaller leagues, had okayed the signing of Stuart Dallas, a midfielder from Crusaders in Northern Ireland, and Jota Peleteiro, a winger playing on loan in Spain's second division for Eibar. The data collection and quantitative analysis at Smartodds were paying off. Together, the squad formed one of the most gifted groups playing in a Brentford team in decades.

Over the years, Brentford fans had watched as skilful teams swept past them on their way to the Championship: sides like Paul Jewell's Wigan in 2005, Roberto Martínez's Swansea City in 2008 and Gus Poyet's Brighton in 2011. Now, finally, it was Brentford drawing envious glances.

The reason for the team's quality was not only down to smart recruitment it was also down to something else: money. Benham had increased his bet on the club – a lot. After the play-off final loss at Wembley, he went even further with his investment. He plugged another £16 million into the club, most of it on the squad. While running up losses in football was not unusual by a club seeking to climb the league, in most other small or medium-sized businesses, the club's widening financial losses would be worrisome. For now, they were something Benham was prepared to accept.[1]

On the training ground in Osterley, Warburton employed a version of the marginal-gains philosophy associated with the Sky cycling team that had recently helped Bradley Wiggins become the first British winner of the Tour de France. Brentford's gut-busting pre-season runs in Richmond Park after a holiday of over-indulgence were over, replaced by a light summer training schedule that kept players fit all year round. During the week, they were tested for lactic acid, which can cause energy-sapping muscle fatigue. On Sundays, players swam laps and did exercises

---

1 Brentford made a loss of £8.7 million in fiscal 2014.

at a public pool to reduce lactic acid after the previous day's game. They wore vests while training, to monitor their heart rate: by tracking heartbeat, staff could see how tired players were and determine when they needed a rest.

Warburton relished the attention to detail and the build-up to the next match. 'I love that adrenaline buzz,' he said. It was, he reckoned, like the preparation in the RBS trading room before the release of economic indicators like trade figures, a moment where traders could win or lose tens of millions of dollars.[2]

At Brentford, each player was given a personal plan, which was printed out on paper and attached to their locker to remind them of weekly challenges and monthly goals. After training sessions, they would split up into defenders, midfielders and forwards, to work on self-improvement techniques. The centre-backs would focus on, for example, how to receive the ball from the goalkeeper and deal with counterattacks when the ball was hit over their heads. Video clips compiled by backroom staff would be shown to the players on an iPad. It was cutting-edge stuff, perhaps more comparable with a Premier League club than a team in League One.

Another shared aspect of Warburton's and Benham's lives was a workplace where performance bonuses were an integral part of employment contracts. Both had benefited from big bonuses in the City. To motivate players, they arranged for what Warburton called 'an aggressive bonus system'. If they met

---

2 Warburton interview, ibid.

targets such as match wins, senior players could increase their weekly pay packet by 20 per cent to as much as £10,000.[3] In pep talks with players Warburton would regularly drop in comments reminding them about the bonuses on offer, encouraging them to chase the financial rewards and the dream of playing in the Premier League so they could achieve a prosperous and secure lifestyle for themselves and their families. According to one player, Warburton's comments spurred the team on.[4]

Brentford won promotion with three games to spare, returning to the Championship for the first time since their single-season dalliance ended in 1993. When a 1–0 home win against Preston exorcised the painful memory of Trotta's penalty miss 12 months earlier, fans swarmed onto the pitch to mob the players. Benham slipped quietly out of the ground with one of his sons. But, dressed in a messy parka and jeans, he was spotted and politely stopped by Billy Grant, who routinely interviewed fellow Brentford supporters straight after each game for the *Beesotted* podcast to ask their reaction to the team's performance. This time, quite unexpectedly, Grant had landed an interview with the team's publicity-shy owner just as Brentford were promoted to the Championship.

Normally, Benham slipped in and out of the ground without any fanfare. He could pass for a normal fan, arriving with his young son. Because there was no parking at Griffin Park on match days, he and other directors parked at Brentford School for Girls, a

---

3 Ted Knutson interview, *The Beesotted Pride of West London* podcast, 21 August 2020.
4 Jonathan Douglas interview, *Ealing Road* podcast, 23 March 2023.

comprehensive school a short walk from the ground. Sometimes, fans would chant, '*There's only one Matthew Benham*' – he squirmed at that; Benham was shy and did not like being in the spotlight. He was fine to deal with one on one if you wanted to discuss something specific, and when he was feeling relaxed he could be funny and candid among friends and colleagues, but he was hardly gregarious. He did not like making small talk with strangers.

Grant teed up his first question. 'You've been supporting Brentford for years. As a Slough Grammar boy, you bunked off school to go to a Nottingham Forest game. You are a hard-core Bees fan. How does it feel today to have taken the team up?'

As fans holding pints of beer, crowded around, Benham looked a little dazed. Supporters hushed the crowds to hear his answer.

Benham paused for a second before responding. 'It feels,' Benham said, 'fucking brilliant.'

Fans around him cheered. The interview was over. One of them planted a kiss on his cheek.[5]

A few months later, when the celebrations had died down and routine daily work resumed, Mark Devlin, Brentford's chief executive, began drawing up a five-year business plan for Brentford. When his preparation was finished, he displayed his PowerPoint presentation to board members in the tiny boardroom at Griffin Park.

While Benham did not sit on the board, most directors were his Smartodds lieutenants, among them Smartodds chief

---

5 YouTube video, posted by *Beesotted*, 15 October 2014.

executive Phil Whall, finance director Cliff Crown and general counsel Nity Raj. They had replaced the likes of lifelong fans Greg Dyke and John Herting, who had advertised his Southall-based ironmongery wholesaler business on advertising hoardings at Griffin Park for 20 years.[6]

When Devlin's PowerPoint came up on the monitor in front of them, some in the room gave a friendly laugh. The title was: 'Getting Premier League Ready'.[7] Brentford had last played in the top division in 1947, before everybody in the room was born. To the assembled group, Devlin's plan sounded more than a little ambitious. The reality was they would start the new season with a handicap over ten Championship teams who were still receiving so-called annual parachute payments of up to £25 million for dropping out of the Premier League over the previous four years. Promotion from League One had already been expensive for Benham, triggering the payment of generous performance bonuses to players and pushing up the previous year's wage bill to just shy of £10 million. Now, in the Championship, life was about to get even more costly. Over the previous few years, Benham had gradually turned his interest-free loans into equity before eventually buying the club outright. He had now ploughed a total of £46 million into the club. The amount of money indicated how successful his professional gambling was, but it was not clear – even to him – how long this type of spending would be sustainable.

---

6 Bees United retained a seat on the board and a golden share that allowed them to veto the sale of the stadium.
7 Author interview with Mark Devlin.

Even the smartest professional gamblers might have a losing streak lasting as long as six months, maybe more, when their bankroll is down for the year, and they begin to doubt their mathematical model. Dotted around the world were other syndicates whose fortunes had ebbed and flowed over the years – before they shut.

In Las Vegas, the Computer Group successfully diversified from American football into other sports such as tennis, baseball and golf. But their sprawling operation attracted the attention of the FBI. To be making hundreds of thousands of dollars by furtive means, the federal agents assumed they had uncovered a major criminal operation. Federal investigators tapped the phones of Billy Walters, who was charged with 'illegal transmission of wagering information'. (Michael Kent, the mathematics brain behind the syndicate, was not charged with any offence.) In fact, what Walters was doing was not illegal. Bookmaking might have been a crime in most US states, but placing a sports bet was not. He was acquitted. However, the court case and subsequent appeal – which cleared him again – wore down the resolve of the syndicate, which split up.

At around the same time as the Computer Group was operating, two men had moved to Hong Kong from Las Vegas to model the outcome of horse races in the metropolis hemmed in by the sea and mainland China. There was an attractive market for licensed betting at the Hong Kong Jockey Club, which took about $10 billion of bets per year, and the sport was relatively easy to model: here were only two oval racetracks and relatively few horses (1,400) and races (800 per year).

One of the first models of Bill Benter, an American, and Alan Woods, an Australian, tracked about 20 inputs, including wind speed and the position of the horse's starting trap.[8] Slaving away over mathematical formulae in an office in a skyscraper, and then betting your savings on fine margins was stressful. In the first year, they burned through most of their £150,000 betting money. The two men eventually fell out and split to form separate operations that were successful: they both went on to win enough to live extravagantly. Benter bought a share in a French vineyard, and Woods splashed out on a Rolls-Royce.[9]

Further down the food chain, there were other full-time gamblers operating out of suburban homes like day traders on the stock market. An insurance lawyer from South Bend, Indiana, developed an algorithm to predict the result of matches on the men's tennis tour and spent 60 hours per week working on his model. Elihu Feustel, who explained to me in 2014 how he operated, employed a computer programmer to trawl the web for tennis data, including service speed and break-point conversions. When his model diverged from the prices of bookmakers, he instructed a trader to place bets of as much as $30,000 per tennis game via an offshore bookmaker. He was able to earn comfortably more, he said, than working in the legal profession, even if he never quite knew the size of his monthly pay cheque. There was also the risk he could end each month in the red.[10]

---

8 Atherton, ibid.
9 Kit Chellel, *BusinessWeek* 3 May 2018.
10 Author interview with Elihu Feustel, 2014; in the US, unlike in the UK, gambling winnings were taxed.

★ ★ ★

By the time Brentford had reached the Championship in 2014, Smartodds employed more than one hundred full-time staff, and the staff syndicate were by now betting whenever they found a big enough edge on club or national games from dozens of countries around the world. (To avoid a conflict of interest, at around this time the Football Association required Benham to sign up to rules that said he could not bet on matches involving Brentford and Midtjylland.) Staff earned a basic salary and, on top of that, a stake in pooled bets. Winnings were paid into a betting account; losses were deducted. Insiders in this niche industry reckoned neither Benham nor the syndicate had had a losing year since the company started and, thanks to pay, winnings and company benefits, employees stayed for an average of six years.[11]

However, in the first years of Smartodds, life was simpler and more profitable. Benham had been just a wealthy personal donor to Brentford, while making a fortune from betting. In those days his average profit margin on each football bet was as much as six per cent and it was possible to make hundreds of thousands of pounds, if not millions, in a single weekend.

Now, however, bookmakers around the world were starting to become more efficient in setting odds, hiring their own quants to help predict match results. As the odds-makers became smarter, Benham's profits declined. According to industry insiders, Smartodds margins had slimmed over the

---

11 Smartodds website, 2023.

years.[12] To stay profitable, Benham and his quants continued to work on their model, making it more sophisticated than ever. Instead of tracking the strength of just a team through Expected Goals, his staff began searching for ways to quantify the value of each individual player to the side by measuring their passing and assists. Some modellers, for example, looked at measuring the pass completion of players relative to crowd noise: the idea was that the noisier the fans were, the more stress the footballer with the ball would be under. If he completed a higher-than-normal ratio of passes under pressure, that was a useful parameter about how good he was. When a manager named his starting eleven an hour before kick-off, Smartodds quants would determine the strength of the team, factoring in the individual value of each player, and calibrate their betting advice accordingly.

In another measure to fight shrinking profits, Smartodds diversified from football and began modelling and betting on other sports such as basketball and ice hockey. The company also sold proprietary analytics to more clients in the gambling industry. But, even after identifying these new avenues to increase revenue, Benham had some money worries.[13]

His plan for Brentford was always to aim high without breaking the bank. The club's mantra since he had arrived was: if we can't outspend other clubs, we have to out-think them.[14] But you could easily burn through tens of millions of pounds in the Championship without seeing any tangible return on

---

12 Professional gamblers familiar with Smartodds model.
13 Interviews with two Brentford directors, who spoke on condition of anonymity.
14 Devlin interview, ibid.

investment – almost all teams lost money as they competed to reach the Premier League.

Benham's financial concerns developed even as he took on a growing number of costly ventures that risked spiralling out of control. The new Brentford stadium could turn out to be a financial burden even if the cost was mainly offset by the sale of Griffin Park and the construction of apartment blocks adjacent to the new arena at Kew Bridge. Stadium budgets had a habit of going over budget.

In another potential drain on his resources, he had also just bought a club in Denmark to test out new ideas which he wanted to introduce at Brentford. He was juggling more and more projects. Until now Cliff Crown had overseen first the bottom line of Smartodds and then Brentford, but Benham felt he needed somebody with a helicopter view.

In 2016 Benham hired a corporate advisor to advise him on how to proceed with his ownership of the football club, and the stadium project. Conor Hayes had a history of guiding companies through financial straits. As a young man, he had made his name as chief executive of an aviation start-up called Ryanair. After decades of one-airline-per-country monopolies, Ryanair had started to eat into the market share of Aer Lingus but was losing money and the owners were talking about the prospect of shutting down. In 1992 Hayes instigated a strict financial reporting system to flag weak spots in the accounts within days, rather than months.

An accountant to his shoe leather, Hayes insisted every single Ryanair flight should make money. If costs exceeded ticket sales on any single flight, his rigid orders were that it should be cancelled, and passengers pushed onto the next available flight. (Any manager ignoring this would be fired.) In his first year in charge, he had nursed Ryanair out of the red. Michael O'Leary, who replaced him as chief executive, described Hayes as a 'company doctor in all but name'.[15] Hayes went on to work for other businesses before becoming a gun for hire. Now, the Irishman, who had recently turned 60, examined the finances of half a dozen Benham-owned companies in the UK, Guernsey and Denmark, and strode around a scruffy patch of land near Kew Bridge in a suit, tie and hard hat.

At his desk, Hayes studied the peculiar economics of the Championship: 99 per cent of the combined clubs' turnover went into player wages.[16] At Brentford it was more than 160 per cent. Hayes recommended finding an investor to buy part of Benham's stake in Brentford and help him sustain the financial losses that were almost a prerequisite of straining to get to the Premier League.

If you wanted to sell all or part of a football club, one of the best-connected brokers was Inner Circle Sports. Over the previous decade, the New York-based advisory firm had helped with the sales of Liverpool, Sunderland, Inter Milan, Crystal Palace and Sheffield Wednesday. Over several months, Inner Circle put Brentford's management in touch with potential investors. Benham invited some of them to the Smartodds

---

15 Michael O'Leary, *A Life in Full Flight*, written by Alan Ruddock.
16 Deloitte Annual Review of Football Finance, 2016.

office, where he and his executives made a pitch about why it would be a good idea to invest their money into a money-losing club in west London rather than other lower league clubs who were offering to sell equity at the time, such as Bundesliga 2 side Union Berlin or fourth-tier Leyton Orient.

As they walked into Smartodds for the first time, the visitors cast their eyes with curiosity over the rows of staff beavering away at computer terminals. They then settled down to hear the Brentford pitch about why they should sink their money into the club. Benham and his lieutenants highlighted how they thought the Smartodds proprietary data would give his team an edge over the coming years. The data being analysed in-house was also collected there; most other clubs used third-party data suppliers and were, to some extent, finding out the same information as each other. During the discussions, they highlighted what they now considered one of the key metrics for the future. They were measuring and analysing how long it took teams to regain possession.

Among those to visit Smartodds to listen to the Brentford pitch was Michael Eisner, a Walt Disney chief executive for two decades. Eisner, in his seventies, was the latest wealthy American to show an interest in British football. He came along to the Smartodds office with his son, Eric. While father and son were impressed with what Brentford were doing, they felt that Benham was looking for a passive investor. Eisner Sr was more interested in using his knowledge and contacts in the entertainment business to run a club himself. He wanted a complete buyout. His discussions with Benham did not extend past an initial meeting. He eventually bought Portsmouth.

A group fronted by Brazil striker Ronaldo, who had retired from playing a few years earlier, also visited Smartodds. The group, which owned a stake in Fort Lauderdale Strikers, went much further with discussions than Eisner had. 'I was very close to buying Brentford,' Ronaldo said.[17] He and others who did the rounds of European clubs for sale were impressed. 'We saw the good, the bad and the ugly,' one said. 'Brentford were one of the more sophisticated.'

In the end, reluctant to cede his autonomy, Benham opted to retain his 100-per-cent stake despite the financial risks involved, and Hayes refocused his attention on making sure spending on the stadium did not exceed what was budgeted.

After buying the patch of wasteland by Kew Bridge earmarked for the new stadium, for several years Bees United had employed an agent to collect rent from businesses in warehouses, lock-up garages and portacabins while building plans remained on the table. There was a lengthy delay because of the 2008 global financial crisis that had led to the initial developer pulling out. It took some time to find a replacement. On the wasteland, some of the small businesses, like the pornographic film maker operating out of a warehouse without a licence, were sent on their way earlier than others, but eventually all of them had to leave to make way for the landlord's grand plan. After 15 years of planning, work began on the Brentford Community Stadium. One day, amid the rattle of trains and traffic noise, Hayes

---

17 Ronaldo interview, *Good Morning, Britain*, 14 October 2022. After talks with Brentford came to nothing, Ronaldo bought Real Valladolid.

noticed a drone whirring above him. Excited by the club's first new home in more than a century, a Brentford fan called Trevor Inns had decided to chart the construction. Because the land was hemmed in by railway lines and the M4 slip road, it was tricky to find a vantage point, so he bought a drone and began to photograph from the sky. Hayes, whose job it was to worry, felt that the drone could crash, interrupt the building process and rack up extra costs.[18]

The size of the new stadium seemed about right for a club like Brentford, but Hayes felt there could be some savings made. He advised Benham to cut his costs by scaling back the capacity from 20,000 to 17,250. Under this proposal, the arena would be smaller, but it would be built in such a way that it would not need any upgrades if Brentford should reach the Premier League. There would be enough space for an array of television cameras to broadcast from Kew Bridge to the rest of the world. In another deal to help balance the books, Brentford signed a stadium-sharing deal with the west London-based rugby union team, London Irish. This was a relatively minor deal, rather than a game changer. In fact, Hayes had concluded, only by reaching the Premier League could Brentford break even and prevent Benham from continuing to haemorrhage money in the Championship.

After reflecting on the stadium size, Benham decided he did not mind too much about the reduction of the capacity. One

---

18 Twitter account of 'Brentford Drone Man', 18 October 2018. The fan, Trevor Inns, carried on regardless, taking over 8,000 photos over the next couple of years.

of his commitments to Bees United before taking over was to maintain Brentford as a community club. The regular crowd for much of the previous 30 years had barely risen over 5,000, only climbing to 10,000 in the Championship. Anyone over and above this coming to the new stadium would, he said, effectively be tourists.[19]

Since completing his Brentford takeover, Benham had longed to transfer more brainpower between Smartodds and Brentford. His traffic-light system for player recruitment continued to work well, but other ideas ran around his head about how to consistently gain an advantage over opponents. He saw the football pitch like the Oxbridge physics graduate that he was: a series of problems waiting to be solved with logic and intelligence. He felt the mathematicians he employed could be adapted to give Brentford an edge. For example, the performance metric they had identified as important – the time taken to recover possession of the ball – could help strategise how aggressively the Bees should press their opponents to increase their chances of victory. Benham wanted the Brentford manager to base his match tactics not only on qualitative judgement. If, for example, the Smartodds model suggested the optimum time to dispossess the opposition should be within 10 seconds, that should be factored into the game plan. Benham's problem was how to sync his two worlds: the archaic ways of English football, and the modern data-based analytics of professional gambling.

---

19 Author interview with source close to stadium project plans.

Back in the spring of 2013, he had been put in touch by a mutual friend with a Dane living in London. The friend thought they would have a lot in common. When Rasmus Ankersen arrived at Brentford's training ground to meet Benham, he tried to make small talk. Brentford were third in League One, just outside the automatic promotion spots. (It was a few weeks before Marcello Trotta's final-day penalty miss.)

'What are the chances of you getting promotion?' Ankersen said.

Benham, no fan of small talk, responded, barely missing a beat. 'There is a forty-two per cent chance,' he said.[20]

Ankersen was from Herning, a town on the remote Danish peninsula of Jutland, where he started his career in football, and had not met someone like Benham before. Professional football was only in its fifth decade in Denmark. While the first club was formed in Copenhagen in 1879, the sport did not catch fire like in Victorian England, existing only as an amateur pursuit. When a professional league was finally launched, Ankersen's hometown team Herning Fremad tempted the then 37-year-old former England captain Bobby Moore out of retirement in 1978 with a 5,000 kroner per match fee (then about £500). The accord was brokered by a Danish newspaper correspondent in London.

Rather than move to Jutland, Moore flew into Billund Airport from London and took a 40-minute taxi ride to the stadium for matches. He did not bother to train with his teammates. Gate receipts increased from the days of the amateur era, but Moore lasted only nine games in what his wife of the time Tina called a 'hopeless project'.[21] After that, Herning and Ikast, a neighbouring Jutland town, settled into a pattern in which they were consistently beaten every year by bigger clubs in Copenhagen. For years, Herning and Ikast were on the receiving end of defeats and not a few jibes.[22] Supporters of the two Jutland clubs felt the urbane folk from Copenhagen thought of them as unsophisticated provincials. The Copenhagen types not only lived in a city with more beautiful architecture, finer art galleries and swankier restaurants, they also won more football league titles and developed more national team players: almost half of Denmark's 1992 European championship-winning squad had played at some point for Brøndby.

The years of mediocrity of Jutland's football inspired the chairmen of Herning and Ikast – a Mercedes car dealer and a carpenter – to consolidate their strengths in a merger to take on the snobs from the capital. FC Midtjylland – which means mid-Jutland – was formed in 1999.

Ankersen's professional career began with this new club, and ended almost as soon as it began because of a knee injury. So, at the age of 19, he took a job with Midtjylland's new academy. It was in a desolate location, according to Ankersen: a couple of grass pitches with cows munching grass on the other side of the fence.[23]

---

21 *Copenhagen Post*, 22 March 2016.
22 In 1987 Ikast came closest to ending the capital's dominance, finishing runners-up to Brondby.
23 Rasmus Ankersen, *The Gold Mine Effect: Crack the Secrets of High Performance*.

Without any pedigree, the academy struggled to attract talent at first, eventually managing to round up a dozen or so teenagers. Among the initial intake was a 15-year-old boy whom no Danish club was much interested in. Ankersen had also seen him play and did not rate him much either. But, anyway, with a lack of alternative teenagers, Simon Kjær got the academy's last spot.

Three years later, the boy nobody wanted to take on was traded by Midtjylland to Palermo for €4 million; Kjær went on to captain Denmark, playing 120 times for the national team.

This story indicated to Ankersen that football and indeed sport in general was in no way linear or obvious when it came to talent development. He decided to take a break from coaching and travel around the world to identify some common factors and then write about them in a book, *The Gold Mine Effect*. He went to Ethiopia and Kenya to study how coaches had developed the world's best long-distance runners, South Korea to see how training methods produced elite women golfers, Russia to track the ascent of women tennis players, Brazil to follow how footballers became so skilful, and Jamaica to see how the fastest sprinters were developed. Ankersen had just published his book when he met Benham and was bursting with anecdotes and ideas. They got on well, swapping contrarian theories about football. 'We just hit it off instantly in this sort of football geek nerd way,' Benham said.[24]

---

24 Benham, Bees United interview, 27 May 2022.

On his travels around the world, Ankersen had visited the athletics club in Kingston, Jamaica, that helped turned sprinter Asafa Powell into the fastest man in the world in 2005. When he arrived there at dawn one day, Ankersen had found a 'diesel-scorched' field, some traffic cones, a gym with no air conditioning, and rusty weights.

In suburban west London, he stood with Benham surveying the handful of side-by-side pitches, the clock-tower pavilion and huddle of portacabins that made up Brentford's training facilities. One of Ankersen's key findings was that success is about mindset, not facilities. A warm feeling spread over Benham as they talked. 'Some of the things he thought were music to my ears,' Benham said.[25]

The following year, the pair had lunch at a restaurant in London's Soho. Benham mentioned he was looking to buy a second club. He wanted a place to use as a testing ground for the kind of ideas that he found some at Brentford were resistant to. Mark Warburton and his inner circle were not as open to incorporating new data-based ideas as Benham would have liked. David Weir, Warburton's assistant, had been a player for 20 years, representing Everton, Glasgow Rangers and Scotland. Frank McParland, the director of football, had spent 14 years running Liverpool's academy. If he was looking for an appropriate club to buy, Ankersen recommended that Benham should consider FC Midtjylland.

---

25 Benham, Bees United interview, ibid.

His former club prided themselves on doing things differently. They were one of the first teams to hire a throw-in coach who could propel the ball some 50 metres into the penalty box; he taught players to use a throw-in not as a break in play but as an offensive weapon. The coach, a former Olympic team bobsledder, was so left-field that he once suggested forwards should study sumo-wrestling techniques. It would, he said, help them avoid markers who clung to them at corners.[26]

When he was at Midtjylland, a more senior coach noticed Ankersen was always questioning the way things were done – and this was fine. He was not told to mind his own business. The club encouraged free thinking.

FC Midtjylland had been promoted to the Danish Superliga in their first season, and over the next decade went on to consistently finish near the top of the table – sufficient to qualify for the Europa League although not quite enough to eclipse both Brøndby and FC Copenhagen. Still, according to a Midtjylland executive, some in Copenhagen remained snooty about the upstart club. 'The people from the capital looked down on us as a bunch of peasants,' he said.[27]

A week after their Soho lunch, Benham flew to Jutland from London, following the route trailblazed by Bobby Moore. He arrived on a private jet at Billund Airport with Ankersen and a couple of Smartodds executives, and they were given a guided tour. The nearly new stadium, next to a main road south of

---

26 Thomas Grønnemark interview, *Football Fanalytics* podcast, 22 September 2021.
27 Author interview with former FC Midtjylland communications director Hans Krabbe.

Herning, was part of a complex built by a private developer that included a conference centre, a concert hall and restaurant.[28] Benham was impressed: the stadium was a century newer than Griffin Park. He liked that the club had connections with 150 smaller amateur teams. This was an efficient way to identify talent and fitted with his beliefs. One of his pledges to Bees United as owner was that Brentford would remain rooted in the community. The group returned to London to mull things over.

Midtjylland looked like it would be a good testing ground for ideas. Danish football did not have the same rigid power structure as he had found in the English game. 'Their culture is a bit more open-minded,' Benham said. 'They have much less hierarchy – [they are] much, much flatter, so anyone can state their opinions.'[29]

There was another element that made Benham think he would be welcome: Midtjylland might have a new stadium to play in, but they were completely broke. The global banking crisis of 2008 had hit the club. After the windfall from Simon Kjær's transfer to Italy ran out there was some capital from a new investor, but that did not go far. They had overstretched themselves: annual costs of about £10 million were double the revenue. Management had no other option than to halt spending on transfer fees. For the 2011–12 season, the only players recruited arrived on free transfers. The club was

---

28 FC Midtjylland took a 25-year lease on the stadium.
29 Benham interview with Bees United, ibid.

scrimping on other costs. Whereas before club officials had piled into the VIP section at FC Copenhagen's stadium for an expensive dinner after an away match, now they ate pizza on the team bus on the three-hour journey home.

The shiny stadium and regular UEFA Europa League football concealed a hollow background, what a club insider called a Potemkin village. 'We were a façade with a logo but not much else.'[30] There was not even a devoted fanbase: match attendances fell to below 6,000. In such a fragile state, there were few barriers to a takeover. Benham agreed to pay the equivalent of about £5 million for a 60 per cent stake,[31] and appointed Ankersen as chairman.

After lawyers finalised the paperwork, all that was left to do was for Benham to return to sign the contract and make a public announcement. When he returned in the summer, there was a relaxed atmosphere. It was a friendly takeover: both sides were happy with the deal. Johnny Rune, the carpenter who had co-founded FC Midtjylland 15 years earlier, was relieved the club's future was now secure, and he had a return on his investment. Benham was comfortable with the management team, who spoke near-perfect English. After exchanging pleasantries, they retired to the bar of the conference centre next to the stadium. As wine and canapés were served, Ankersen, Rune and communications director Hans Krabbe talked about the next day's news conference, and Benham excused himself.

---

30 Krabbe interview, ibid.
31 Borsen.dk, 13 August 2014.

It was the middle of the World Cup in Brazil. That evening Argentina were playing Belgium in the quarter-finals. On the other side of the room, Benham settled down to watch the match on a television monitor on the wall, while scanning a laptop computer and talking into his mobile. When Krabbe walked over to see if he wanted anything, he looked over Benham's shoulder and asked what he was doing. 'Matthew showed me a 1.0 number on the screen and explained that meant he was betting £1 million in Asia,' Krabbe said. 'He asked me to get him a Diet Coke.'

For the next hour or so, he left Benham alone. Benham did not like to be disturbed during games. When he was working – and football was work – he preferred silence. One of Benham's favourite books was *Thinking, Fast and Slow* by Daniel Kahneman, who explained how 'ridiculously over-optimistic people are about their ability to predict [the future]'. He had given copies of the book to Smartodds staff. If a bystander spouted an opinion about who would win a match it was usually based on the flimsiest evidence. 'I don't like to talk during games,' Benham said.[32] 'It might sound snooty, but a bunch of people talk a lot of crap.'

Later, Krabbe heard that while sat in front of a laptop Benham had used Smartodds modelling to make 80 bets during that evening. As well as betting on Argentina's 1–0 win, he wagered on another quarter-final in which the Netherlands beat Costa Rica on penalties.

---

32 Matthew Benham interview, *11 Freunde*, April 2013.

Benham and Ankersen had been in the conference complex for several hours when they finally emerged after midnight. They were in an even more convivial mood than when they had arrived. Sharing jokes, the English among the party were surprised to walk out into the Scandinavian summer night and find the sun had not set.

Over the coming days, gossip swirled among club staff that Benham had paid for his acquisition of FC Midtjylland thanks to his World Cup trading that evening.[33] To have won £5 million on two quarter-finals is feasible, although he would likely have had to successfully stake more than £2 million on each of the two matches. Some of the bets he made during the games could have been a form of insurance to protect his position.

At the news conference the next day, Ankersen did most of the talking. Benham, always uncomfortable public speaking before an audience, did some one-to-one interviews instead. A buyout of a Superliga club was big news in Denmark, making the evening news, with analysis from a sports business expert who said the takeover elevated Midtjylland to a new level. In Britain, the news barely raised an eyebrow, even among Brentford fans. The ins and outs of the Danish football league were hardly the subject of pub chatter.

Soon afterwards, Benham arranged for the team and staff to fly to London to visit Smartodds. Among the group was team captain Jakob Poulsen, who had returned to Midtjylland for a second stint during that year's January transfer window. Players

---

33 Author interview with Krabbe, former FC Midtjylland communications director.

looked at the banks of television monitors and computers in the former warehouse in Highgate Road with a bemused air. They had heard about the big data plans of Benham and were a little spooked. Back in Jutland, even the term 'Key Performance Indicators', or KPIs, was not a familiar term to some staff. As they were being shown around the Smartodds office, Poulsen, 31, approached a man a few years younger than him whose eyes were fixed on a computer. 'What have you got on me?' Poulsen asked.

The younger man swivelled around in his chair. 'Ah, you're Jakob,' the young Smartodds man said. He pulled up a file, which he showed to Poulsen. There was a mass of data, including how many passes the midfielder had made over the previous year with his left and right foot, how far he had run in each game, and all his goalscoring chances rated.

Poulsen was stunned. He took two steps back and said, 'Wow!'[34]

Benham's staff had already begun searching for players to strengthen FC Midtjylland before the takeover was finalised, with Benham setting aside £2.5 million for spending in the summer transfer market: half the transfer budget of FC Copenhagen and Brøndby.

Within a few days of Benham's acquisition, the club had signed a little-known Finnish midfielder from Greuther Fürth, a club in Germany's second tier that had just lost to Hertha Berlin in the play-offs. The staff liked Tim Sparv because of what the

---

34 Krabbe interview, ibid.

data said: he was an influential midfielder in a team which was underrated based on its position in the league. Greuther Fürth won more when he was in the side than when he was not.

Sparv was happy to sign for a forward-thinking club. The only problem was: no one had informed the Midtjylland head coach Glen Riddersholm about his qualities. In fact, when a club press officer was preparing a media release and asked him for a quote about why he liked the new recruit's style of play, Riddersholm explained that would be difficult: he knew nothing about him. He was not just bemused; he appeared a little angry.[35] At FC Midtjylland the head coach was no longer in charge, the data was.

---

35 Author interview with source who worked at FC Midtjylland.

Chapter 10

2015: Jersey Road, Osterley

In their first season in the second tier for 22 years, Mark Warburton was leading Brentford to a standout year. Jota, the Spanish winger with a wiry frame, was one of the stars of the team: he was a gifted dribbler, hugging the touchline before suddenly slaloming towards the box and unleashing a ferocious shot. He had an easy smile, pop star looks, and was dating a former Miss Seville.

Everything was going better than anyone could have hoped. In November they won all of their league games, beating Derby County, Nottingham Forest, Millwall, Fulham and Wolves to equal their previous record winning streak in the second tier in 1935. In a memorable moment, they beat Fulham 2–1 with an injury-time winner: Jota darted in from the wing and scored with a 20-yard shot. After they hammered Wolves 4–0 for their fifth straight win, Warburton was understandably bullish.

'People talk to me about coming into this division and looking to survive, but that's nonsense,' he said. 'Our aim isn't just to stay in this division.' In another shot in the arm for Benham, Brentford did the double over Brighton, putting one over his nemesis Tony Bloom. By February Brentford were fourth. The club had gone from League One to the doorstep of the Premier League in barely a year. And they were playing breathtaking passing football, no longer the rudimentary heave-ho style supporters had watched for years. Yet something still irked Benham.

As with previous managers, Benham wanted to be able to discuss and test new ideas to help the team. Some of these ideas were his own, others came from Smartodds staff. Warburton, however, remained not as receptive to these ideas as he would have liked. The data Benham had seen showed Brentford performed poorly at set pieces which, according to analysis, could add 15 goals a season – a rich seam of extra points. At the start of the season, Benham had offered Warburton the chance to work with an Italian corner specialist who had worked in Serie A and had a playbook with more than 4,000 routines from corners and free-kicks. Not now, Warburton had said. They would get around to it later.[1] By mid-season, even if they were in the play-off spots, Brentford were one of the worst three teams at set pieces in the Championship.

Warburton was by no means lazy. He got to training before dawn, would sometimes work 14-hour days and had meetings

---

1 Ted Knutson, *StatsBomb* podcast, 9 June 2021.

on Sunday mornings with Weir, his assistant. Maybe his brain was not wired the same as Benham's, who believed the team could be a couple of places higher in the league if they scored more goals from dead-ball kicks. Brentford were, in Benham's mind, leaving points on the table. He could not understand Warburton's reluctance: if set pieces could make up 30 per cent of goals, as the data showed, why not practise them? It was like a student going to sit exams without bothering to study for one-third of the syllabus.

Then, by January, they had another difference of opinion. While Brentford were a highly impressive fifth in the table, the Smartodds 'Justice Table' suggested they were riding their luck and should be six places lower in mid-table. Some points had come by virtue of late goals. As well as Jota's winner against Fulham, a last-minute goal by Stuart Dallas had given them a 2–1 win over Derby. While statisticians might consider these extra points to be good fortune, Warburton chalked them up to players being motivated. More than once, Warburton and Benham discussed this. 'How can you measure motivation?' Benham asked.[2] Warburton conceded that you could not, but stuck to his belief that team spirit was a key component of success.

With a view to strengthening the squad in the mid-season window, and improving on the virtual position of 11th place that was based on the Expected Goals calculations of the Smartodds staff, Benham suggested a couple of potential signings based

---

2 Street and Lane, ibid.

on broader research. Warburton pushed back: adding new players was not a good idea; with things going so well, he did not want to upset the team's mojo.[3] Believing Benham's gripes were more of an intellectual debate than anything, and with Brentford enjoying their best position in the Football League since the 1950s, Warburton seemed to have got his way and turned his attention back to his weekly routine. Brentford continued to knock over much bigger teams and stay in contention for promotion to the Premier League.

By now, football analysis in England was gradually becoming more sophisticated, even if it was only taken seriously by a small group of teams. At Liverpool, where Bill Shankly was once regarded a manager with almost mystical powers, management set up a data science department led by a man with a doctorate in theoretical physics from Cambridge University.[4] This approach was encouraged by American owner John Henry, who had become a billionaire thanks to an algorithm he came up with to predict swings in the soybean market.[5]

Henry also owned a baseball team, Boston Red Sox, which had long employed data analysts. One of them, Bill James, had previously written about baseball data while doing nightshifts as a security guard at a pork and beans factory. James wrote an annual review that poked holes in conventional wisdoms. In 1977, when quantitative analytics in sport was almost unheard

---

3 Knutson, ibid.
4 Ian Graham's stint at the club lasted from 2012 to 2022.
5 *New York Times*, 22 May 2019.

of, the first edition of *The Bill James Baseball Abstract*, which he self-published, sold 75 copies.[6]

A generation later, bloggers began to post statistical analysis about European football on specialist websites. On some days, one of the sites, StatsBomb, would struggle to get more than a couple of hundred daily views. In the first year, its Twitter account had fewer than a thousand followers. The site's American founder Ted Knutson said in a post at the time that there was still a long road of data evangelism ahead in European football. Statisticians in football were routinely ignored by the game's insiders, many of them ex-professional players. Apart from Liverpool and one or two others, Knutson wrote, 'Europeans often first shout, "Shut the fuck up!" because they don't think stats matter, or that they ruin the purity and sanctity of the beautiful game. Obviously, the Americans are right, but it will take a good many years before we get anywhere near the level of data availability and acceptance that, say, the NBA has right now.'

As a young man, Knutson had used sports statistics to bet as a professional gambler. He went on to take a job at Pinnacle Sports as the offshore bookmaker sought to expand a mainly US client base. While working there, Knutson was diagnosed with testicular cancer, requiring surgery and chemotherapy.[7] As he recovered, to occupy himself he took up a couple of hobbies: he bought an electric guitar and started to look at football statistics.

---

6 Michael Lewis, *Moneyball: The Art of Winning an Unfair Game.*
7 Ted Knutson, StatsBomb website blog, 28 June 2023.

So consumed did he become with the data in the game that he left his guitar virtually untouched. Statistics, until then largely gathered by professional gamblers but hidden from the public domain, were being made available by Squawka.com and other websites. Using these statistics, Knutson did some analytical writing about Manchester City on a website called Bitter and Blue, but did not want to limit his thinking to a single club. So, in 2013, he founded a blog.[8]

The readership of StatsBomb was small but enthusiastic, and some of the readers who followed its blogs via Twitter worked in football, so it was a way for budding analysts to advertise their work to professional clubs. Benham liked what he read and hired Knutson as Brentford's head of performance analytics, along with a small cell of mathematicians that he wanted to supplement the brainpower already at his disposal. Knutson took a desk at Benham's office in north London. He brought with him other StatsBomb contributors including a Polish computer scientist with a background in modelling biological parameters, a skill set important for pharmaceutical companies.[9]

Marek Kwiatkowski's route to working for a Championship club was, like Knutson's, through the prism of Twitter. After devouring the work of other amateur analysts on the platform, in 2014 he joined with the handle @statlurker and began to contribute to StatsBomb, evangelising about the untapped potential of analytics in football.

8 The account of the start of StatsBomb is from Ted Knutson's blog on the company website, 28 June 2023.
9 Marek Kwiatkowski worked remotely from Switzerland.

The Brentford cell's job was to help sift through masses of data to uncover insight that could give Brentford an edge, not only in the transfer market but also in the way they played football. Benham did not broadcast the recruitment, perhaps because he knew that it might not be well received: data geeks from the United States and Poland were going to give tips on tactics to the British, the people who invented Association Football.

At English clubs, the performance and analytics staff were typically considered near the bottom of the hierarchy. If the training ground was a country estate, the first-team coach was the lord of the manor, and the analysts worked out of sight under the stairs. Not that Knutson, a cheerful type, was at all aware of these British social norms. Once, during a training session, he drew some tutting and raised eyebrows by casually leaning against a goalpost. It was, one writer said, an etiquette breach equivalent to mooning at the Queen.[10]

In Benham's eyes, of course, the stats guys were almost as important as the players. Soon, Brentford and Midtjylland were paying almost £1.2 million between them for Smartodds quantitative analysis to help them with recruitment decisions and to improve performance – the equivalent of the combined annual wages of three first-team Brentford players.[11] The money was well spent based on the £2.5 million profit the team had made from trading midfielder Adam Forshaw to Wigan at the start of the season, two years after he arrived from Everton on a

---

10 Michael Calvin, *Living on the Volcano: The Secrets of Surviving as a Football Manager.*
11 Companies House filing, 2016; £800,000 came from Brentford and £375,000 from Midtjylland.

free transfer. The jury was still out on how much quants could improve football performance tactically, but if they were being used in other industries to make strategic decisions it seemed logical that they could benefit Brentford.

Warburton's latest Saturday afternoon scalp as manager in early February was Leeds United, who Brentford rolled over 1–0 at Elland Road, completing the double over the Yorkshire team. The next morning as Warburton was reflecting on the game in his portacabin office over a coffee with Weir, they came across a report in the *Mail on Sunday* saying Brentford had approached Paco Jémez, the coach of Spanish club Rayo Vallecano. Jémez had rejected an offer to join the Bees, the report said. Stunned, Warburton contacted Benham seeking an explanation.

At the Smartodds office in north London the following day, Benham explained to Warburton why he was looking for someone who would be more open to listening to the findings from data analytics and incorporating them it into decision-making. With the two men at a crossroads in their professional relationship, the differences between them appeared irreconcilable. As a temporary fix, Warburton agreed to Benham's proposal to stay on for the last three months of the season.[12]

The news leaked out. Benham's was a difficult decision to fathom. Why would Brentford fire their manager during its best season in more than 60 years? For a column in the *Guardian*,

---

12 Mark Warburton interview, Coaches' Voice website, undated.

Daniel Taylor studied the cuttings about Brentford – 1930s success, failed 1960s takeover by QPR, six decades of going nowhere. Now, just as they were enjoying some rare success, this. If, Taylor wrote, Benham did not reverse his decision, he was opening himself up to accusations of being another club owner 'with more money than sense'.[13]

As the news spread Brentford were at home to Watford. Striker Andre Gray hit the opening goal and immediately ran over to embrace Warburton on the touchline. Gray's teammates gathered around to show their support for the now lame duck manager. Warburton urged his players to rally around him in the final stage of the season and show that the decision to replace him was wrong. The club issued a statement, seeking to downplay the conversation with Jémez, implying it was misinterpreted as a job offer. 'Football,' the statement said, 'is sometimes called a village, and in a village, gossip and rumours can spread like wildfire, whether or not such rumours are true.' The damage, however, was done. Benham stayed away from the training ground, where there was lingering ill feeling about the role of Smartodds in the football side of the club.

Uncomfortable with public scrutiny about his methods in newspapers, radio phone-ins and fan forums, Benham sought to make clear that he was not a barmy physics graduate as some liked to portray him. Data analysis was only one part of the club's thinking, he said. They used statistics only to help shape decision-making. It was a misconception that *everything* was

---

13 *Guardian*, 14 February 2015.

based on data. During Warburton's last weeks, Brentford's strong form continued, and they finished fifth to reach the play-offs, but were well beaten in the semi-final by Middlesbrough, losing 5–1 on aggregate and missing out on an opportunity to reach the Premier League.

FC Midtjylland coach Glen Riddersholm was a son of Jutland. He was born on the west coast of the peninsula, which had a history tied up with fishing and farming in a desolate landscape where wolves once roamed. His first job in football was coaching Ikast, one of the teams which morphed into FC Midtjylland. He had an innocent face, piercing clear blue eyes, and a hunger to gain an edge in the dog-eat-dog world of football.

He was the first youth-team coach at Midtjylland in 1999, working with Rasmus Ankersen in the academy before moving up the ranks to become assistant coach, and then first-team manager. He described the club as being close to his heart. Like many colleagues, he felt executives and fans of Brøndby and FC Copenhagen were condescending towards Jutland's upstart football team. 'They felt that we were a pebble in their shoe,' he said.[14]

After so long as a coach there, Riddersholm was in step with Midtjylland's innovation. He liked how they had a psychologist who assigned them a colour based on their character to help understand each other better and develop as individuals. (Riddersholm was marked as red – because he was

---

14 Author interview with Glen Riddersholm.

ultra-competitive.) At home, even their wives noticed positive changes.

While he was used to coming at football from new angles like this, Riddersholm was surprised what Benham had in store: the Englishman told him at their first meeting how he planned to do things. 'Glen, you can lose five games in a row, that's OK,' Benham said, as he explained how he would evaluate Midtjylland's progress using data analytics.[15] More important than results – whether a team won, lost or drew – were the 'Expected Goals', the metric which helped Smartodds determine underlying form; the index they were so confident was accurate they used it to gamble millions of pounds every week. Benham would, he told Riddersholm, judge him on xG.

As Riddersholm went into the changing room at half-time, he would hear a ping on his mobile phone with the xG of both teams. Another text message arrived from Smartodds after the game: this time it was the Danish Superliga 'Justice Table' that showed him where Midtjylland should really be. Sometimes, after a spell of bad luck, their position was better than they merited. Conversely, the alternative table could act as a canary in a coalmine, indicating when performance was in decline despite a healthy points tally. According to Benham's envoy, Ankersen, the table could lie by as much as 15 points.

Ankersen brought in more original thinking, such as data to identify the exact places on the pitch where Midtjylland players

---

15 Ibid, Riddersholm's recollection of the meeting.

were more likely to score from. This research showed, among other things, that it made more sense to keep possession until you were inside the penalty box before shooting. A kicking coach with a sports science master's degree was integrated into the training schedule, along with an NFL expert, a pundit on Danish television, who showed them how American football teams created a playbook: this helped with planning corners and free-kicks.

Once, when the players had gathered in what Ankersen dubbed the 'set-piece lounge' to brainstorm about corners, Benham listened in via Skype from London. Sharing his screen, he showed a YouTube video of a corner routine from the 1990s and asked whether Midtjylland might use it. Instead of thinking, 'Mind your own business,' the group of players were impressed by how invested this quiet Englishman was in the project.[16] Most of the time, though, Benham remained in the background, removed from the daily grind. After a convincing victory, Riddersholm might get a short text message from him: 'Really good job, congratulations.'

It was mid-December, about halfway through the season, when Riddersholm went to Madrid for a short holiday with his wife during a break in the league. He started a diary, sensing that this would be an important year in his life, and noted down the team was doing so well he thought they would win the league. Benham had not only strengthened the squad with investment he had also brought even more innovative thinking.

16 Tim Sparv interview, *Guardian*, 27 July 2015.

Riddersholm did not switch off in Spain, taking a taxi out to the suburbs to watch a game between the youth teams of Real Madrid and Atlético Madrid. He was particularly impressed by a young Atlético player and mentioned his name to Ankersen. 'He could be one for us,' Riddersholm told his colleague.

A week later Riddersholm received a document of more than 20 pages from Smartodds about the young player that analysed his performance and went as far as describing the jobs of his parents and some problems he'd had at school. 'The level of information was amazing,' Riddersholm said. 'It was like a new world opening up.' Based on the player profiling, Midtjylland decided not to make an offer to sign the player. It would, he found out later, turn out to be the right decision.

Helped by their NFL expert and hours of training-ground practice, Midtjylland's work on set pieces began to pay off: they were scoring a higher ratio of set-piece goals than any other team in the league, adding goals in their challenge for the title. Tim Sparv, the signing based on Smartodds analytics whom Riddersholm was not consulted about, turned out to be a success: he was a calm presence in the centre of the defence who read the game expertly.

As the Warburton affair played out in London, Midtjylland were poised to win their first league title in their short 16-year history. With a few games of the season left, a 2–0 home win against closest rival FC Copenhagen had almost sealed the championship. Benham, who was in the crowd for that game, found himself getting a whole lot more love in Denmark than in England. 'Matthew,' said one Midtjylland player, 'is the x-factor.'[17] Copenhagen, which had won eight of the last 12 titles, were beaten by Benham's team by four points.

Happy but exhausted, Riddersholm resigned within weeks.

It was not, he said, Benham's new approach to football that wore him down. Reportedly, a tense relationship with sports director Claus Steinlein caused his departure. However, the season had been the best of his career. Football was a frenetic business, and he swiftly moved on to another club. There was barely time to pause and reflect, but when he retired and would be drinking a glass of rum in his Jutland summer house, he would look back and savour the memories.

Amid the brouhaha in London, Midtjylland's success appeared to give Benham confidence that his methods were on the money. He appointed two men who were in tune with his thinking. Phil Giles, the Smartodds quant with a first-class degree in mathematics, became co-director of football with Rasmus Ankersen. Their remit covered both Brentford and Midtjylland. Ankersen had been around professional football much of his life, even if he was by no means a traditional thinker. Appointing Giles was more unusual: in fact, it was one of the most contrarian decisions in modern-day British football.

Giles's primary experience in the game – apart from being a Newcastle United season ticket holder – was working at Smartodds. Nevertheless, after eight years at the company, Giles had deep experience of finding meaning in millions of football

---

17 Erik Sviatchenko, quoted in the *Guardian*, ibid.

data points. His work with fellow quants had already proved useful for Brentford's recruitment by identifying exceptional talent lower down football's ecosystem. The previous year, they had helped with the decision to sign Andre Gray, then at fourth-tier Luton, for as little as £450,000. After a season at Griffin Park in which he scored 16 goals in the Championship, Gray was transferred to Burnley for about £8 million.[18]

Crucially, as well as understanding intricate mathematical models, Giles also had a knack for breaking down complex data and explaining it in layman's terms to coaching staff. In his soft Geordie lilt, he was approachable, unassuming and low maintenance. His office in Osterley was a whitewashed room that could have passed for a prison cell: there was a narrow window, and the only adornments on the walls were a series of electrical fittings.

Giles and Ankersen would work with a new coach. Marinus Dijkhuizen came from Rotterdam's tiny third club, Excelsior, which had a 4,500-seat ground and played on artificial turf because they could not afford under-soil heating for a grass pitch. During the interview process, Dijkhuizen had agreed to work with data analytics but, just to make sure he knew what he was getting himself in for, he was asked to sign an eight-clause document agreeing not to ignore Giles and Ankersen. One clause effectively said: no idea can be brushed aside without argument.

Benham also brought in the Italian with the playbook of 4,000 set pieces whom Warburton had overlooked. Gianni

---

18 Transfer fees based on Transfermarkt.com data.

Vio hailed from Venice, the breathtaking historic gem with crumbling pastel façades, intricate bridges, gondolas and no football heritage to speak of. He had previously worked in a UniCredit bank in Mestre, across the water from Venice.

Vio got his break in football after writing *The Extra 30 Per Cent*, in which he set out his philosophy about how a club could increase its goal tally by one third from set pieces. His book piqued the interest of Walter Zenga, the former Italy goalkeeper, who hired him as a consultant while he was coaching in the Middle East. As Vio's reputation spread, he went on to work in Serie A, for Catania, Palermo and AC Milan. In Italy he became known – thanks to his white beard, and ability to turn corners into goals – as *il mago*, the wizard.

In Osterley, amid the thunderous noise of Boeing 747s descending, Vio's wisdom was introduced to English football for the first time. He was employed as a consultant to teach Brentford the benefits of sowing chaos in the penalty box. In the build-up to a corner, as many as five players might run into the penalty box in a zigzagging movement, as much to distract the defenders from the trajectory of the ball as to make space for a shot or header. Many of the corners were in-swingers hit towards the five-yard box, where the defence was most vulnerable. Often in the organised chaos, the ball would be bundled into the net. It was not as beautiful as Venice's St Mark's Square, with its golden mosaics, Gothic colonnades and soaring bell tower, but, eventually, Brentford began to score more from set pieces.

In another routine, five players stood to one edge of the penalty box, out of the sightline of the goalkeeper and defenders so, as they rushed towards goal, their opponents did not know whether to look at the ball flying across the penalty box or at the oncoming attackers. In this way, Brentford got a 96th-minute equaliser against Ipswich.

Sometimes, corners were taken quickly before the defence arranged themselves: this earned a headed goal against Charlton. Then, there were the stage-managed routines that the team had worked on in training. A week after Christmas, at Birmingham City, Brentford players stood in two rows in front of the defensive wall in a shape like a Christmas tree. As Alan Judge stepped up to take the free-kick the first wall splintered, with three players running around the back of the other two walls. Then, in the climax of the carefully crafted move, Judge shot wide of the post.

Players generally found corner drills dull and repetitive. To try to interest them, Manchester City staff showed players motivational videos with clips of match-winning goals; they gave them creative licence to devise their own routines.[19] Brentford tried a different approach: a performance bonus was written into player contracts that meant with each goal from a free-kick or a corner, they would get a cash bonus. By midway through the season, the team had banged in ten goals from set pieces and lifted their ratio of goals from set pieces to 27 per cent, from 12 per cent.[20]

---

19 Author interview with Ed Sulley, former Manchester City analyst.
20 Sky Sports website, 8 January 2016.

By then, Dijkhuizen had gone, fired after just eight games. On a September morning, he was asked to come in at 8 a.m. In a conversation he said lasted one minute he was told his services were no longer required.[21] It was probably the shortest managerial stint of any Brentford manager, excluding caretaker managers. During a pre-season tour of Portugal, things had started badly. There was no chemistry between the Dutch coach and the British players, who had got on so well with Warburton. They questioned his methods, complaining that he was not doing enough fitness work to prepare them for the new season. In the league, Brentford started poorly, winning only two of their first eight games.

Little was more inviting for a tabloid journalist than when a plan appeared to be going spectacularly wrong: the gleeful hack could portray it like a scene in the television farce *Only Fools and Horses* when south Londoner chancer Del Boy comes up with what he perceives as a clever scheme. 'After four games, Brentford are bottom of the Championship,' Martin Samuel wrote in the *Daily Mail*, 'but do not worry. This is only the real league table, the one that actually decides relegation; no doubt at Brentford there is another table on expected goal value, or some other worthier calculation, that informs them it is all going swimmingly.'

Dijkhuizen had arrived at Brentford with chaos behind the scenes. Not only had Warburton and his staff departed without a succession plan but they had taken their scouting

---

21 Dutch broadcaster NOS website, 28 September 2015.

network with them to Glasgow Rangers. That summer, 23 players left Brentford: everyone from top scorer Andre Gray to a group of 20-year-olds. Meanwhile, other young players were returning in droves to Griffin Park following loan spells across Britain.

Ted Knutson found himself with considerably more responsibility than when running a blog with a couple of hundred daily views. New to the club, he had no idea who some of the younger members of the squad were. His inbox was a mess. When he was forwarded an email from the brother and agent of Jack O'Connell asking what Brentford's plans were for their 21-year-old centre-back who had spent a few weeks on loan at Rochdale the previous season, he thought: 'Jack who?'[22]

Knutson and his colleagues were allotted a £10 million bankroll to sign reinforcements, along with a couple of rules: no transfer fee over £2 million for a single player, and no base salary over £8,000 per week.

Dijkhuizen's firing added a new layer to his working life: Knutson was given a brief to search for a manager who would embrace analytics but would get on better with the mainly British squad who were used to passionate coaches not cool continental types. He looked at coaches in Major League Soccer and in Denmark, both seen as more open cultures which were more likely to accept data analysis. On the shortlist was a man called Thomas Frank.

---

22 Knutson interview, *The Beesotted Pride of West London* podcast, 21 September 2020.

Chapter 11

2021: Brentford Community Stadium, Kew Bridge

Thomas Frank was in his third season at Brøndby when he was first contacted by Brentford co-director of football Rasmus Ankersen. Frank was having a hard time in his first high-profile job. He had cut his teeth coaching Denmark's youth teams when Morten Olsen was the coach of the senior team and advocated a short passing style like Ajax and Barcelona. Impressed by Dutch Total Football, Frank copied the style with teenagers, and this earned him the reputation required to land one of the biggest jobs in Danish football.

Brøndby were football aristocracy, but the last of their ten league titles had come a decade earlier and fans were restless. In 2015 Frank could only lead them to third, 16 points behind Matthew Benham's *Moneyball* team, FC Midtjylland. When I asked a Danish football executive about Frank at around this time, he said not to expect much from him. Frank, he said, was not a coaching star in the making.

Jan Bech Andersen, the Brøndby chairman, was not a fan either. He had witnessed the team's 6–1 elimination by PAOK from a Europa League qualifier and their latest capitulation in the Danish championship. With a minority stake in the club, Andersen was influential, but he did not call all the shots. In the depths of the Scandinavian winter, he logged onto a fan forum using his son's account and the pseudonym 'Oscar'. And then he lashed out at Frank. He typed into the chat that he was ignorant and inexperienced. 'Another coach should be able to get more out of the squad', he wrote. 'I'm convinced we'll see changes very soon.'[1]

Shortly after the identity of Oscar emerged, Frank resigned.[2] By then, Brentford had turned their attention elsewhere, and hired Dean Smith as their manager. Smith, who played more than 500 Football League games for Walsall, Leyton Orient, Hereford and Sheffield Wednesday as a centre-back, was selected partly for his knowledge of 'English football culture', which Rasmus Ankersen said would help him connect with Brentford's mostly British squad. He was also picked for the attacking style he had pursued as manager of Walsall in League One, and his openness to innovation. Before taking the job, Smith was told the same thing as his Dutch predecessor: you cannot dismiss the findings from quantitative analytics without

---

1 These Football Times website, 14 March 2022.
2 Ekstrabladet.dk, 9 March 2016.

a discussion. 'It's about having hopefully a lot of smart people in the same place who can add their opinions and perspectives,' Ankersen said. Smith, who had once been West Midlands school chess champion, did not see that as a problem. He still played chess regularly, saying it helped him with football tactics.[3] Smith established a stronger rapport with the players than Dijkhuizen, maintaining the blend of attacking football from the Warburton era. In his first season in charge, Brentford finished ninth in the Championship, nine points off the play-off positions, scoring a division-leading 72 goals. However, they had a worrying propensity to implode, leaking 65 goals: the team was a work in progress.

It was also a transitional period for Brentford's team of quants. A time for reflection. Benham decided he had tried to change too much, too soon. Benham disbanded the analytics cell led by Ted Knutson. It wasn't that the cell was failing to come up with good ideas it was just that, in Benham's push to assemble a lot of smart people, there were too many voices at Brentford shouting to be heard. He decided to streamline decision-making, leaving Phil Giles to request and sift through data insight from north London and relay key data to coaching staff in Osterley.

By his own admission, a few of the recruits Knutson had identified did not live up to expectations. Philipp Hoffmann, an old-school centre-forward who was 6 foot 5 inches tall, hit four goals in two years before being traded to a team in the German

---

3 Dean Smith interview, Sky Sports website, 21 February 2021.

second division. 'We made a bunch of mistakes,' Knutson said.[4] Some arrivals worked out better: midfielder Ryan Woods played 122 games in four years before joining Stoke City for a £5 million mark-up. Sergi Canós – signed initially on loan from Liverpool – became a fan favourite. Brentford spent the next couple of seasons, developing as a Championship team, exciting to watch, if frail in defence.

After taking a few months to decompress from his travails at Brøndby, Frank and his wife discussed moving abroad with their three children to experience another culture. One day, he received another call from Ankersen asking if he would be interested in working as Smith's assistant at Griffin Park. Frank agreed to come to London for an interview. His wife was excited by the prospect of a move to London, and a position where he would not have as much pressure. When she phoned him to find out how the interview had gone, Frank was less than enthusiastic. Becoming an assistant coach, he said, would be a step backwards in his career trajectory. He heard the disappointment in her voice.[5] After a second interview, Frank changed his mind. He was warming to Brentford. Griffin Park was archaic, and the training ground was what he later called a 'shithole', but he liked their front-foot style; it was the way he liked to play. And he saw that the club, while modest, had an ambitious owner and a smart strategy. To the delight of his wife, he took the job and moved his family home to south–west London.

---

4 *The Beesotted Pride of West London* podcast, 22 August 2020.
5 Thomas Frank interview, *The Coaches' Voice* podcast, 3 February 2022.

Brentford's decision to shut down the academy and start a B team was another unorthodox move. Apart from an extended period when the youth team was shut down to save costs after the failed QPR takeover plan, there had been teenaged trainees at Brentford since the 1960s. Every Premier League and Championship club had an academy. However, despite an operating cost of £1.5 million, only a tiny minority of academy players ever made it to the first team, either because they were not the right fit, or because they were poached by more powerful clubs. Among the teens headhunted before Brentford could command a transfer fee was Ian Poveda, a winger born in London to Colombian parents. Manchester City were required to contribute just £30,000 to Brentford towards the costs of training him, two per cent of the academy's annual overheads.[6]

The B team model had some precedent among the biggest clubs in continental Europe. In Spain, Real Madrid had a B team, Castilla, which they used to give match practice to youth-team players: in the 1980s they blooded a freckle-faced 19-year-old called Emilio Butragueño. He was promoted to the first team within a couple of years, becoming known as *El Buitre* – the Vulture – for scavenging in the penalty box: he scored 171 goals for Real Madrid's first team.

Brentford's B team would have a different approach, collecting players released by Premier League clubs like Arsenal, Chelsea and Manchester United; players Brentford felt still had plenty of potential. These were talented footballers who had not

---

6 Jay Harris, the *Athletic*, 18 July 2022.

quite made it in the world's most competitive league. Instead of trying to bring through academy talent, Brentford would gather more mature footballers and, if everything went to plan, integrate them into the first team.

At Brentford, part of Frank's remit was to oversee the evolution of young players from the new B team. Player development was his forte: he had almost 20 years of experience, five with Danish national youth sides at under-16, under-17 and under-19 levels. He was passionate about coaching. Also, fitting the Brentford mould, he was patient and process-orientated, even if his long hair and wild eyes made him look a little like the rock star Iggy Pop.

Dean Smith tried to shore up Brentford's leaky defence by employing high pressing in the 2017–18 season, with forward Ollie Watkins, who arrived from Exeter City at the start of the season, among those encouraged to harry opposition defenders in the final third of the pitch. Brentford conceded a more respectable 52 goals and, for the third season in a row, finished within a few points of the play-off positions. In the autumn of 2018 Smith – a supporter of Aston Villa since boyhood – was lured to manage his hometown club and, after two seasons as his assistant, Frank was promoted to head coach. Brentford were sitting seventh in the Championship when he was appointed: Frank looked tanned, relaxed and ready for his new job.

According to some accounts, his appointment was preordained: it was a role he was said to have been promised if Smith left. Brentford had started the season well, even if they had not recorded a win in the five games before Frank's appointment. The weakness was still the defence: Brentford could dominate with more than 70 per cent of possession and still lose. And, just as Frank took over, they started losing a lot. They lost six of their next seven games.

Supporters began to raise doubts about Frank's appointment during this period. 'Is he inspiring me? No,' said Dave Lane, a veteran Brentford commentator and co-host of a fan podcast. 'I don't think he is the right fit for the head coach. If we lose the next two games Frank will have to be a miracle worker to keep his job,' Lane added.[7] Brentford lost one, drew one. They won only one of their first ten games with Frank as head coach and found themselves two places above the relegation zone. Frank had started worse than Marinus Dijkhuizen.

Amid gripes from supporters, the mood was pushed much lower at Osterley because of matters unrelated to what was happening on the pitch. In the early hours of a Monday morning, during Frank's first weeks as head coach, Brentford technical director Robert Rowan died in his sleep.

There might not have been a more popular figure at the club than the young Scotsman, who a few years earlier had arrived for his first day at the training ground in Osterley in a clapped-out Vauxhall Corsa with all his belongings in the boot. Rowan had first tried to get into football at the age of 19 by analysing the 2009 Champions League final between Barcelona and Manchester United and sending his report by post to dozens of

---

7 Beesotted podcast, 26 November 2018

clubs across England and Scotland. He addressed each envelope to: 'the Manager'. His analysis was sharp enough to get him some work with Celtic's under-18 team and later with the Scottish Football Association, but it did not work out at Hampden Park, and he dropped out of the game for a while. But by then he had a network of contacts in football, including Brentford assistant coach David Weir. It was while working at a branch of Lloyd's Bank in Rosyth, Scotland, that Rowan received a call on his mobile from Brentford technical director Frank McParland.[8]

At the time, Rowan was ushering a customer out of the bank and he raced down to a toilet cubicle to take McParland's call. He was invited to an away match at Blackpool and got on well with the Brentford entourage. Not long after that, aged 23, Rowan travelled south to take a job as Brentford's scouting co-ordinator. He set his alarm for before 4 a.m., loaded up his battered Vauxhall Corsa with his possessions, and started on the ten-hour drive down to London. He had nowhere to stay, so he headed for the training ground. Weir would put him up at his home for his first few weeks in London.

Rowan was bright, friendly and enthusiastic to learn, insisting on spending one day a week at the Smartodds office. He was the perfect fit for a club searching for new ways of gaining an edge. 'If you wanted to build a Brentford person you would make him like Rob,' Nity Raj, the company lawyer who sat on the Brentford board, said.[9]

---

8 The account of Rowan's arrival at Brentford draws from a profile on www.nutmegmagazine.co.uk, September 2016.

9 Nity Raj interview, the *Athletic* podcast, 'Access All Areas: Brentford', 24 July 2023.

When Warburton was fired, Rowan found himself in the middle of a schism between Benham's approach and that of McParland, who had hired him. He stayed on and was appointed as head of operations, a role which included overseeing the launch of the B team. In February 2018 he was promoted again to technical director. Over the next few months he could be seen on the training pitch exchanging ideas with Thomas Frank. The day after a game against QPR, he went to bed early because he had a speaking engagement at a conference with Frank the next day. Rowan's heart stopped during the night: he died because of a cardiomyopathy episode at the age of 28.

Players and coaching staff gradually managed to pull themselves out of their grief at Rowan's death. By working together as a team, they dedicated their objectives achieved to his memory: a model Brentford staff member and friend. Between the Christmas period and late February, the team only lost one out of ten games and got themselves out of their early-season slump. Among other initiatives to pay tribute to him, Brentford have since named their training ground in Robert Rowan's honour.

For the best part of 15 years, Matthew Benham's gambling operation had remained robust, protected by the gambling lust in Asia. Smartodds had no exposure to the UK's economic climate, unlike the retail firms that worked out of the same building. Provided Asia's centuries-old habit continued, he would have a market from which to make money. In more recent years Benham had experienced some anxieties, but nothing compared with what hit in the winter of 2020.

Before the global spread of Covid-19, of course, nobody knew what was coming. On one of the back pages of an edition in the first weeks of the year, the *Economist* reckoned China's swift response to the virus may have 'nipped things in the bud' and stopped it spreading abroad.[10] The following week, the first case was detected in Europe, and the virus soon engulfed northern Italy. With nobody sure what the future held, people tried to be careful: with a nervous laugh, they tapped shoes or elbows together by way of greeting. Football executives huddled to discuss whether to halt games or carry on. Soon, the decision was taken for them: governments suspended sports.

As sports stopped, so did sports betting. The hundred or so staff at Smartodds had no way of earning revenue. The watchers had no games to analyse, the quants had no new data to process, and the traders had nowhere to trade. The only football games still being played were in remote outposts such as Belarus, Nicaragua and Turkmenistan. In Bangkok, one of the epicentres of the Asian football betting market, some gamblers continued to bet on illegal pursuits such as cockfighting and underground lotteries. There was a smattering of other niche sports still going: Australian greyhound racing, Russian ice hockey, and a darts competition in which professionals – used to duelling in halls packed with boisterous lager-drinking fans – tussled via dartboards in their homes in contests livestreamed on betting websites.[11]

---

10 *Economist*, 16 January 2020
11 Asian Racing Federation 'bulletin', 29 July 2020.

At Brentford, most executives reckoned Covid-19 would soon blow over – apart from one, with a background in statistics. For his Ph.D at Newcastle University, he had studied pandemics. The reproduction, or R number, emerged as the key metric for measuring how fast the disease was spreading: it measured the average number of people infected by an individual with Covid; this showed whether the pandemic was gathering pace or relenting. In a management meeting, Phil Giles said he thought it would take months or even years to play out.[12]

Within two weeks of football stopping, and taking the advice of Giles, Brentford were among the first clubs in the Championship to negotiate wage deferrals with players. Meanwhile, Smartodds furloughed staff: with most football stopping, there were not enough games to bet on. As Covid continued to ravage public health and the economy, Benham ran down the company's cash pile in the bank to pay running costs. He claimed government financial aid made available to UK companies to retain staff.[13] By April Smartodds employees had accepted a temporary reduction in pay; by June, the business had laid off 18 members of staff.[14]

At Kew Bridge, builders had almost completed the Brentford Community Stadium, and – whether there was a pandemic or not – it was nearly time to move homes. The club was on course to leave Griffin Park after 116 years. The ground, once

---

12 Phil Giles quoted in the *Daily Mail*, 9 August 2021.
13 Companies House; Smartodds claimed £600,000 of funding.
14 Companies House, ibid.

an orchard, would be converted into housing and, in time, the Princess Royal, one of the four corner pubs, would close for business.

The pub had once served as the club's headquarters and, for a few years from 2005, Brentford had leased it from Fuller's. (After Brentford left, a planning application was later submitted to turn it into an Armenian church.) In Braemar Road, the two-bedroom home which Terry Hurlock bought with a mortgage for £24,000 in 1980 was little changed but, in line with London's booming housing market, was now worth more than £600,000. Round the corner in Ealing Road, the Bricklayers Arms – once the local of Stan Bowles – had closed recently and been transformed into three tightly packed cream-coloured terraced houses. London was continuously changing, adding new layers over old ones. Gone but not forgotten. The name of the pub remains etched in stone in a semicircle above the three homes. One hundred metres down the road, the Coral bookmaker once frequented by Bowles remained in business, one of a dwindling number of betting shops in London as gambling moved online.

Over months, plans were made to give Griffin Park a grand send-off, with a light show and fireworks. Players and fans of different generations would say their farewells. The pandemic also wrecked those preparations. When the Championship returned in June after a three-month shutdown, there was still a public health crisis and gatherings were prohibited. Brentford's last game at the ground in late July would have to be played without any supporters.

For the time when fans could return, a new ground awaited. The Brentford Community Stadium had been fitted with a visual blizzard of 17,250 purple, yellow, red, black and white seats to create the illusion of being full – even if it was not. Some christened it 'the Lego Stadium' because those colours looked a bit like Lego bricks – and there was a certain symmetry to that: the toy company was based in Billund, in the middle of Jutland.

There were clear sightlines from every seat, an improvement on the old ground where iron stanchions got in the way. There were dozens of smart but functional corporate hospitality boxes decked out like the interior of a three-star Ibis hotel, with flat-screen televisions, modern upright furniture and minibars. Instead of a pub on each corner, there were a couple of apartment blocks on the same site, and an advancing line of café franchises selling lattes and cappuccinos: to the south and east there was a Costa Coffee.

As head coach, Thomas Frank brought straight-talking, infectious enthusiasm, and a white board he carried around to give impromptu coaching tips. The players liked him and so, in turn, would supporters. He had survived the early wobble and his team was in now in a good place. After an 11th place finish in his first season, the behind-the-scenes work to strengthen the defence resulted in three signings in the summer of 2019 that anchored the team: Ethan Pinnock, Christian Nørgaard and Pontus Jansson. In attack there was the BMW formation of Saïd Benrahma, Bryan Mbeumo and Ollie Watkins. The team moved around the pitch as a unit, playing with such high intensity that a tactics website called it 'heavy metal football'.[15]

After a decade of trial and error – some of it carried out quietly in Jutland, and some amid the tut-tutting of British media – Matthew Benham seemed to have got what he wanted. Brentford had a healthy mixture of data analytics and coaching. There was a process in place: in very basic terms, the quants helped find the under-appreciated assets in the player transfer market, and the club helped polish them into stars. Also behind the scenes, Brentford had as many as 30 video analysts picking apart games in the build-up and during matches.[16] In groups, they studied live data on laptops and fed key pieces of information to Frank and his coaching staff. Perhaps most pleasing for Benham in this increasingly slick operation was that Giles, Ankersen and Frank, his most senior football personnel, were a mix of humility and intelligence, keen to pursue his obsession with finding an edge.

Now Frank was pleased with the performance at both ends of the pitch. After a 5–0 win against Sheffield Wednesday he said his players 'defended with their lives'. Because of a three-month suspension caused by Covid, the last nine games of the 2019–20 season were in the summer, with drink breaks in each half. In a match at Griffin Park, as players drank electrolytes from bidons and sucked sachets of energy gel, Frank brought his white board, along with red and yellow circular magnets,

---

15 Themastermindsite.com, 24 May 2021.
16 Thomas Frank interview, *The Coaches' Voice*, ibid.

onto the pitch midway through the second half. He moved the magnets around to show how to break through the Charlton defence. Brentford scored two late goals to win 2–1.

These final games were played without fans to limit the spread of the pandemic. Watching the action via a livestream, they looked and sounded more like training games. You could hear the shouts of players echoing around the empty ground, and the thwack of the ball being struck. Only a few journalists and team directors were allowed into the ground. Benham and Brentford board members sat on red plastic tip-up seats at Griffin Park, following protocol by staying a couple of metres apart.

In these extraordinary times, the Smartodds quants were handed a conundrum. For years, home advantage had been factored into their modelling because data showed teams playing in their own ground had an edge, but was this now suddenly redundant because there were no fans to cheer them on? The quants scrambled to try to recalibrate the proprietary model and remain one step ahead of the bookmakers. This was the kind of insight they uncovered on a regular basis. It would emerge over time that in empty stadiums, home advantage shrank, but did not disappear altogether. One study found that, without fans, the home-win rate of teams in the Championship fell to 38 per cent from 43 per cent during the pandemic.[17] This was an important differential if you were a syndicate betting millions of pounds each day.

17 Dane McCarrick, Merim Bilalic, Nick Neave, Sandy Wolfson, 'Home Advantage During the Covid-19 Pandemic: analyses of European football leagues', July 2021 https://www.ncbi.nlm.nih.gov/pmc/articles/PMC8422080/.

Syndicates also found games flowed more freely without fans. When players were fouled they rolled around on the grass less; they were swifter taking free-kicks; and goal celebrations took less time. All of which meant the ball was in play more and thus there were marginally more goals.[18] For syndicates like Smartodds that gambled on the total number of goals per game (a common bet in Asia) this was another significant change caused by the pandemic.

None of these underlying details had a negative impact on Brentford's results. During the travails that the pandemic brought to daily life, Frank was coaching the Bees to the edge of the Premier League and providing a welcome distraction to supporters. They won their first seven games after the resumption of the league – beating Fulham, West Bromwich Albion, Reading, Wigan, Charlton, Derby and Preston. Recording their best run in the second tier, they stormed up the table to within a point of second place. After his side become the latest victim, Preston manager Alex Neil offered his appraisal of the Bees. Brentford, he said, 'rip teams apart'. If they could beat Stoke in their penultimate game, they would be promoted to the Premier League.

They lost to Stoke.

If they could beat Barnsley in the last game, they would be promoted.

They lost to Barnsley.

---

18 Author interview with industry source. The goals tally was important for the so-called over-under market in Asia that was based on the number of goals per game.

Brentford were pitched into the dreaded play-offs again.

In the semi-finals, they rallied from a defeat away at Swansea to win 3–2 on aggregate, marking the last ever game at Griffin Park with a victory. It was meant to be a rousing farewell to the old ground, but instead was more of a personal one for Benham, who had acquired it with Bees United for £1 when nobody else wanted to buy it. After the game, he walked out onto the pitch for the last time, dressed in blue Nike trainers, grey jeans and an unzipped jacket. In the deserted stadium he had a last kickabout. Trying to recreate Marcello Trotta's last-day miss in 2013, he launched shots from the penalty spot at the crossbar.

The play-off final – against Fulham, whom Brentford had already beaten twice – took place in a near-empty Wembley stadium in August; the final day of a season that had begun 367 days earlier. It was Brentford's third chance to win promotion to the Premier League. They lost, 2–1 in extra-time.

As player transfer fees surged in tandem with the booming £5 billion television rights market, clubs continued to recruit players based on hunches and sentiment. There was little data science involved when some of the biggest European football clubs went shopping for talent. Sometimes, even when there was painstaking research, old-school owners and managers ignored it. Once, a Premier League club owner commissioned a consultant to draw up data analytics to forecast the value of a striker. In the owner's office the consultant measured in granular detail the extent to which the potential signing would add value to the team. When his presentation was over, the owner came up with his first question: 'That's all very interesting, but is he any fucking good?'

Harry Redknapp was another data sceptic operating at the top of the game: as manager of Southampton, he had once turned to his performance analyst after a loss and said, 'I'll tell you what. Next week, why don't we get your computer to play against their computer and see who wins?'[19]

In fact, never had it been as important to use data to support decision-making. In the old days, most players arrived at Griffin Park on a free transfer. Now some came for millions of pounds and left for tens of millions, so it made more sense than ever to make sure you signed players who would fit into the squad. The summer before the outbreak of Covid was perhaps the most successful in terms of recruitment in Brentford's history, Brentford signed six players for a combined total of about £25 million that would become part of the team's central axis for several years: as well as the defensive trio of Pinnock, Jansson and Nørgaard, goalkeeper David Raya, midfielder Mathias Jensen and forward Bryan Mbeumo arrived. The following year they sold forwards Ollie Watkins and Saïd Benrahma to Aston Villa and West Ham, respectively, for more than £50 million.[20]

The buy low, sell high strategy meant Brentford were one of the most effective clubs in the transfer market across the whole of Europe. Their net gain from transfers between 2015 and 2021 was some £100 million. One of the few clubs that

---

19 *Guardian*, 9 March 2014.
20 www.Transfermarkt.com data.

was more effective in the market was Tony Bloom's Brighton, thanks to the quants at Starlizard.

In Camden, a 30-minute walk from Smartodds, Bloom's company inhabit a glass-fronted four-storey building in a quiet road off the tourist drag, overlooking Regent's Canal. Security cameras point at the entrance. Bloom, owner of homes in Sussex and Australia, where his wife is from, had converted a block of flats into the office, although there was still some residential space: when in London, he lives above the office in a penthouse apartment.

After signing non-disclosure agreements, new Starlizard employees were introduced to the Dixon–Coles model as part of their in-house training – and told to make themselves feel at home. Inside the open-plan office they'd discover a gym with a punch bag, treadmills and spinning machines, as well as a canteen serving breakfast, lunch, and dinner every day of the year, including Christmas Day.

Like Brentford, Brighton had access to highly sophisticated analytics to measure how tens of thousands of players from around the world would perform in English football. It is difficult to compare two such publicity-shy organisations but, according to one industry insider, Bloom's syndicate was somewhat bigger, betting larger sums in Asia than Benham's. Certainly, by virtue of being in the Premier League since 2017, Brighton had more financial resources than Brentford.

Part of the art was finding players who were not necessarily eye-catching but were efficient and contributed more to the group than sometimes the naked eye could see.

Vitaly Janelt, who arrived at Brentford in 2020, had played for VfL Bochum in Germany. While his individual on-the-ball performance data looked unexceptional in a team that finished eighth in the Bundesliga 2, his contribution to the team made him stand out. Janelt had a knack of being in the right place on the pitch. At 21, his reading of the game was exceptional, and he was still developing. With a cool composure to match his blue eyes, he was likely to get even better. Perhaps nobody else had seen this: Brentford signed him for just £500,000.

Goalkeeper David Raya arrived from Blackburn just after they finished in the bottom half of the Championship. Aside from his defensive skill, he looked as comfortable with the ball at his feet as many outfield players. Data showed he was one of the top-five Championship goalies at creating assists at Blackburn.[21] At Brentford, he would flourish as a playmaker, initiating scores of moves and helping to provided far more value than his modest £3 million fee.

With so many of their forwards leaving for fat fees to the Premier League, Brentford had to recruit frequently; they had a database with the statistics of 85,000 players that was consistently being updated. At any one time, this was whittled down to a smaller target group of 5,000.[22]

In League One, at Peterborough United, they spotted a striker who had dropped down the divisions from Newcastle United and looked like a classic lower league target man – but

---

21 www.Fbref.com.

22 Lee Dykes, Brentford technical director, interview for the *Athletic* 'Access All Areas: Brentford' podcast.

one who, according to the Smartodds modelling, was much more than that. Celtic and Rangers had also approached Ivan Toney, but they wanted him as a backup striker, with a role mainly on the substitutes' bench. Thomas Frank told him that, based on the club's statistical analysis, he would score 20 goals in the Championship with Brentford. On that basis, if he joined Brentford and they did not get promoted to the top division, he would be poached by a Premier League club. In the end, the modelling was way off the mark: Toney scored 31 goals, a Championship record.

New players arriving at Brentford were surprised by the tactical precision required of them. They were told where to position themselves at goal kicks and corners; they were instructed at what distance they should stand from their markers; and they were advised on how many seconds to hold onto the ball before passing out of defence. In artistic terms, it was like painting by numbers, rather than daubing a canvas with broad brushstrokes. It took time to adapt during the frenzy of a match, but new recruits began blending each requirement into their game.[23]

Brentford did not run on maths alone. There was also an element of free spirit that new recruits found refreshing: they were told to be bold. When there was a corner the centre-backs always went up to the opposition's penalty box; when the team was winning by a single-goal margin they were encouraged to

---

23 Ben Mee interview, the *Athletic* 'Access All Areas: Brentford' podcast, ibid. Mee joined Brentford in 2022 from Burnley, who he said had a more 'off the cuff' tactical approach.

keep attacking. Also, you only had to look at the number of Danish players in the Brentford squad – eight, at one point – to realise the personal opinions of the coaching staff were also factored into decision-making. When defender Mads Roerslev joined from FC Copenhagen it was largely based on one reason: Brian Riemer, Thomas Frank's assistant, knew him.[24]

Brentford began the new season in the unfamiliar surroundings of the Brentford Community Stadium. The changing room was fancier than at Griffin Park: the interior was wood panelled, and each player had a cream-coloured leather seat to himself. The fittings were worthy of a five-star West End hotel. The reception was as sleek as an advertising agency office, and there was a glass lift to take you up to the VIP boxes flanking one side of the pitch. When I first visited, on an invitation by one of the directors, a gentleman in his seventies stepped into the lift with me. We looked at each other. I said, 'This can't be Brentford, can it?'

That autumn, Frank's team kept their momentum of the previous season by going on a 21-match unbeaten run. There were so many games squeezed into the season that, at times, coaching staff said they did not know which day of the week it was. Nevertheless, based on their xG ranking, Brentford were the division's best team, even if results dropped off a couple of times. With Toney proving a handful, they finished third and entered the play-offs, again.[25]

---

24 Benham interview, Bees United, 27 May 2022.
25 'Brentford FC', Companies House; in their 2021–22 filing Brentford said they were virtual xG champion in the Championship the previous season.

By now, with the pandemic eased, a restricted number of fans were able to attend games and experience the new arena. They would find they had better seats, more legroom, superb acoustics and excellent sightlines. When catering was permitted again, the food was more upmarket: Danish coffee, vegetarian burgers, Shiraz wine – and, in a nod to Hounslow's Asian community – samosas.

Before the second leg of the semi-final against Bournemouth, Frank gathered with players in the pristine changing room. He showed them two short clips: a tactical video and a motivational video and then, unusually, he gathered them in a huddle. He pointed at the calmer players, Ethan Pinnock and Mathias Jensen, and told them to be more aggressive. He fixed his eyes on the more hot-headed Sergi Canós and Pontus Jansson, telling them to stay cool. Then he left and got to work on the restricted crowd of 4,000. Channelling his inner Martin Allen, he ran around the perimeter of the pitch, throwing his hands up and down to fire up fans.

Brentford trailed 1–0 from the first leg but had home advantage, and the fans responded. Everything was meticulously planned. Then, five minutes in, Bournemouth scored. Frank turned around and kicked an ice box in frustration. 'Stay cool, Thomas,' he told himself. For a few seconds he managed to compose himself. Then he kicked the ice box again.[26]

Frank's team also responded. Ivan Toney scored after 16 minutes with a penalty and, as Brentford dominated,

26 Thomas Frank interview, *The Coaches' Voice* podcast, 3 February 2022.

Bournemouth had a player sent off.[27] Janelt levelled the aggregate score. With ten minutes left, Brentford substitute Marcus Forss made it 3–2. As a sign of his status in the organisation, during matches Phil Giles sat to the left of Matthew Benham. As teammates ran to mob the goalscorer, Benham turned to Giles and swore. Confused, Giles questioned why his boss was peeved. That goal meant, Benham said, another week of stress and misery.[28] The next weekend at Wembley stadium, the whole season – nine months of planning and hard work – would be on the line again.

The play-off final, against Swansea, went more smoothly than Benham had imagined. Brentford took the lead with a penalty by Toney after ten minutes, went 2–0 up after 20 minutes and were dominating. Yet even with probability modelling showing they had a 70 per cent chance of winning, Benham remained nervous. When it came to matches, his fandom overtook his analytical, process-driven thinking. At half-time he was too tense to sit down, pacing up and down. He had mentally prepared himself to lose. Even when Swansea had a player sent off with 25 minutes left, Benham thought the worst: how terrible is this going to be if we don't go up now?

It was only with 30 seconds remaining he was able to assume what was going to happen: Brentford would play the following season in the Premier League.[29]

---

27 Chris Mepham.
28 Street and Lane, ibid.
29 Street and Lane, ibid.

★ ★ ★

Over a couple of summer days in 1968 Paul McCartney wrote 'Hey Jude' in his top-floor music room at home in Cavendish Road, St John's Wood.[30] The song, originally titled 'Hey Jules', was written for John Lennon's six-year-old-son Julian to console him about the break-up of his parents' marriage.

The song, which starts as a monologue, ending as a communion with more than a dozen musical instruments, was, according to McCartney, renamed after a character in a musical. However, Beatles biographers note that Jude is the patron saint of lost causes.[31] Since the 1960s the song had been played at Griffin Park more than a thousand times, mostly in the third and fourth divisions.

McCartney was a master of composing singalong tunes thanks to family gatherings around a piano in Liverpool; 'Hey Jude' was recorded in a backstreet studio in Soho and voted best song of 1968 by *New Musical Express*. The lyrics – '*Take a sad song and make it better*' – illustrated the power of hope and were woven into memories for Brentford fans. Even hearing the first few bars would transport you to Griffin Park on a Saturday afternoon.

Every now and again, fans would debate on having the song as the club's unofficial anthem. When one contributor to a fan message board suggested replacing it with something more exciting, the first supporter to react responded: 'Close this thread immediately.'[32] It was true the song had been popularised

---

30 'Hey Jude', John Lennon and Paul McCartney, Sony/ATV Tunes LLC.
31 James Campion, *Take a Sad Song . . . The Emotional Currency of 'Hey Jude'*.
32 Griffin Park Grapevine, 21 May 2013.

into chants by other football clubs, and even England cricket fans. So could Brentford really lay claim to it? But for older fans it still felt inextricably linked with the club.

In British football, 'Hey Jude' had some notable peers. As a student in Manchester, I stood on the Kippax at Manchester City's Maine Road as fans sang 'Blue Moon', a love song which Frank Sinatra covered.[33] In the early 1990s City trained on a patch of land with chicken-wire fence on the edge of Moss Side and played awful football in the bottom half of the Premier League while Manchester United dominated the division. The rendition of 'Blue Moon' was one of the highlights of City home games, reflecting undying loyalty and longing for better days: *You saw me standing alone, without a dream in my heart.*

In Edinburgh, Hibernian had their heyday in the 1940s and 1950s and had a sad-to-happy song of their own. In 2016, I watched on YouTube 30,000 Hibs fans singing The Proclaimers' 'Sunshine on Leith' after they beat Rangers to win the Scottish Cup for the first time in 114 years.[34] The Hibs motto became more apt than ever at this point: *When in doubt just keep in mind our motto, persevere.*

On a Friday evening in August 2021, Brentford's moment finally arrived; in their new stadium they were opening the Premier League season, against Arsenal. It was a sellout and live on television in more than a hundred countries. In the

---

33 Original version written by Richard Rodgers and Lorenz Hart, published by EMI Robbins Catalog Inc.

34 'Sunshine on Leith', written by Charlie and Craig Reid, Chrysalis Records. The Proclaimers are from Edinburgh, perhaps making the Hibs song more fitting than those of Brentford and Manchester City.

ground were middle-class season-ticket holders from Ealing and Richmond, Asian families who had never been before, more women and children than ever. One of the objectives of new director Preeti Shetty, the club's first Asian board member, was to try to make sure the club was representative of the local community. Brentford did not release details of the demographics of the new season-ticket holders, but it was clear from the faces in the crowd that by arriving in the Premier League they had attracted a more diverse following than ever. There was even the odd hipster from the Netherlands and Denmark.

Unsettling Arsenal with over-the-top balls, throw-ins into the penalty box and energetic pressing, Brentford prevailed: Sergi Canós banged in a goal from ten yards out and, after a goalmouth scramble, Christian Nørgaard's header sealed a 2–0 victory. Amid the pinch-me celebrations, there was an encore of 'Hey Jude'. As the song was reaching its crescendo, a television camera panned to a 74-year-old man in the crowd.

Bryan Godfrey's grandfather had been a fan in the early days of Griffin Park. Godfrey was born the year when Brentford were last in the first division. From 1952, the year Brentford's form imploded and they began to fall down the divisions, five-year-old Bryan would come by bus with his sister and father from the family home in Acton, wearing a red-white bobble hat and knitted scarf. The three of them had got off at the gasworks and walked to their place at the front of the Ealing Road terrace.[35]

---

35 *Push Up Brentford!* film interview with Bryan Godfrey.

As Godfrey stared into the distance, lost in his thoughts, he mouthed the chorus to 'Hey Jude' and tears streamed down his cheeks.[36]

---

36 The image was posted on TikTok and liked more than 1 million times. Godfrey, in an interview later, blamed the tears on the glare of the floodlights.

Chapter 12

Amex Stadium, Brighton

With promotion to the Premier League and a new stadium it felt like almost everything had changed at Brentford Football Club – from the installations to the fanbase. When I visited the directors' box in 2021 for a match against Everton, there were guests present including England manager Gareth Southgate, Bill Kenwright and his partner the actress Jenny Seagrove, and the venture capitalist Dharmash Mistry.[1] Matthew Benham was nowhere to be seen.

The owner left the diplomacy to Cliff Crown, his finance director who had become club chairman. Crown had the right patter for such an occasion. He gave a short speech welcoming the guests before they tucked into a three-course meal, grabbed an espresso in a paper cup, and took their seats as the game was

---

1 Dharmash Mistry was a Premier League non-executive director.

getting underway. Bundled up in a scarf, Benham watched the game with his family from the anonymity of his personal box.

Brentford soon found that things might be all right in the Premier League even with a team mostly made up of players recruited in the Championship for little more than £25 million. Tactically, they had decided they could not outplay the world's best players; instead, they aimed to throw them off their game, pressing high, mixing in long balls, and using set pieces to seek advantage. In that first season in the Premier League there was a rocky patch in the autumn, but they rebounded to finish in mid-table. Among the highlights, they drew 3–3 with Liverpool, beat West Ham home and away, and trounced Chelsea 4–1 at Stamford Bridge.

That season, they posted a record £25 million profit. It was the first financial return for Benham after putting more than £100 million into the club. Off the Great West Road in Osterley, the white portacabins at the training ground received a paint job – a matt-khaki-and-grey finish – and a new slicker logo of a bee adorned the wall of the redbrick cricket pavilion. It was only the following year that staff moved into a new set of containers. Over two floors, there was a hydrotherapy suite, a cryotherapy unit, a plunge pool and a balcony overlooking the pitches.[2]

Brentford, for the first time, became bigger than Smartodds in terms of staff numbers and revenue. So, after a decade in charge, could Benham lead the club to further progress? More Premier

---

2 Portakabin media release, 30 September 2022.

League clubs were starting to deploy data scientists to improve performance, although most were playing catch-up. After Brentford's analytics cell led by Ted Knutson was disbanded in 2015, one of their members wrote an article saying it was time to look past the 'isolated factoids' like passing, tackling and shooting, and look at what happened on the pitch as a sequence of events: a team's 'possession chain'.[3] Instead of trying to meld together 11 footballers using intuition, a quiet movement had started towards fitting them together using maths by measuring their contribution to each goal scored and conceded.

Two systems engineering professors at George Washington University who had worked as consultants for, among others, NASA, Shell and the US Air Force were among those developing this thinking. Reckoning 40 per cent of player transfers were unsuccessful, they came up with a formula to measure the value of a footballer to a team's performance. Their academic paper did not receive much interest in the game, apart from by those who were the deepest thinkers.[4] Since Benham had got involved with Brentford, there had been scores of academic papers on football to dissect.

For Brentford and Brighton, two of the world's most sophisticated football teams, there was a never-ending quest to improve performance; to assist them, they had turned to advanced player-tracking software and machine learning.

---

3 Marek Kwiatkowski, StatsBomb website, 2 September 2016.
4 Ali Jarvandi, Shahram Sarkani and Thomas Mazzuchi. 'Modelling Team-Compatibility Factors Using a Semi-Markov Decision Process: A Data-Driven Framework for Performance Analysis in Soccer', 2012.

Artificial Intelligence could spot patterns that coaches could not and so, for a while, the owners of both clubs had been hiring quants who had AI expertise.[5]

Of course, as football traditionalists point out, football games cannot be won with computer programs. Academic research has confirmed a strong link between higher wage bills and superior performance in the Premier League: so even if you have smarter backroom staff with cleverer insights, you will tend to lose against the teams that can afford the most skilful athletes. However, you can still apply brainpower to try and bridge the financial gap.

Even 20 years after their falling out, there was still lingering animosity between Matthew Benham and Tony Bloom. Over the years when Brighton played at Brentford, Bloom did not turn up to shake hands with his former colleague in the directors' box, instead taking the train to London Victoria, making his way to Griffin Park, and watching from the away fans' terrace.

When Brighton played Brentford in the Championship at Griffin Park in February 2017 Bloom went along in a party of family and friends, including his wife and son. Wearing a black puffer jacket with the Brighton logo and a blue–and–white scarf, Bloom jumped up and down in celebration with his son when Brighton scored two goals in four minutes to level the game; that season Brighton were promoted to the Premier League.

---

5 Smartodds website, April 2023.

For more than four years they would not play Brentford, but eventually they would face each other again, reigniting the Bloom–Benham rivalry. Brighton won their first two Premier League games, but Brentford prevailed in the next one. In April 2023, their fourth meeting in the top flight, I watched as the two teams faced off at the Amex Arena, near Brighton.

With a 65 per cent bigger wage bill, Brighton were more likely to finish higher up the Premier League table. They had a squad including Moisés Caicedo, uncovered from a football outpost in Ecuador, who would soon be transferred to Chelsea for a British record fee of £115 million. However, Brentford were master tacticians and disruptors. They had identified weaknesses in the Brighton defence and had spent the week practising to exploit them.

A few weeks earlier, Brentford had prepared to unravel Liverpool in the same way. At corners, instead of jostling for the best position around the penalty spot, Brentford players had done something Jürgen Klopp's team were not expecting. They ran in the direction of the corner-taker, Mathias Jensen. The idea was to flick on the ball into the goalmouth where, statistics showed, there was a higher probability of a goal. Brentford scored on the way to a 3–1 win.

Klopp saw dark arts in Brentford's methods. 'If you singled out every situation [in the mêlée before a corner kick] you would find five fouls but because it's so chaotic, nobody sees it,' Klopp said. It was as though Liverpool players had lost their wallets to a gang of professional pickpockets. During the game at Brighton, Brentford had less than 28 per cent of ball possession, yet their training-ground preparation helped them score three goals. Roberto de Zerbi, the Brighton manager, was so frustrated that at one point he smashed an iPad on a tripod to the ground. The game ended 3–3.

In the Premier League table, Brighton finished sixth. Brentford were ninth, their highest finish since 1938, and the first year in eight decades that they had ended the campaign in a higher position than Chelsea.

At the start of Brentford's third season in the Premier League, and after Rasmus Ankersen had departed to lead a takeover of Southampton, Benham sold FC Midtjylland. The sale, to Anders Holch Povlsen, a retail billionaire, valued the club in Jutland at about £50 million. Not for the first time, Benham had transformed a barely solvent club into an attractive asset. Yet he remained a relative pauper compared to most of the other 19 Premier League owners whose numbers included two sovereign wealth funds worth many hundreds of billions of pounds. According to one ranking, the former Slough Grammar schoolboy was the least wealthy of them all.[6]

---

6 *Sports Illustrated* put Benham's wealth at $300 million, less than half of the next richest owner, 8 January 2023.

Epilogue

Afootball team's top goalscorer is often the most emblem-atic figurehead after the manager, and so it was with Ivan Toney at Brentford. While he had gone under the radar for much of his career, dropping down the leagues for several years, he had now risen back up to the top: he had looked accomplished in League One, the Championship and now the Premier League. In fact, he was becoming one of the most effective Premier League strikers. So, in November 2022, when he was charged by the FA with 232 counts of betting on football, the news was what tabloid journalists would once call a 'Fuck me, Doris' moment: a conversation starter over cornflakes between the average British couple reading their daily newspaper.

Over five seasons, and while contracted to Newcastle, Peterborough, and Brentford, Toney was accused of using multiple betting accounts, either on his mobile phone or via a third party. The bets under the scope of the investigation began when Toney was a 20-year-old on loan at Scunthorpe United and ran until four months after he joined Brentford, aged 26. They were made during a period in which his older cousin, Nathan Hicks, a non-league footballer who was a few years older than Toney, had admitted breaking betting rules.[7] Eleven of Toney's wagers were for Newcastle to lose, although he did not play in any of those games and there was no suggestion of match-fixing. On nine occasions he backed himself to score in matches he was about to play in.

Toney had started betting at 15. At one point he opened a William Hill online account, made four bets in a day, and then shut the account down, according to the FA. It's not clear which other bookmakers he bet with, or the amounts he staked. He would not have had to be particularly successful with his betting strategy to draw the attention of bookies. From staking £700 on 18 games, according to one report, his cousin Nathan had come away with a net loss of £12.97.[8]

One day, one of the bookmakers Toney had an account with informed him he had become part of a so-called 'Threat Matrix' – company jargon which sounded like the title of an action movie rather than what it was: a procedure to investigate customers.

Every pay cheque Toney received he would pay bills and expenses and allocate a segment of the money for betting. As his

7 'The FA v Nathan Hicks', written ruling published 14 June 2023.
8 *Daily Mail*, 26 May 2023.

salary increased, he allocated more money to gambling, aware that there would be another cheque coming the following month. 'I thought to myself, "If I lose this, that's fine,"' he said. Without realising it, he was moving towards addiction.[9] In those early years, he thought he could stop when he wanted, but later said he was not sure: he would have been 'frail' when trying to muster the resolve to stop, he admitted.[10]

FA executives had countered what they perceived to be the threat of gambling since the early years of the organisation. In 1892 the FA introduced a rule that any player betting on a football match in which he played in would be guilty of serious misconduct. This was partly to ally with the Church of England in a societal debate over gambling. A few years later the FA stiffened the punishment to an automatic life ban; an amateur Norwich City player was found guilty simply for filling out a football pools coupon at the factory where he worked.[11]

While attitudes towards betting had softened over the years, FA punishments remained strict to deter match-fixing. In fact, it widened the restriction in 2014, prohibiting players from not only wagering on their own club, but on football anywhere in the world.

When a potential infraction was identified – often by a UK-licensed bookmaker with a duty to pass information to the authorities – the FA's powers to investigate were almost on a par with those of the Metropolitan Police. FA officials could

9 Ivan Toney interview, *The Diary of a CEO* podcast, 21 August 2023.
10 Toney interview, ibid.
11 B. G. Smith's sanction was reported in the *Edinburgh Evening News*, 21 March 1924.

call a player in for questioning, as well as order him to hand over bank records and his mobile phone. Just as the FA stiffened rules for players in 2014, they relaxed them for club owners. This was something of an ethical puzzle that some – including Toney's lawyer – felt needed more explanation.[12]

Under new provisions, the syndicates run by Benham and Bloom could continue gambling, provided they kept within an agreed set of boundaries that was not disclosed publicly and, once a year, informed the FA of their business activities through an external audit.[13]

Meanwhile, Toney found himself on the wrong side of the regulations. He was instructed to hand over statements from three bank accounts, and relinquish his phone to be imaged, allowing the FA to trawl through voice and text messages and betting app activity.[14] One FA interview lasted five hours, longer than the average police interrogation. FA investigator Tom Astley questioned Toney. 'Can you tell the FA what you understand about the FA's betting rules, Ivan?' he asked Toney.

'Can't bet on football,' Toney said.

'Is that something you've known . . . when was it you first become aware of that?' Astley said, fumbling his question.

'Yes, you guys used to come at Peterborough when I was there to say you can't bet on football.'[15]

---

12 Nick de Marco QC, quoted in the *Guardian*, 24 September 2023.
13 *New York Times*, 11 August 2017; the precise boundaries were not made clear.
14 'The Football Association and Ivan Toney', written ruling published on the FA website, 23 May 2003.
15 FA written ruling, ibid.

Toney was popular at Brentford, and not just for his goals: he had an easy smile and a bank of one-liner jokes which he often tried out on the communications team on Monday mornings as they filmed players arriving for training. On the pitch, Toney was difficult for Premier League defences to handle. He was powerful, smart at shielding the ball, and cool under pressure. He converted 28 penalty kicks in a row, using the same technique: he entered a Zen-like state, took a couple of steps, and banged the ball into the net. Even as he was under investigation, he continued to emerge as one of the Premier League's top strikers.[16]

By March 2023 Toney had 16 goals in 27 Premier League games. He was behind only Manchester City's Erling Haaland and Tottenham's Harry Kane for goals scored, and ahead of Liverpool's Mohamed Salah. England manager Gareth Southgate said it was not up to him to make a moral judgement on Toney's betting charge and, in any case, he had not been found guilty of anything yet. He picked him for Euro 2024 qualifiers against Italy and Ukraine.

On the last Sunday in March, Toney came on as an 81st minute substitute at Wembley Stadium, watched by his mother and other family members in the stands, becoming the first Brentford player to represent England since Leslie Smith in 1939. He replaced Kane and played for barely ten minutes, but it was a landmark for himself and Brentford.

Afterwards, in the dressing room, Southgate handed Toney a scarlet velvet cap with white stripes and a tassel as a memento

---

16 Toney finished the season as the top scorer after Erling Haaland and Harry Kane.

to mark his debut. Stitched into the cap was the Three Lions logo and the number 1,272 that underlined how he was part of a select group of England footballers.[17]

'I couldn't think of a better ground than Wembley for my debut,' Toney said. He reflected on more than a decade in football, including a long, winding journey through the lower leagues of the game. He'd been released by Leicester City as a schoolboy, made his debut in League Two at hometown club Northampton Town at 16. Then, having been signed by Newcastle United, between the ages of 19 and 22 he was sent out on loan to Barnsley, Shrewsbury, Scunthorpe and Wigan Athletic before being released. He ended up at Peterborough in League One, then Brentford.

The more Toney was in the limelight, the more his betting case interfered with his personal life. He was barred from a restaurant and had his car insurance revoked; when he was filling up his car at a petrol station, accompanied by his wife and three young sons, one man shouted, 'Are you putting a tenner on today's game?' Young men took delight in mocking him. '*Toney, Toney, what's the odds?*' Southampton fans yelled at one game. Manchester City fans chanted, '*Ivan Toney, he should have cashed out.*' To share the joke with a wider audience, they posted the songs on social media. Betting culture was more intertwined than ever with British football and marketing by bookmakers aimed at young men with disposable cash.

---

17 The FA had recently introduced a cap to place England players in chronological order dating back to 1872.

As Toney was making his first bets as a young man, televised matches featured a blizzard of adverts from gambling companies. Over the festive period of 2017, the *Daily Mail* counted a total of 322 during coverage of 26 Premier League games. In one game alone, there were 23.[18] Some of the adverts which appeared on player shirts were in Chinese characters and featured the number 8. In Mandarin, the number sounds like the verb 'to make a fortune'. (In China, car owners paid a premium to put '8's on personalised number plates.) Such companies were marketing to the Asian betting market; other advertisers targeted British punters.

Not only would Toney have repeatedly seen betting logos while watching games on Sky Sports and BT he would also have been familiar with some because he had worn them on his shirt. At Newcastle his black and white shirt carried the branding of 'Fun88'. That was not the only time he had crossed paths with the betting industry: in League One and the Championship, he had won the Sky Bet player of the month, and now at Brentford he wore the logo of 'Hollywood Bets' on his red and white shirt. None of the British betting companies was bigger than Bet365. It was often on television with a well-known frontman in tough guy actor Ray Winstone who, in a broad Cockney accent, encouraged you to, '*Have a bang on that.*'

One of the football insiders best placed to comment on Toney's case was Paul Merson, a popular pundit with Sky Sports.

---

18 *Daily Mail*, 17 January 2018.

Merson had made his first bet aged 16 when he was a trainee at Arsenal. After training on a Friday in 1984, he picked up his wage slip from youth-team coach Pat Rice. The slip, in a brown envelope, said he had earned £100 for the month. Merson and fellow trainee Wes Reid went to Barclays bank in Finsbury Park, north London, to take their money out. As they left the bank, Merson turned to Reid. 'What are you doing now?' he asked.

'I'm going into William Hill,' Reid said. 'Do you fancy it?'

Inside, Merson burned through his wages in ten minutes. On the way to his family home in Greenford, he scratched his face on a brick wall and told his mother he had been mugged.[19] That night, Merson recounted in his autobiography, *Hooked*, that he lay in bed promising himself he would not do the same again – but he found himself longing for pay day and the same buzz. It had been what he described as an out-of-body experience, where all his worries about making it as a professional footballer had disappeared, even if only for a few minutes.

After breaking into the Arsenal first-team squad, Merson justified his betting habit by telling himself he had not had to work nearly as hard as his parents – his father was a coalman and his mother an office cleaner – and therefore the pay cheque that he was earning was expendable.

It was around this time, aged 18, he was sent out on loan to Brentford. He arrived at Griffin Park in January 1987. Brentford were in the bottom half of the third division. Stan Bowles

---

19 Paul Merson, *Hooked: Addiction and the Long Road to Recovery*.

had retired from football but still lived around the corner. Terry Hurlock had recently left, but Francis Joseph was still at Brentford along with younger brother Roger. The club's latest recruits, both signed a few months earlier, were Mickey Droy and Steve Perryman, both aged 35. They were winding down careers that had reached their pinnacles at Chelsea and Tottenham and had been brought in before Christmas to add experience.[20]

At Brentford, the older players were kind to Merson, but the club was on a losing streak: as he watched from the bench, they lost 4–1 at Port Vale, dropping to within five points of last-placed Newport County. Before the team bus had arrived back in London, chairman Martin Lange had informed manager Frank McLintock he had lost his job; Perryman was appointed player-manager. Merson was in the starting line-up at home to Fulham the following weekend, setting up a goal as Brentford came from behind to draw 3–3.

By now Brentford's home crowd had dropped to 3,032. Merson, playing like a seasoned professional, according to the *Middlesex Chronicle*, was an asset as they beat Carlisle 3–1 for a first league win in more than two months. He was in his element, dribbling down the right flank, dinking in crosses and shooting from outside the penalty box. Brentford were unbeaten in Merson's first six league games in the team and began to move up the table. After a win at Bolton a Brentford player came off the pitch and, without having a shower, threw

---

20 Droy signed from Crystal Palace and Perryman from Oxford United.

on his clothes and dashed to an off-licence. He returned with a crate of beer for the journey back to London.

By sinking a couple of beers on the team bus, Merson found his social inhibitions among his new teammates disappeared. In Brentford's cosy pubs, he could hardly get enough beer. He could down 12 pints in a session. For the older players, Merson was talented, cheeky and fun to be around.[21]

After eight games at Brentford, Arsenal recalled him. He returned to Highbury full of confidence. In those days drinking and betting were seen through a different lens, and not considered as harmful, especially if they did not affect a player's performance on the pitch. Merson went on to play more than 300 games for Arsenal, winning two league titles in three years, as well as the FA Cup, League Cup and Cup Winners' Cup. He was capped 21 times for England.

It was only after his career had ended that he openly discussed his addictions as a player, to which at one point he'd added cocaine.

Two months after his England debut, Toney returned to Wembley. The stadium, with a statute of Bobby Moore in the main entrance, also served as the London offices of the Football Association. There was modern furniture, glass-fronted meeting rooms, flat-screen computers, and a space that jarred with all this minimalism: a small library jammed full of odd-shaped books of varying ages.

---

21 Merson, ibid.

Arriving on a May morning for a hearing ('The Football Association and Ivan Toney') besides the Brentford striker were 16 people including four King's Counsels, two of which sat on the adjudicatory panel while the others represented the two parties. Toney's was Nick De Marco, who happened to support QPR. The hearing would last most of the day.

Although Toney admitted to making 232 bets, De Marco said there were mitigating circumstances and called a psychologist to give evidence. Speaking via video link, Damian Hopley diagnosed Toney as having an impulsive/compulsive disorder, based on research carried out by a company which had analysed his betting habits.[22] The FA legal team questioned the validity of Hopley's claim because the company had not interviewed Toney.

The adjudicatory panel, however, accepted Hopley's diagnosis. The player had a lack of control over his betting, the chair of the FA panel ruled, noting he now bet on other sports and casino games but was planning to have therapy.[23]

In the 35 years since Paul Merson had played for Brentford in the third division, football and gambling had evolved at a fast pace, but he felt like he understood the way Toney's mind worked. Banning him from betting would not solve anything. Referring to the FA adjudicatory panel, Merson said, 'They all sit behind their desks and don't have a clue about the brain, and they go, "Oh, we'll do this, we'll do that."'[24] He knew as well

---

22 Trace Data Science.
23 David Casement, K.C., quoted in FA ruling, ibid.
24 Paul Merson interview, Sky Sports, March 2023.

as anyone that betting – 'having a bang' – was not necessarily fun. 'It is,' Merson said, 'the worst addiction in the world.'

In May 2023 Toney was fined £50,000 and banned from football for eight months. The betting he was charged with mostly preceded his time at Benham's club and was unrelated to the world of professional syndicates, but all the same it was an awkward addendum to the rise of Brentford Football Club that exposed the dark side of gambling and could not be easily explained away with numbers and statistics, or even an academic paper.

Appendix

Brentford Football Club, Football League division by year:

1889–1920: Regional UK and London metropolitan competitions

1920–1933: Division Three (South)

1933–1935: Division Two

1935–1939: Division One

Second World War

1946–1947: Division One

1947–1954: Division Two

1954–1962: Division Three (South; renamed Division Three from 1958)

1962–1963: Division Four

1963–1966: Division Three

1966–1972: Division Four

1972–1973: Division Three

1973–1978: Division Four

1978–1992: Division Three

1992–1993: Division Two

1993–1998: Division Three

1998–1999: Division Four

1999–2007: Division Three (renamed League One from 2003)

2007–2009: League Two

2009–2014: League One

2014–2021: Championship

2021–present: Premier League

Brentford Football Club, controlling shareholders (and profession) by year:

1889–1901: Sporting association led by management committee

1901–1962: Limited company owned by multiple shareholders

1962–1967: Jack Dunnett, solicitor and Member of Parliament

1967–1980: Limited company owned by multiple shareholders

1981–1997: Martin Lange, property developer

1997–1998: David Webb, footballer and football club manager

1998–2005: Ron Noades, property developer and football club owner

2005–2012: Bees United, not-for-profit trust overseen by supporters

2012–present: Matthew Benham, professional gambler

Bibliography

Ackroyd, Peter. *Thames: The Biography*, 2008

Ankersen, Rasmus. *The Gold Mine Effect: Crack the Secrets of High Performance*, 2012

Atherton, Michael. *Gambling: A Story of Triumph and Disaster*, 2006

Biermann, Christoph. *Football Hackers: The Science and Art of a Data Revolution*, 2019

Bower, Tom. *Broken Vows: Tony Blair, The Tragedy of Power*, 2016

Bowles, Stan. *Stan Bowles: The Autobiography*, 2005

Burchill, Jonathan. *A Pub on Each Corner: Stats and Facts from Griffin Park, the Home of Brentford FC for 116 Years*, 2021

Campion, James. *Take a Sad Song: The Emotional Currency of 'Hey Jude'*, 2022

Clegg, Gillian. *Brentford Past*, 2002

Clegg, Gillian. *Brentford Through Time*, 2011

Clegg, Gillian, *Brentford and Chiswick Pubs*, 2005

Dodds, Christopher and Marks, John. *Battle of the Blues: The Oxford & Cambridge Boat Race from 1929*, 2004

Forrest, Brett. *The Big Fix: The Hunt for the Match-Fixers Bringing Down Soccer*, 2015

Glanvill, Rick. *Chelsea FC: The Official Biography, the Definitive Story of the First 100 Years*, 2005

Hammond, Carolyn and Hammond, Peter. *Brentford, Then & Now*, 2006

Hennessy, Peter. *Having It So Good: Britain in the Fifties*, 2006

Higginbotham, Danny. *Rise of the Underdog: My Life Inside Football*, 2015

Hill, Jimmy. *The Jimmy Hill Story: My Autobiography*, 1999

Hilmes, Oliver. *Berlin 1936: Sixteen Days in August*, 2018

Jackson, Dan. *Positively Brentford: A Pictorial History of Brentford FC, 1896–1996*, 1997

Jenkins, Simon. *A Short History of London*, 2019

Jennings, Paul. *The Local: A History of the English Pub*, 2011

Kucharski, Adam. *The Perfect Bet: How Science and Maths are Taking the Luck Out of Gambling*, 2017

Lane, David and Croxford, Mark. *Harry Curtis: Brentford's Golden Era*, 2020

Lee, Richard. *Graduation: Life Lessons of a Professional Footballer*, 2012

Lewis, Michael. *Moneyball: The Art of Winning an Unfair Game*, 2003

Marshall, James. *The History of the Great West Road*, 1995

Merson, Paul. *Hooked: Addiction and the Long Road to Recovery*, 2021

Mullery, Alan. *Alan Mullery: The Autobiography*, 2007

O'Hanlon, Ryan. *Net Gains: Inside the Beautiful Game's Analytics Revolution*, 2022

Pugh, Martin. *We Danced All Night: A Social History of Britain Between the Wars*, 2008

Reid, Jamie. *Victor Chandler, Put Your Life On It: Staying at the Top in the Cut-Throat World of Gambling* (authorised biography), 2021

Schoenfeld, Bruce. *Game of Edges: The Analytics Revolution and the Future of Professional Sports*, 2023

Smith, Rory. *Expected Goals: The Story of How Data Conquered Football and Changed the Game Forever*, 2022

Spurling, Jon. *Get It On: How the '70s Rocked Football*, 2022

Sharpe, Graham and Bose, Mihir. *William Hill: The Man & The Business*, 2015

Street, Tim and Lane, David. *The Brentford Revolution: The Bees' Rise from the Basement to the Premier League*, 2022

Tippett, James. *The Expected Goals Philosophy: A Game-Changing Way of Analysing Football*, 2019

Twydell, Dave, Chapman, Mark and Hirdle, John. *Brentford: 1989–1999, Ten Traumatic Years*, 1999

White, Eric, with Haynes, Graham, Westbrook, Ian and Jex, Rob. *100 Years of Brentford*, 1991

Wilson, Jonathan. *Inverting the Pyramid: A History of Soccer Tactics*, 2008

Acknowledgements

I would like to thank the following people for their generous help in researching this book: Barry Ashby, Troels Bager Thøgersen, Jamie Bates, Alan Bird, Brian Burgess, Kathy Burton, Iñigo Calderón, Mark Devlin, Greg Dyke, Gareth Farrelly, Chris Gammon, Terry Hurlock, Rob Jex, Hans Krabbe, James Ludden, Christine Mathews, Andrew Mills, Ken Monro, Stewart Purvis, Glen Riddersholm, Jane Ruddell, Charlie Sale, Chanchal Saroya, Nevin Saroya, Brian Statham, Ed Sulley, Thomas J. Taulé and Edward Whitaker. I would also like to thank many other people from both the football and gambling industries who preferred not to be named.

David Walker and Peter Duff read earlier drafts with fresh eyes and provided sound advice. Dave Lane and Mark Croxford's book *Harry Curtis: Brentford's Golden Era* was an excellent primer about the club in the 1930s. *Push Up Brentford!*

An Oral History of Brentford Football Club helped with the memories of fans since the 1950s, as well as Martin Allen's epic time as manager in the 2000s. *Bees, Battles, Buckets and Ballot Boxes*, an online publication by Bees United, mapped each step of the move from Griffin Park to the new stadium by Kew Bridge. A *Beesotted* podcast interview of Ted Knutson recorded in 2020 provided insight into the club's transition towards using more data analytics.

Finally, a hat tip to the local historians who dig up and share so much of the rich past of Brentford, both the town and the football club. If you want to explore further, the Brentford High Street Project website is a good place to start, as is Jonathan Burchill's book *A Pub on Each Corner*.

Index

100 Famous Football Systems
159

100 Years of Brentford 1, 174

Accessories Electrical
Supplies 86
Adie, Kate 110
Alexander, Gary 178
Allardyce, Sam 197–8,
200–2, 204
Allen, Martin 142–5, 153–4,
172
Andersen, Jan Bech 264
Ankersen, Rasmus 231–5,
237, 239, 252–7, 263–6,
276, 296

Arsenal 31(n), 40, 66–7, 69,
70, 71, 75–6, 79, 288–9,
304, 306
Artificial Intelligence 294
Asaba, Carl 121, 124
Ashby, Barry 124
Asian betting market 6–7,
163–4, 181–90, 208,
221–2, 271–2, 278
Asian handicap 184
Astley, Tom 300
Aston Villa 50

Barnes 56–7
Barnsley 278
Bastin, Cliff 76

Batchelor, Horace 159–60

Bates, Jamie 114, 117

Beane, Billy 175

The Beehive 50

Bees United 133–5, 139–42,
144–6, 150–3, 166–7, 192,
228, 230, 236, 279, 310

Benham, Matthew 6–7, 15,
145–51, 153–5, 160–7,
174–80, 188–93, 206–20,
223–31, 233–40, 244–6,
248–51, 253–8, 265,
271–3, 276–9, 286,
291–6, 300, 310

Benrahma, Saïd 275, 280

Benter, Bill 222

Berlin Olympics 77–8

Bet365 303

Bird, Alan 166, 176–7, 191

Birmingham City 178, 259

Black, Fischer 148–9

Blackburn Rovers 71, 282

Blair, Tony 137–9

Blindell, Ron 104, 105

Blissett, Gary 111, 113

Bloom, Harry 180

Bloom, Tony 6–7, 179–81,
186–91, 244, 281, 294–5,
300

'Blue Moon' 288

Blundell, Harry 53

Blunstone, Frank 18

Bolton 50, 70, 197–206, 305

Boston Manor House 61,
61(n)

Boston Red Sox 246

Bournemouth 122, 285–6

Bowles, Stan 23–6, 28–9,
31–6, 110–11, 114,
147–8, 274, 304–5

Bradd, Les 105

Bragg, Wally 84, 84(n)

Bray, Ken 91

Brentford Community
Stadium 139, 153, 225,
228–30, 273–5, 284–5,
288–9

Brentford Dock 38, 42, 49,
61, 107–8, 110

Brentford Nylons 11–12, 13,
125

Brentford Rowing Club
45–7, 48, 50, 52, 54

Brentford Supporters' Club
104

Brice, Gordon 98

Bricklayers Arms 31, 33,
35–6, 39, 274

Brighton & Hove Albion 7,
179–80, 191, 244, 281,
293–6
Brøndby 232, 235, 252,
263–4
Brook, Rhidian 19
BSkyB 117, 119
Bullivant, Terry 175, 193
Burgess, Brian 139, 142,
145, 153
Burton, Richard 18–19
Bury 15, 90
Bushy Park 86–7, 87(n)
Butragueño, Emilio 267
The Butts 37, 49, 110

Caicedo, Moisés 295
Calderón, Iñigo 179–80
Callaghan, Fred 22, 26–7, 35
Canós, Sergi 266, 285, 289
Cardiff 90
Carlisle 205, 305
Carson, Johnny 18–19
Carter, Dave 172, 172(n)
centenary book 124
Championship 226, 243–52,
257, 265–8, 275–86, 294
pandemic 273–4
parachute payments 220

promotion 218
Chancerygate 153
Chandler, Victor 181,
184–8, 189
Chapman, Herbert 67
Charlton 259, 277, 278
Chelsea 12–13, 67–8, 67(n),
69, 70, 71, 74(n), 141–2,
204, 292
Clitherows 61, 61(n)
Clough, Brian 25, 127,
147–8, 176
Coles, Stuart 3–5, 7, 160,
162, 281
Comic Relief 165
Computer Group 155–8,
161, 221
Conn, David 141–2, 146
Coty 59, 109
Covid pandemic 272–3,
276–8
Crown, Cliff 165, 167, 220,
225, 291
Crystal Palace 117, 127–8
Curtis, Harry 64–6, 69–75,
78, 83–5, 88

Dagenham & Redbridge
191–2

Dallas, Stuart 215, 245

Dare, Billy 85

Davis, Frank 96, 100

De Marco, Nick 307

Denmark tour 84

Derby 176, 243, 245, 278

Devlin, Mark 219–20

Diaz, Cameron 19

Dijkhuizen, Marinus 257,
   260–1

Division Four 100–1, 103,
   124, 130–1, 175
   see also League Two

Division One 70–6, 78–85

Division Three 16, 21, 25,
   28, 31, 62, 65, 69, 100–
   1, 111, 116–19, 123–4,
   132, 143–4, 175
   see also League One

Division Two 70, 85–95,
   111

Dixon, Mark 3–7, 187, 281

Docherty, John 112

Dodge, Bill 46–9, 53

Dodgin, Bill 22, 100

Doncaster Rovers 89–90,
   211–12

'Don't Tell the Wives Club'
   166

Douglas, Jonathan 210

Droy, Mickey 305, 305(n)

Dudley, Frank 95–6

Dunnett, Jack 100–5, 133,
   310

Dyke, Greg 122–3, 141,
   145(n), 152–3, 166, 178,
   220

Eisner, Michael 227–8

Eriksson, Sven-Göran 143

Euro 2024 301

FA Cup 12–13, 51, 56,
   78–9, 83, 89, 112, 132,
   144

Farnfield, Reverend Herbert
   56

Farrelly, Gareth 203

Fashanu, John 112

Fenton, Ted 98

Ferguson, Alex 197–8, 200

Feustel, Elihu 222

Finney, Tom 90–1

Firestone 19, 59, 60, 109

Football Association 51–2,
   57, 79, 297–300, 306–8

Ford, Anna 110

Forde, Mike 201–2

Forshaw, Adam 210, 249
Forss, Marcus 286
Forster, Nicky 120, 177–8, 193, 205
Frank, Thomas 261, 263–4, 266–9, 271, 275–7, 283, 285
Freeman, Alan 13
'FT Index' 120
Fulham 49, 50, 97–8, 243, 278, 279, 305
Fuller's 41, 54, 134(n), 274

gasworks 14, 39, 46, 64–5, 82–3, 108
Gayle, Marcus 114
German tour 76–8
Gibbons, Jackie 85, 86–8, 89–91, 94, 96–7
Giles, Phil 160–1, 160(n), 256–7, 265, 273, 276, 286
Gilham, Peter 120, 144, 174
Gillette 59
Glanville, Brian 116
Goddard, Stanley 108
Godfrey, Bryan 289–90, 290(n)

Godfrey, Kevin 114
Goebbels, Joseph 77
Gomm, Harry 50
Gomm, William 50
Grabban, Lewis 178
Grant, Billy 218–19
Gray, Andre 251, 257, 261
Great West Road 11, 19, 59–62, 68, 86, 104, 109, 119, 171, 292
Green, Mr 164
Greenwood, Ron 93–7, 98–9
Gregory, John 103
Gresham, Thomas 173
Griffin Park 7, 12, 14–15, 18, 20–1, 23, 27, 33–4, 56, 64–5, 86
1990s 107–35
2000s 137–67
Bees United plans 134–5, 139–42
building 54–5
end of 273–4, 279
expansion 62–3, 71
first match 55
'Hey Jude' 120, 174, 287–8
muddy midfield 90

Noades' proposed sale
128–9
sale 225
Wendy House 119
Grimsby 84

Harris, Tom 153
Hartlepool 130–1, 133, 144
Hayes, Conor 225–6, 228–9
Hearts 72–3
Henly's car showroom 60
Henry, John 246
Herning Fremad 231–2
Hertha Berlin 78
Herting, John 220
'Hey Jude' 120, 174, 287–8,
289–90
Hibernian 288
Hicks, Nathan 298
high pressing 92, 268, 292
Hill, Jimmy 85–6, 88–9,
93–4, 96–9
Hitler, Adolf 76–7
Hoddle, Glen 113
Hoffmann, Philipp 265–6
Holdsworth, Dean 113
Holliday, Jack 77
Hong Kong Jockey Club
221–2

hooliganism 15, 20–1
Hopkins, Idris 76
Hopley, Damian 307
Hreidarsson, Hermann 130,
132
Hungary 82(n), 97
Hurlock, Terry 26–8, 29,
30–2, 35, 112, 274
Hurst, Geoff 98

Inner Circle Sports 226–7
Inns, Trevor 229, 229(n)
Interactive Gaming 190

James, Bill 246–7
James, Joe 65–6, 83
Jameson, Derek 24
Janelt, Vitaly 282, 286
Jansson, Pontus 275, 280,
285
Jémez, Paco 250, 251
Jensen, Mathias 280, 285,
295
John, Elton 21
Johnstone's Paint Trophy final
205
Jones, Vinnie 112, 132
Joseph, Francis 20, 28–9,
35–6, 305

Joseph, Roger 305
Judge, Alan 259
Justice Table 162, 208, 245, 253
Jutland 231–41, 252, 256, 275, 276
see also Midtjylland

Kahneman, Daniel 238
Kamara, Chris 27–8, 35
Kane, Bob 65, 84, 89
Kane, Harry 301
Kent, Michael 156–8, 221
Kenwright, Bill 291
Kew FC 48
Kjær, Simon 233, 236
Klopp, Jürgen 295
Knutson, Ted 247–9, 261, 265–6, 293
Krabbe, Hans 237–8
Kray twins 115
Kwiatkowski, Marek 248

Lane, Dave 269
Lange, Martin 22–3, 25, 27, 110, 116–18, 119–20, 121, 122, 129, 305, 310
Lawther, Ian 103
League Cup 116, 147, 178

League One 175–80, 190–3, 205, 217, 231, 244
see also Division Three
League Two 175
see also Division Four
Lee, Richard 177, 178
Leeds 13, 74, 250
Lennon, Julian 287
Levy, Reuben 63–4
Lewington, Ray 129, 130
Lewis, Michael 175
Lilleshall Hall 93
Lionel Road 134–5, 153
Littlewoods 63
Liverpool 13, 23, 71–2, 246, 292, 295
Livingstone, Ken 152–3
London FA 51
London Irish 229
London War Cup 83
Long, Luz 77
Longson, Sam 176
Loring, Keith 119
Lucozade sign 109, 109(n)
Lyall, John 98
Lyons, Eddie 30, 30(n)

Macaulay, Archie 84
McCartney, Paul 120, 287

McCulloch, Dave 72–4, 75

McLaren, Steve 200

Macleans 59, 109

McLeod, Roddy 52–3

McLintock, Frank 305

McParland, Frank 234, 270–1

Manchester City 34, 78, 90, 204, 211, 248, 259, 267, 288

Manchester United 67, 78–9, 123, 197

Marshall, Ian 203–4

Mathews, Christine 26, 32, 118

Mbeumo, Bryan 275, 280

Mears, Gus 67

Mears, Joseph Theophilus 67–8, 68(n)

Mercers' Company 173–4

Merson, Paul 303–6, 307–8

Midas Way Ltd 150

Middlesbrough 75, 111, 252

Middlesex FA 51–2

Midtjylland 232–3, 234–41, 249, 252–6, 263, 296

Milk Cup *see* League Cup

Millennium Dome 137–8

Mills, Andrew 175, 176, 192–3

Millwall 15, 20, 22, 40, 112, 243

Mistry, Dharmash 291

Molyneux, Dick 53

Moneyball 175

Monk, Freddy 90

Moore, Bobby 98, 231–2, 306

Morley, Ebenezer 56–7

Neil, Alex 278

Neilson, Robbie 178

NextGen 190

Nicholson, Bill 112, 126

Noades, Ron 117, 127–34, 140–2, 150–1, 310

Nørgaard, Christian 275, 280, 289

Nottingham Forest 25, 147–8, 219, 243

Notts County 14, 104–5

Oatway, Charlie 131

O'Connell, Jack 261

O'Connor, Kevin 212

O'Flanagan, Kevin 86

O'Leary, Michael 226
Olsen, Morten 263
Osterley 26, 61, 113, 125, 142, 171–4, 193–4, 216, 257–8, 265, 269, 292
Owens, Jesse 77
Owusu, Lloyd 130–1
Oxford–Cambridge boat race 44–5

Pambakian, Harry 11
Patel, Neerav 130, 131
Paton, Johnny 85–6, 93–4, 99, 99(n)
Peleteiro, Jota 215, 243, 245
performance analysis 175, 195–6, 198–204, 206–10, 224, 227, 230, 244–50, 253–7, 264–5, 276–8, 279–83, 293–4
performance bonuses 217–18, 220, 259
Perryman, Steve 127, 305, 305(n)
Peterborough 111, 282
Peters, Martin 98
Pinnock, Ethan 275, 280, 285

Plymouth Argyle 55, 69, 104
Pond-Jones, Peter 104
the pools 63–4, 158, 160
Port Vale 305
Portsmouth 20, 70, 83, 227
Poulsen, Jakob 239–40
Poveda, Ian 267
Povlsen, Anders Holch 296
Premier Bet 188–90
Premier League 2, 93, 220, 286, 288–9, 291–6
Preston 79, 90–1, 218, 278
Price family's backyard 81–2
Priestley, J. B. 59–60
Princess Royal pub 274
Pritchard, Alex 215
Professional Footballers' Association 98–9, 132
Prozone 198–9, 200, 202, 204
Puskás, Ferenc 97

Quality Street Gang 34
Queens Park Rangers 12, 13, 18, 23–4, 33, 34, 38, 51, 101–4, 111

racism 20–1, 77, 125–6
Radley Smith, Eric 18
Raj, Nity 220, 270
Raya, David 280, 282
Reading 69, 278
Real Madrid 199, 267
Redknapp, Harry 280
Reep, Charles 87–8, 89–90, 91–3, 98
Reid, Bobby 74, 75, 76
Reid, Wes 304
Richards, Dai 74
Richmond Park 29, 117–18, 193, 216
Riddersholm, Glen 207(n), 241, 252–6
Riemer, Brian 284
Roerslev, Mads 284
Rogers, Eddie 145(n)
Ronaldo 187–8, 228
Ronaldo, Cristiano 194
Rondo 205
Rosebys 13
Rosenblatt, Michael 13
Rösler, Uwe 205–6, 210, 212
Ross, Bobby 103
Rothschild, Charlotte de 40, 42, 53–4, 61, 134

Rothschild, Leopold 40, 53–4
Rothschild, Lionel de 134
Rous, Stanley 79
Rowan, Robert 269–71
rowing 43–7, 48, 50, 52, 54
Rowlands, Martin 130
Rowlatt, Judge 164
Rune, Johnny 237
Ryanair 225–6

Samuel, Martin 260
Saroya, Chanchal 125–7
Saroya, Nevin 126–7, 130–2
Saville, George 215
Schlupp, Jeffrey 178
Scholes, Myron 148–9
Scott, Andy 174–9, 190–3
Scott, Billy 76(n)
Seagrove, Jenny 291
Sexton, Dave 33
Shanks, Don 24, 34
Sheffield United 90, 95
Sheffield Wednesday 276
Shetty, Preeti 289
Simon, Louis Paul 64, 68–9, 84
Simpson, Alan 104

Smartodds 150, 153–5,
    160–6, 190, 206–10,
    212, 215, 219–20, 223–
    4, 226–8, 230, 238–40,
    244–6, 249–51, 253–7,
    271–3, 277–8, 282–3,
    292–3
Smith, Dean 264–6, 267–8
Smith, George 13
Smith, Leslie 75–7, 76(n),
    78, 83, 84, 301
Smith, Paul 124
Smith's Crisps 60, 109
Southampton 95–6, 130,
    144
Southend 103
Southern League 50–1, 56
Southgate, Gareth 291,
    301–2
Sparv, Tim 240–1, 255
Speed, Gary 202, 204
spiels 32
Spurs see Tottenham Hotspur
Starlizard 190, 281
Statham, Brian 112–13, 124
Statham, Jason 132
StatsBomb 247, 248
Steinlein, Claus 256
Stoke 278

'Sunshine on Leith' 288
Surban, Jason 130
Swaisland, Tony 123
Swansea 147, 154, 279, 286
Swindon 113
Swordfish 184–5
Syon House 37–8
Szczepanski, Lukasz 209(n)

Tampa Bay Buccaneers 201
Tanasijeviæ, Dobrivoje
    16–23
Taylor, Bob 120
Taylor, Daniel 251
television 99–100, 182–3
Thomas, Dave 114
'Threat Matrix' 298
tiki-taka 179
Toney, Ivan 283, 284,
    285–6, 297–303, 306–8
Toshack, John 147
Tottenham Hotspur 53, 69,
    70, 112, 116, 126–7
transfer market 52, 70, 210,
    249, 276, 279–83
Trotta, Marcello 211–12, 279

Valdano, Jorge 199–200
Venables, Terry 28

Viduka, Mark 209(n)
Vio, Gianni 258
Vulliamy, Ed 111

Wakeman, Rick 21
Walker, Paul 27
Walters, Billy 157–8, 221
Warburton, Mark 190,
    192–5, 204–6, 210, 215,
    216–18, 234, 243–6,
    250–2, 257, 260–1, 271
Watermans Arms 44
watermen 43–6
Watford 21, 251
Watkins, Ollie 268, 275, 280
Webb, David 110, 113–15,
    116–17, 120–4, 128, 310
Weir, David 234, 245, 250,
    270
West Bromwich Albion 50,
    278
West Ham 15, 26, 40, 51,
    98, 292
Whall, Phil 165, 220
Wheatley, Walter 'Bill' 18

White City 34–5
White, Eric 109, 174
Wigan 278
Wilson, Jonathan 92
Wimbledon 112, 127, 132
Winterbottom, Walter 93,
    94
Wise, Dennis 112
Wolves 243
Woods, Alan 222
Woods, Ryan 266
World Cup 98, 101, 183,
    186–8, 189, 238
World War II 83
Worshipful Company of
    Mercers 173–4

Yamaichi Securities 148,
    149
Yeovil 212
Youth Training Scheme
    (YTS) 127, 130, 267

Zenga, Walter 258
Zerbi, Roberto de 296